CULTURAL
FOUNDATIONS
OF
EDUCATION

An Interdisciplinary Exploration

CULTURAL
FOUNDATIONS
of
EDUCATION
An Interdisciplinary Exploration

By THEODORE BRAMELD

Foreword by Clyde Kluckhohn

GREENWOOD PRESS, PUBLISHERS
WESTPORT, CONNECTICUT

Library of Congress Cataloging in Publication Data

Brameld, Theodore Burghard Hurt, 1904–
     Cultural foundations of education: an interdiscipli-
nary exploration.

     Reprint of the 1st ed. published by Harper, New York.
     Includes bibliographical references.
     1. Educational anthropology. I. Title.
[LB45.B7 1973]   370.19'3   73-7070
ISBN 0-8371-6904-6

Originally published in 1957 by Harper & Brothers, New York

Reprinted with the permission of Harper & Row, Publishers,
New York

Reprinted by Greenwood Press, Inc.

First Greenwood reprinting 1973
Second Greenwood reprinting 1977

Library of Congress catalog card number 73-7070

ISBN 0-8371-6904-6

Printed in the United States of America

To Ona

CONTENTS

    TIME AND HISTORY IN CULTURE-THEORY   86

    CLASSICAL EVOLUTIONISM   89

    CONTEMPORARY EVOLUTIONISM AND THE CULTURE-
        HISTORY SCHOOL   91

    CULTURAL ORDER AS HISTORY-AND-SCIENCE   95

    RECENT PHILOSOPHIES OF CULTURAL HISTORY:
        METHODOLOGICAL   100

    RECENT PHILOSOPHIES OF CULTURAL HISTORY:
        SUBSTANTIVE   103

    THE TEMPORAL ORDER OF CULTURE: OPPORTUNITIES
        FOR EDUCATION   112

PART III—The Problem of Human Process

7. Cultural Process: Preview of the Problem   121

8. Some Major Concepts of Cultural Process   126

    DISCOVERY AND INVENTION   126

    DIFFUSION   127

    ACCULTURATION   129

    ASSIMILATION   131

    INNOVATION   133

    FOCUS   135

    CRISIS   136

    CAUSATION AND PREDICTION   141

    "EDUCATION AND THE CULTURAL PROCESS":
        RELATIONS OF THEORY TO PRACTICE   148

9. Personality in Cultural Process   157

    THE CULTURE-AND-PERSONALITY FRONTIER   157

    THEORIES OF LEARNING AND PERSONALITY   158

    THE CONCEPT OF PERSONALITY: RECENT EMPHASES   165

    MODAL PERSONALITY, NATIONAL CHARACTER, AND
        CULTURAL CHANGE   169

FOREWORD

By CLYDE KLUCKHOHN, *Professor of Anthropology,*
Harvard University

A GENERATION AGO John Burnet wrote that if current trends continued a specialist would be able to talk on his subject to only a few people in the world. Indeed, before long, he would find that he could converse only with himself, and then the new Dark Ages would be upon us. Professor Brameld's book is an impressive counter-attack upon the intellectual celibacy of the contemporary world. With a sweep and a sophistication that command respect, he brings to educational theory substantial ideas and facts from anthropology, philosophy, psychology, sociology, and other fields.

Anthropologists must feel complimented that he has made their principal contribution to the mainstream of thought (the concept of culture) central to his exposition. I shall not pretend that I am satisfied with every detail of workmanship in the technical matters I know best nor that I am persuaded by every aspect of his systematic theory. On the other hand, I must say with equal honesty that I have learned, as an anthropologist, from his synthesis and his critique. In no sense has he passively absorbed and accepted anthropological notions about culture. Nor has he—as have some who have attempted to introduce this concept into other subjects—simply borrowed a vocabulary at the surface level. On the contrary, he has examined (with philosophical skills which few anthropologists command) the underlying premises of culture theory and their linkages.

Much verbal assent is given these days to the proposition that "generalists" are needed. Yet the usual tendency for the specialist who has agreed to this proposition is to quarrel loudly with major and minor issues that bear upon his own particular conceptual territory. I do not propose to follow this example. Rather, I shall add a few comments of my own upon the relations between anthropology and education.

Formal connections are recent, although by now there are anthropologists upon the faculties of several of the leading graduate schools of education. It is obvious, however, that the interests of education and of anthropology converge at the core of both subjects. For each is fundamentally concerned with humanly created techniques of living, the attached norms and values, and the transmission of techniques and values. The problems of "eclectic aimlessness" and "vicious relativism" are as inescapable for the contemporary anthropologist as they are for the teacher or the theorist of education. These problems assume somewhat different dimensions for members of the two professions. The anthropologist may not feel that, as an anthropologist, he must make that "normative commitment to the purpose of transcultural freedom" which Professor Brameld urges upon education. But the intellectual issues must be faced equally in both disciplines. And each group should learn from the empirical experience and analytical progress of the other.

Dr. Brameld in his fundamental enquiry has certainly drawn from what is most relevant in anthropology. One notes especially the massive influence of our leading figure, A. L. Kroeber. Most anthropologists agree today that if the distinctiveness of cultures rests upon their principles of selectivity, in terms of which certain "paths" are consistently selected from the many that are "objectively" open, one can hope to understand these principles only insofar as one grasps the key values of each culture and sees these in the context of those broad pan-human values that are universals or near-universals. Education likewise, whether its emphasis be upon the enrichment of the mind or upon the formation of character, must see values—their perpetuation and the constant critical scrutiny of them—as at the heart of its problem.

Some readers may find Professor Brameld's anthropological viewpoint disturbing. It may appear to challenge "common sense" and even to threaten the stability of some familiar, cherished values. His analysis makes enormously complex the question "What is human nature?"—a question to which the "practical" man and the conventional teacher find it convenient to have a simple answer. On the other hand, Brameld's position does not open the way to a complete and chaotic relativism. Nor does it exalt the irrational and non-rational aspects of human behavior. On the contrary, it advocates an extension of the areas which reason can understand and perhaps to some extent control by the search for discoverable regularities. An education so based may help a little to halt the flight to the irrational, the terrified retreat to the older orthodoxies which we have seen on a mass scale in this century.

In our world where varied peoples and cultures now find themselves in uncomfortably close contact, it is the function of anthropologically-oriented education to supply, on a smaller scale and in a scientific manner, the perspective which philosophy has attempted in a global and unscientific manner.

Such education, as Professor Brameld rightly insists, must be founded upon the fundamental professional training and scholarship in depth of educators. An outstanding example of this kind of training is that of the examination and interpretation of culture theory set forth in the present book.

PREFACE

EDUCATION WILL attain the status of a profession comparable in proficiency and standards with professions such as law only when it incorporates within its training program the richest, most authoritative experience and knowledge available from all relevant fields of human achievement.

That education has not attained such a status is apparent to anyone familiar with curricula and practices of the great majority of American teacher-training institutions. The only scientific discipline, for example, that is everywhere formally studied is psychology, though even this discipline receives inexpert or limited treatment by many such institutions. Thus the "science of education," a movement inaugurated more than a quarter-century ago, has meant primarily the measurement of mental processes and abilities by methods borrowed from physical science. The quantifying of intelligence and the mechanizing of tests and examinations have been its dominant achievements.

While the "science of education" continues to exert legitimate influence, it is criticized for its narrowness as well as for many of its claims. A shift has been under way for some time to counterbalance the psychological over-emphasis by comparable attention to the natural and social sciences, the arts and philosophy. The "foundations of education" are a consequence of this shift: increasing numbers of teachers' colleges are establishing courses that try to provide substantial knowledge of the natural world, of the behavioral sciences, of literature and other fine arts, together with critical interpretation of the assumptions, conflicts, and aims of modern civilization.

This important shift is far from achieved, however. Among all the sciences, psychology remains the most common requirement in education. Educational sociology, philosophy, and similar fields are still regarded as of subordinate importance if they are studied directly at all. A committee of the American Philosophical Association has reported, for example, that "there are 700 or more colleges training teachers which offer no philosophy whatever." Without question, the new field of educational anthropology is ignored by a still larger number. One may doubt whether the average prospective teacher, through no fault of his own, could clearly define anthropology, much less demonstrate familiarity with its subject matter or its significance for his professional work.

And yet, ironically, the key concept of anthropology—culture—is perhaps the most overworked term in current educational literature. Like the term, "felt needs," which cluttered the textbooks a decade or two ago, "culture" is now the rage. Even psychology textbooks usually say something about it, if only to confuse their readers by failing to elucidate its meaning. The popularity of the term exemplifies the professional educator's most chronic occupational disease—his penchant for clichés and catchwords that sound important but are, in fact, deceptive substitutes for intellectual precision. This is what happened with "felt needs": everybody talked about gearing the teaching process to them, about building the curriculum out of them, but few ever stopped to analyze "felt needs" so that the phrase made scientific sense. The same hazard now confronts educators intrigued by "culture." What it means to those most competent to tell us, and whether it actually is as significant as we are enjoined by its sloganizers to believe, cannot be determined from typical usage among educators.

Typical usage is not, of course, the same thing as universal usage. A growing minority of authorities in education, especially those most responsible for encouraging the foundations of education, are aware of the pitfalls in careless treatments as well as of the complexities in careful ones. They would agree, therefore, that the task facing professional education in the study of culture is to open its doors wide to the most reliable, most expert, sources that they can discover and to select from these sources the most exciting implications for education that they can ascertain. They would agree, too, that this task is anything but a quick or simple one. They know that culture is an idea of many colors and many shapes, that, far from being the exclusive franchise of any one discipline, its value has been enriched by at least a dozen. Among these disciplines, anthropology is the most focal. Yet, in view of the scope and depth of the idea, they would expect other fields to contribute abundantly, including psychology itself.

For these reasons this book is subtitled "an interdisciplinary exploration." It suggests that the foundations of education cannot be properly studied as separate courses put up in separate packages of knowledge—psychology here, social science there, philosophy somewhere else. Granting that specialized subject matters are likewise necessary, these belong on a different level of the curriculum in teacher education. They do not belong in foundational courses that should provide a comprehensive as well as fundamental outlook upon education as a crucial enterprise of culture.

The study of culture, furthermore, is first of all the study of its theory. The impatience and short shrift with which theory is regarded by run-of-the-mill teachers' colleges is an academic scandal. Over and over, we are told that teachers must have "know-how" to practice in their classrooms; for this they need skills and the facts that go with skills. Of course they do need these. But they need much more. If they are to perform their role effectively and responsibly, they require a framework of principles—carefully wrought principles—that alone can provide skills and facts with durability and purpose. Prolonged attention to theory does not lead to poorer or weaker but to better and stronger practice. To help teachers *apply* the theory of culture to their everyday work is, in one sense, the first objective of this book. But there is no shortcut to this objective. Shortcuts are exactly the danger that the profession of education, if it is ever to become a *profession,* must learn to avoid.

The mandate to construct a theory of culture for education is confronted by difficulties that might not arise equally elsewhere. Assuming that anthropology is the main, though far from the only, source from which we must draw, anyone who investigates its subject matter discovers quickly that its theoretical formulations, though abundant, are remarkably heterogeneous. One explanation is that anthropology, a comparatively young discipline, has hit its stride during a period in the evolution of the social sciences when stress has been upon first-hand, empirical research. While earlier anthropologists were devoted to general theory, most of those responsible for elevating their subject to the rank of a major social science have concentrated upon theoretical systematization much less often than they have upon specific examination of cultural phenomena—and then frequently they have done so after rather than before their data have been gathered and explained. Some of the most influential anthropologists in recent years have also avoided much attention to theory for fear of regressing to armchair speculations which, as scientists, they wish to supplant. It has been necessary in this book, then, to consider the theoretical contributions of many anthropologists as well as of other scholars of culture, and to coordinate their diverse views into a design that cannot be attributed to any one authority.

To "keep the record straight," however, it should be noted that after having developed the threefold conceptual scheme of the following pages, I became acquainted with a work suggesting a partly parallel scheme. I refer to *Structure and Function in Primitive Society,* by the notable British anthropologist A. R. Radcliffe-Brown. Certain resemblances of this work to my approach were called to my attention by the anthropologist M. G. Smith when I visited the University College of the West Indies. But even Radcliffe-Brown, though his interest in theory was exceptional, cannot be considered as primarily a systematizer: like others of comparable stature and influence, he was during his lifetime still more absorbed in circumscribed empirical investigations. In any case and in fairness to him, his concepts of "structure" (resembling most closely my concept of "order") and of "function" (resembling my concept of "process") are by no means identical with those I adopt. Nor does he single out the concept of "goals"—the third angle of my schematic triangle—for sustained attention.

My reason for anticipating here the design of this book is to emphasize not only that no one anthropologist would wish to be held accountable for it but, as will be apparent to all anthropologists, that it has been developed by an adventurer into their own domain rather than by a fellow-specialist. Concern with the systematization of theory is more in accordance with the habits of one trained, as I have been, in the field of philosophy. This book aims to utilize philosophy as a bridge connecting the theory of education as a central institution of organized human life and the nature of culture as a central concept of the social sciences. In so far as it fulfills this aim, it is addressed not only to educators who wish to understand the systematic relations of culture to their field, but to social scientists and philosophers who wish to understand the systematic relations of education to theirs. With all three groups in mind, I have as often as possible adopted terminology familiar to an interdisciplinary audience.

The design of this book has likewise governed both the inclusion and the omission of materials. It makes no claim to being an exhaustive interpretation of culture-theory. Rather, it selects those features that seem most likely to enlighten the philosophy and practice of education. Readers are urged to consult the *References* for many fuller and more authoritative treatments.

This design governs the sequence of interpretation as well. The introductory Part highlights the timeliness of the problems selected for examination. Each of the next three Parts begins with a "preview" of the central issue, followed by chapters all of which first interpret the appropriate phase of culture-theory and then develop certain educational implications that emerge from that phase. The final Part recapitulates some of the principal ideas of the book as they bear upon teacher education.

Readers may be aided still further if they appreciate the logic of the plan by which we proceed from broader to narrower areas of attention. We begin with the term, human, as the all-embracing concept, but almost immediately we turn to the three large categories of human experience mentioned above: order, process, and goals. These categories, too, are then dealt with selectively—that is, in terms of their cultural components. Finally, we ask what education may mean when viewed through the lens of each cultural category. The plan is thus one of progressively sharper focus upon the diffused landscape of humanity.

A more personal note is also called for. Over a period of years I have been developing a theory of democratic education that could give consistent and dynamic direction to the schools of America and of other countries in an age of revolutionary change. In the course of developing this theory, which is still far from satisfactory, it became clear to me that no educational philosophy could hope to perform such a service unless it included in its formulations the thought and research of the human sciences. Among these, the field that deals most painstakingly with the nature of culture seemed likeliest to prove essential; for, though I was far from proficient in anthropology, I was reasonably sure that both its inclusiveness and its fecundity would warrant whatever effort I could expend in its study.

For the most part, my expectation has been fulfilled. The theory of education which I advocate, and which of course has influenced my choice of materials as well as my judgments of them, has been further strengthened and further substantiated. At the same time aspects of this theory have in turn been modified and qualified. In particular, I have been made more aware of how little we know in the human sciences, yet how rapidly our knowledge is developing— so rapidly that some parts of this book will properly require amendment or correction almost before it appears.

But though this interpretation of culture-and-education is shaped by deep personal need and by personal conviction, I have tried also to respect the canons of objectivity in considering the ideas of every culture-theorist from whom we shall learn. In this effort, as well as in all others, the advice and assistance of the following anthropologists, historians, educators, and philosophers have been invaluable: Ethel M. Albert (Harvard University); Ethel Alpenfels (New York University); Kenneth D. Benne (Boston University); David Bidney (University of Indiana); Theodore Blegen (University of Minnesota); George S. Counts (Columbia University); Merle Curti (University of Wisconsin); H. Harry Giles (New York University); A. Irving Hallowell (University of Pennsylvania); F. Ernest Johnson (Columbia University); Felix M. Keesing (Stanford University); William H. Kilpatrick (Columbia University); Ward Madden (Brooklyn College); Maurice Mandelbaum (Dartmouth College); Robert McKennan (Dartmouth College); Margaret Mead (Museum of Natural History); Ashley Montagu (New School for Social Research); Charles Morris (University of Chicago); Louis Raths (New York University); R. Bruce Raup (Columbia University); Harold Rugg (Columbia University); B. Othanel Smith (University of Illinois); George D. Spindler (Stanford University); Lawrence G. Thomas (Stanford University); and John W. M. Whiting (Harvard University). In addition, two anthropologists have given even greater time and attention to problems of my study: Joseph Bram (New York University) who read the manuscript and offered excellent advice, and Clyde Kluckhohn (Harvard University) who guided me with patience and acumen. To my students at New York University, the University of Puerto Rico, Dartmouth College, and the William Alanson White Institute of Psychiatry where I first explored the theme of this book: my gratitude for criticism and stimulation. My wife helped me at every step of the way; the dedication is only the slightest token of my indebtedness to her.

I express appreciation also to the editors of the *Harvard Educational Review, Educational Theory,* and Stanford University Press for permission to incorporate materials of mine that they have published; to the officers of Baker Library, Dartmouth College, for having so cooperatively made its resources available to me in the preparation not only of this book but of others as well; to Provost Donald Morrison for having arranged for me to spend a semester at Dartmouth College; to Ordway Tead, of Harper and Brothers, who has encouraged me at the same time that he has been my friendly critic; and to the Wenner-Gren Foundation for Anthropological Research and its Research Director, Paul Fejos, for having provided grants that enabled me to devote uninterrupted time to the investigation of which this book is both an ending and a beginning.

Theodore Brameld

PART I

THE PERSISTENT PROBLEMS OF EDUCATION IN CULTURAL PERSPECTIVE

CHAPTER ONE

CULTURE: THE CONTEXT OF EDUCATION

THE NEED FOR RE-EXAMINATION

IF AMERICAN EDUCATION is ever to emerge from the confusion and disagreement in which it is now floundering, it will have to admit that it is incapable of doing so under its own steam. The reason lies, of course, in the character of education itself—an institution deriving its meaning and energy from the surrounding environment of things and of men; an institution therefore that is able in turn to affect that environment only in so far as the latter has first provided the conditions and resources of education's own operation.

An example is the current crisis in American school facilities. Despite the lip-service of devotion that most of us are always ready to pay public education, we as a people are notoriously unwilling to match verbal tributes with pecuniary payments. The result is that we have failed to heed the warnings of administrative experts, reiterated endlessly, that the extraordinary increase in the American birth rate would quickly bring about an appalling shortage of school buildings, equipment, and teachers. The tragedy predicted is now upon us in full force: millions of children unable to protest are victimized by overcrowded, even unsanitary conditions, by worn-out or insufficient supplies of tools, laboratory materials, and books, and by poorly trained, makeshift, overworked staffs.

And yet in long range the present American situation is but a minor instance of the general rule of education's dependence upon its encompassing environment. The rule may be supported by every known record, beginning with the most primitive efforts of nonliterate tribes and extending to all areas of the ancient, medieval, and modern world. Every people known to history has created some kind of educational program and has determined the conditions under which it is allowed to function. To be sure, shockingly large populations are today still deprived of formal schooling: well over three-fourths of all the people of India, to take but one country, can neither read nor write. This is not to say, however, that these populations are being deprived of education. They still receive prolonged acquaintance with and practice in the skills, habits, beliefs, traditions, and values of the respective groups into which they are born and which establish the rules and routines that they must learn to obey and utilize. Nor are the countries that are able to maintain formal school systems different in these basic ways. Here, at any rate, education in Spain or the Soviet Union is not unlike that in Norway or the United States.

To assert that every educational endeavor has always been and continues to be the servant, the agent, and the product of its natural and human environment may appear obvious. Not obvious, however, are the far-reaching inferences. For example, one whole section of influential educational theorists rests its case largely upon the more or less explicit belief that, just because education is determined by the tribe, the community, or the state, its central function is therefore to teach the young how to conform with and adjust to the tribe, the community, or the state. Another section discovers a different implication: it finds evidence for the viewpoint that education often plays a creative role in modifying, even in reconstructing, the environment from which it is derived. Each section admits a degree of validity in the other's position; hence neither is in fact as unqualified as any summary statement suggests. The difference in emphasis, nevertheless, is important enough to produce varying consequences not only in theory but in practice.

Thus in hundreds of rural areas as well as cities of America the guiding if seldom enunciated philosophy of the school system is primarily one of "fitting into" the given pattern of economic, social, religious, and ethical life by tacit acceptance of habits, mores, and beliefs practiced and cherished by the more powerful, articulate sections of the local population. Other school systems are beginning to question such a philosophy as inadequate and unsound. Somewhat more self-consciously than the first group, they claim that the business of education is also and even more properly to deal critically and experimentally with inherited, tradition-encrusted values, attitudes, and practices. While this second approach remains as yet more on the theoretical level than on that of everyday practice, anyone familiar with recent trends not only in America but in countries like England admits its growing influence upon the content of curricula, upon methods of learning, even upon the control of education.

Neither camp of interpreters, however, is sufficiently sensitive to the real matrix of the dispute—namely, the nature of the environment of which we have spoken as the prime conditioner of education's limitations and restrictions as well as of its possible creative opportunities. With some important exceptions—most of them perhaps in the second of the two camps—there has been little sustained or critical examination of that environment from which, after all, education now as always receives its justification for existence. In a sense, such lack of exertion is understandable: no less than other public institutions, education is so beset with its own internal troubles, so enslaved by the job of keeping its huge, cumbersome machine going in the face of one new shortage and demand after another, that it seems to have little energy or patience left for anything other than emergencies.

Yet, if education is to perform the service that it ought to perform in an age such as ours, this preoccupation with short-term practice, with internal and academic issues and techniques, will have to be corrected. Dissatisfaction with untrained school administrators, with incompetent teachers, with colleges of education abounding in dubious "busy-work," with universities characterized by polyglots of unrelated courses, with outmoded facilities on all levels—such criticisms as these, whether always justified or not, can be met only when and if those deeply concerned with education are willing to reappraise its place, its work, and its purpose in a setting much more encompassing than education itself.

INTRODUCTION TO THE MEANING OF CULTURE

To speak of the setting of education is simply an unprecise way of pointing to the nature of that total environment which it now becomes our business to delineate more carefully. Ultimately, this total environment includes everything in nature—the stars, atmosphere, terrain, and the birds and beasts. All these are relevant, for without them there could be no human species, and hence no human institutions. For our purpose, however, we may consider them as a kind of backdrop for the drama itself. The action proper takes place on the stage of experience which man himself has fashioned through his amazing ingenuity, his fears, his dreams, and his wants.

This stage is the culture. It is from the stuff of culture that education is directly created and that gives to education not only its own tools and materials but its reason for existing at all. It follows that if we are ever to come to grips with the bewilderments, strains, contradictions—in short, the most persistent problems—that confront education in our "time of trouble" we shall first have to come to grips with pervasive problems on that level of the environment which hereafter shall be called the culture. What, then, more precisely does "culture" mean?

Those experts who now consider this question to be their special province of investigation—I shall take the liberty of calling them "culture-theorists"—would be the first to insist that the answer is far from complete. The astonishing influence of the concept in recent years, not only in anthropology where it has been central, but in such fields as sociology, psychology, history, and philosophy, has produced a great deal of controversial interpretation of what originally appeared to be a simple idea. Since the aim of subsequent chapters is to utilize such interpretation as it bears upon basic problems of education, I confine myself here only to a reconnaissance of that vast domain of nature that culture symbolizes.

At the outset, it is necessary to distinguish between, on the one side, the more traditional honorific idea of culture as the cultivation or pursuit of perfection, of the graces of learning and gentility, and, on the other, the more recent objective idea of a "way of life" prevailing in any particular society. Both ideas are legitimate. As will be noted later, some interpreters now seem to be groping for a synthesis of the two in a way that could scarcely have been considered until both of them had reached their own levels of mature meaning.

The more traditional notion is also, of course, the one we tend to associate with education in the classical sense. To be "cultured" and to be "educated" are here identical. Either way, one who attains this happy state is presumably familiar with the noble achievements of the arts, of thought—in short, of the "finer things of life."

The first influential notion of culture in its more recent sense can be marked, interestingly, by an exact date: 1871. It was only then, considerably less than a century ago, that the Englishman, Edward

B. Tylor, offered in the first sentence of the first page of his famous *Primitive Culture* the one definition that has doubtless been quoted more often than all others combined. "Culture or Civilization. . . ," he says, "is that complex whole which includes knowledge, belief, art, morals, law, custom, and any other capabilities and habits acquired by man as a member of society."[1]*

It is worth examining this definition, for today we still find wide respect for it at least as a point of departure for more precise and extensive treatments. It includes seven more or less distinct components. Notice first the phrase, "complex whole." Tylor is hinting that culture, however multiple its parts, possesses some kind of unity, perhaps even pattern or design. Second, it embraces an array of psychological achievements that are not so much visible in the form of material objects as they are expressions of emotional and mental life. Third, observe however that culture may very well also include such material objects—those of art, say, or those of morality as manifested in the conduct of visible groups (the family, for example). Fourth, the stress is upon the kind of behavior that manifests a certain regularity and continuity—customs, capabilities, habits —not discrete or momentary events. Fifth, unlike the older definition which implies an invidious comparison with the "uncultured" or "untutored," there is no sign of something better or worse: culture is a reality to be viewed objectively and impartially, although concerned with morality and art as parts of that reality. Sixth, since it is regarded as a totality of characteristics that man *acquires* from his surroundings, it is not to be found in his genes or other hereditary equipment. Finally, culture is not created by man out of his solitary genius: he must live in a society—that is, with other human beings— if he is to acquire culture.

Although practically every word in Tylor's definition invites analysis and research, the one that at first glance seems most innocent is, in fact, the most elusive—the simple word, "man." If we think of man in the image of an individual person, we need to ask, for example, just what may be his relationship to the culture within which he must live. Granting, as all experts do, that without man there would be no culture, how far is he its creator and its master? How far is he its product and its pawn?

* References can be found beginning on page 305.

"Society," another innocent-sounding term in the definition, is only a little less provocative. One is surprised by the frequency with which it still seems to be used as loosely synonymous with the term "culture," even by social scientists. But as Tylor implies in his definition, and as most scholars now agree, the two terms by no means point to identical phenomena. Of course, culture in a sense is the product of society, just as it is of the individual. Both are necessary to the existence of culture. A product, however, is not the same thing as its producer any more than milk is the same thing as a cow, and how best to specify the precise relation between society and culture remains a matter of dispute.

The contention that lower animals, such as bees and buffalo, organize societies (defined here as aggregates of interrelated individuals) but do not organize cultures has been found to be a useful distinction as far as it goes. A more subtle distinction on the human level is provided by the notion of "situation": a society is the situation in which human beings find themselves when they are associated with one another, as in a family, a tribe, or a town. It takes on the character of culture when it is found also to acquire common values and skills that are cherished and transmitted by society. Obviously the two terms are not separate in the experience of human groups except for purposes of scientific differentiation. Yet while cultures presuppose societies, not all societies presuppose cultures As a level of human experience, culture functions over and above that merely of society. Even while it continues to be a society, it is not reducible to a society.

The implications of Tylor's definition extend further. The terms "knowledge" and "belief" imply that culture embraces philosophy, religion, science, as well as folklore and superstition. It includes moral beliefs, standards of good and evil and of right and wrong; it therefore leads straight to the complex field of values—a field which, inasmuch as art is explicit in Tylor's definition, would also encompass the values of beauty and ugliness.

Even more inclusive is his phrase, "other capabilities and habits." Here the door is left wide open, and his successors have been glad to accept his invitation to enter. A few of the miscellaneous capabilities that are listed by them are crafts, skills, industry, etiquette, symbolism, instruction, painting, points of view, and goals. As for his term "habits," its importance is nowhere more cogently reiterated than in the compact, Tylor-influenced definition of that towering anthropologist of American scientific history, Franz Boas: "Culture embraces all the manifestations of social habits of a community, the reactions of the individual as affected by the habits of the group in which he lives, and the products of human activities as determined by these habits."[2] This definition is noteworthy too for its recognition of the role both of society and the individual in culture, and for its inclusion of objects and institutions—that is, "products"—along with more psychological experiences.

Mention of psychological experiences opens up a huge area scarcely explored by Tylor himself, or even by Boas half a century after. Only within perhaps the past two decades have culture-theorists tried systematically to come to grips with the meaning of such experiences for their own field. Some, such as the British anthropologist, A. R. Radcliffe-Brown, and the Polish-British anthropologist, Bronislaw Malinowski, have stressed the "functional" character of culture in ways sometimes suggestive of the psychology associated with the views of William James and John Dewey. Others, such as the antropologically-slanted psychoanalysts, Géza Róheim and Abram Kardiner, have interpreted culture by means of Freudian postulates. Still others, especially Americans such as Clark Wissler, reflect the influence of behaviorism. Finally, the gestalt viewpoint, so influential in recent years, is sometimes apparent in culture-theory—in, for example, the most distinguished American anthropologist since Boas: Alfred L. Kroeber. But regardless of what psychological viewpoint individual experts happen to prefer, few would exclude as irrelevant to their interpretations one or more of such common psychological phenomena as adjustment, problem-solving, needs and wants, learning, and symbolizing. And no expert would deny that always at the root of cultural experience is the inherited biological-physiological-neurological equipment of the human being.

At the opposite pole, so to speak, from the individual is the area marked by Tylor's term, "complex whole." Here theory and research extend further back, but it is also one of the chief problems of culture-theory today—the problem of what systems of relationship, if any, can be discovered within cultures, or between cultures, that would provide them with some sort of unity and pattern. Its audacity no doubt accounts for the fact that philosophers dared to tackle this question earlier than did anthropologists, the more cautious scientists of culture. It is startling to realize, for example, that the German philosopher of culture, G. W. F. Hegel, who died in 1831, still exerts influence through the two most powerful revolutionary and counter-revolutionary systems of the twentieth century, the communist and fascist; both find in his thought different but equally fundamental grounds for their respective doctrines. Within less than fifty years a number of other philosophers of culture, such as the German, Oswald Spengler, and the Englishman, Alfred Toynbee, have endeavored to organize the great cultures of all time into huge constellations. In America, three systematizers of culture may be mentioned, all of whom are contemporary: the philosopher of science, F.S.C. Northrop; the philosopher of art, Lewis Mumford; and the philosopher of society, Pitirim A. Sorokin. Other recent thinkers of first rank, both European and American, have also contributed much if sometimes in less unified fashion, to mention only John Dewey, Alfred North Whitehead, Vilfredo Pareto, Karl Mannheim, Ernst Cassirer, José Ortega y Gasset, and Benedetto Croce.

Not that anthropologists have ignored the problem of the "complex whole." During the nineteenth century, when "the science of man" was just emerging and remained intertwined with other disciplines (philosophy and sociology, especially) systematization was still more the rule than the exception. Most prominently, Auguste Comte and Herbert Spencer tried to organize culture in a series of ascending evolutionary levels from the less to the more "civilized." But the speculative and deductive nature of much of their effort, and that of their many followers, produced an understandable reaction. If anthropology were ever to become a mature science, it would have to deal not with sweeping generalizations about culture but with much more limited patternings or clusterings that might emerge from multiple, empirical data gathered firsthand and tested by carefully controlled techniques. This was the position advanced perhaps most persuasively by Émile Durkheim in France, by Radcliffe-Brown in England, and by Boas in America.

It is possible, however, that anthropology is now at the threshold of another synthesis no less important than the one earlier mentioned as likely to emerge from a synthesis of the honorific and scientific views of culture. This second synthesis would encompass both the empirical and grand-scale approaches—a difficult feat which at least one American anthropologist, Kroeber, has already attempted to accomplish. Others have paved the way through their growing interest in the question of just what it means to assert, for example, that every true culture has its "way of life," its indigenous pattern not only on the explicit level where it is consciously expressed, but on the implicit, half-conscious, emotional and perhaps mythical level as well.

Two final implications in Tylor's definition deserve a word of pre-liminary comment—the first, his use of the term "civilization" as synonymous with "culture"; the second, the term "custom." As to the first, culture-theorists are perhaps even looser in their terminology than they are in regard to the relations of society and culture. To be sure, anthropologists today largely agree with Tylor that civilization and culture mean the same thing. They do not think of "civilized" as superior to "primitive": if they use the latter term at all, they refer rather to groups outside the mainstreams of Western and Eastern culture that possess institutions, beliefs, habits, and skills different from those of the mainstreams. Indeed, because of the invidious connotation of "primitive," anthropologists now use the term less frequently than the term "nonliterate," which merely suggests that certain cultures or civilizations possess no written language. Such an objective meaning is not nearly so common, however, among historians and philosophers of culture, or even sociologists. Thus Spengler and Toynbee, although they disagree on the meaning of civilization, still agree that it marks an advanced stage in the evolution of culture. In this volume I follow Tylor and his anthropological disciples, because nothing is gained from the bias that the "civilized" are of course superior to the "primitive."

As for "custom," one of the most cogent definitions since Tylor is that of another outstanding anthropologist, Edward Sapir. It is, he says, "the totality of behavior patterns which are carried by tradition and lodged in the group, as contrasted with the more random personal activities of the individual."[3] Three elements seem to stand out in this definition: behavior patterns, tradition, and group. The first ex-presses again a gestalt quality: customs are characterized by a harmo-nious, organic interrelationship of human experience—of people functioning together in terms of common interest. The second suggests the potent influence of the past, of the social heritage, but in an active, practical sense: the tradition of Christmas, although very old, is still something we *do*. The third suggests that customs are never confined to occasional individuals, or to accidental collections of individuals; they have a quality of continuity and solidarity about them that only a community could make meaningful or vital.

This is about as far as we can go in our opening survey of that level of the environment which it is so necessary for us to comprehend if we are to comprehend, in turn, the problems of modern education that emerge from it. Any culture-theorist would rightly criticize the survey for being not only a bare skeleton of the meaning of culture, but an incomplete one. One of the most serious questions that could still be raised concerns the criteria or differentiae of culture. This too is a question difficult to meet to everyone's satisfaction —above all, the expert's—since from period to period the criteria change. In the past decade, for example, emphasis seems to have been much more upon the factor of learning than it was earlier. A few culture-theorists have insisted that the differentiating feature is the symbol—the instrument by which man is able to communicate and thereby to make such phenomena as custom possible. Most experts, however, tend to agree that no one or even two criteria sufficiently characterize culture. The majority, rather, seem to believe that several are essential—another tribute to the genius of Edward B. Tylor.

THE IMPORTANCE OF VALUES

As we return now to the persistent problems of education fed by the springs of culture, one criterion should be singled out for a moment's special attention. This is the criterion of *value*. Few culture-theorists deny any longer that responsible studies in culture must take account of guiding beliefs about the good and bad, the right and wrong, the beautiful and ugly, that always exercise tremendous power in the conduct of every human group united by custom, law, and other habits acquired by man as a member of society.

This point becomes peculiarly relevant because education too is immersed in values. This is not to say that it is always cognizant of the values it aims to teach to its charges; on the contrary, what is called above the "implicit" culture is exemplified by the often vague, haphazard way that education endeavors to incorporate them into its activities. Nor is such ineptness true merely of nonliterate cultures: if we need an example of how literate cultures seem to grope in their efforts to articulate and implement their values, we need only cite one of the most literate—America itself.

Indeed, however sharply the legion of critics of our American educational system fails to agree on many propositions, there is one on which agreement seems wide: our schools and colleges, by and large, are neither consistent nor clear about the values they are obliged presumably to instill in the young. They are not consistent because the tensions epidemic to economic, moral, religious, political, and other institutions of our time inevitably infect also our teaching or learning about values. And they are not clear because in so far as American education has tended to regard its chief business as that of conveying information and training in skills it has tended to store its values, so to speak, in the educational attic. The result is that values—those associated, say, with the Declaration of Independence or the Bill of Rights—are more often taken for granted, or at best treated with a kind of sentimental deference, than critically and constantly reinterpreted as of importance to the whole theory and practice of education in a democratic culture.

Education is always normative in character. It is always governed by norms—that is, standards—deriving their own meaning from values inherent in the life of people organized in cultures. Yet a strong case could be made for the contention that education is racked by chronic problems that have failed of solution precisely because their deeply normative character is assumed or entirely ignored. If this is so, then one of the urgent tasks confronting education, and doubtless its single most perplexing one, is to face its problems in the marketplace of values where, if anywhere, the traffic of education and of culture meet and intermingle. It is here that education most openly reveals itself to be what it has always been beneath the surface of its commonplace routines: an institution concerned first and last with helping human beings learn how to live up to the norms of a given culture.

Three great clusters of problems here converge. Each is of as wide a circumference as the culture itself. Each is a multitude of problems, so multiple that one invariably oversimplifies by reducing them to a single problem. Each of them is ancient, but likewise wholly modern. Each reaches out toward the other two, interweaving with them at a hundred points. And each, while constructed straight from the facts and events of everyday cultural experience, is also normative.

Let us group them around three familiar but provocative terms: first, *the problem of human order;* second, *the problem of human process;* and third, *the problem of human goals.* Remaining chapters are concerned both with examining their import for education as they derive from and impinge upon culture, and with pointing toward whatever solutions may be justified on the basis of that examination. Meanwhile, it is helpful to anticipate something of their significance in the preliminary fashion already attempted for the concept, culture.

CHAPTER TWO

THREE GREAT PROBLEMS OF EDUCATION·AND·CULTURE

THE PROBLEM OF HUMAN ORDER

ALTHOUGH THE problem of order is as old as humanity, and although it will always remain in one way or another a partially unsolved problem, nevertheless it looms before us today in unprecedented—no, threatening—forms.

Consider, for example, the contrast between contemporary and medieval order. In the Middle Ages, not only was the tempo slower and arrangements of living simpler; in addition, most men found themselves established from birth in so permanent a niche within so permanent a social and religious structure that whatever modicum of freedom they might still have possessed was well determined by others far in advance.

The waning of medievalism and the waxing of the modern era gradually changed this kind of order both in terms of actual experience and in terms of the philosophies that were developed to justify and to hasten the transformation. Order was still accepted. But more and more it was regarded rather as a means to the value of individual freedom than as a value in and of itself. The state, for example, was tolerated as a necessary evil—as a coercive power required by transgressors within and aggressors without—but scarcely as an institution worthy in its own right.

Now we are witnessing another shift. The negative view of the state, though still influential, is being challenged as never before in modern history. Fascist totalitarianism openly declares that, since unity and strength of the totality are the one supreme good, individual freedom must always be subordinate to or absorbed by the state. Soviet totalitarianism, while in theory repudiating the state as an ultimate good, has sought in much of its practice both to increase its power and to exact absolute devotion to its allegedly beneficent authority.

Nor is totalitarianism the only force that is fast refashioning the character and meaning of order. In the democracies, too, the traditional stress upon free individuals as independent beings is now qualified by a different stress upon corporate and public enterprise. The "welfare state" of, say, the Scandinavian countries and of the New Deal period in America; the recognition among all but the most myopic of conservatives that laissez-faire will no longer do (counterbalanced, to be sure, by puzzlement among liberals as to what will do instead); the agonizing struggle to build a United Nations in the face of bitter resistance; most pervasive of all, the gropings of countless citizens in many cultures, including our own, for some way to satisfy their half-conscious yearning to belong, to be needed and appreciated as members of a more purposeful whole than their own constricted lives have satisfied—here is ample testimony that the problem of order is severe.

Education, too, suffers from involvement in the problem. Take as one illustration an issue that at first glance may seem remote: the issue of integration. I am not thinking at the moment of the racial integration constitutionalized by the Supreme Court of the United States (although, if there is one normative principle upon which every anthropologist cited in this volume would agree, it is the principle of full integration of Negro and white children in public and private schools). I am thinking primarily of integration in the form of fresh, exciting curriculum designs. The problem is: What criteria of order can we discover, if any, that would serve to provide the young adult in general education with a sense of unity, of meaningful relationship, between himself and the world that is revealed to him through learning? Or, negatively, by what kind of integration could education succeed in liquidating the outmoded, anxiety-generating, bewildering hodgepodge of credits, courses, and requirements that still remains far more typical than atypical of the high school and college of our day?

All sorts of schemes have been concocted and several have been tried. Whether any have been proved successful is debatable: if widespread dissatisfaction with the present status of general education is any indication, certainly they have not.

In appraising these plans, in trying to decide why they seem so much less effective in practice than they had appeared to be on paper, both critics and defenders have usually neglected to look in the right place. I suggest that the search for renewed order in education is conditioned, first of all, by the search for renewed order in the culture; that just as the latter presents many marks of instability, so too does the former; and that one main reason for genuine concern among leaders of education to help the student find his bearings again is that the culture has helped him to lose them. The one question, nevertheless, that almost no leaders have pursued relentlessly is whether they can ever hope to crystallize a unifying and dynamic principle of integrated education so long as they fail, as they are failing, to construct that principle upon and from the order of culture—upon and from groups, races, nations living and working in concentric circles of relationship; upon and from the institutions that, within each culture, function on rising levels of authority and scope; upon and from the temporal and thus historical development of these relations and levels. Here is a question that we shall examine with considerable care.

Or take a different illustration: the problem of order as it underlies the curriculum of the social studies. To what extent is it defensible to teach young people to believe that all economic, political, historical, religious, and moral experience is governed by objective and inviolable law; that the past, present, and future are linked together in a sequence of events that could not possibly be otherwise; and that all the diversities and perversities that appear on the fluid surface of cultural life are, beneath that surface, carefully meshed parts of some universal whole?

This question, too, is far from academic. Behind it lies not only one of the most controversial issues in all social science—the issue, namely, of what it means to assert that human relations are bound by some sort of ordered objectivity—but also the practical issue of what attitudes young people are to develop toward the course of history, toward the power of institutions, toward the sanctions of ecclesiastic or political authority, toward the sway of tradition and custom. Are they to be taught that the true answer and the wisest attitude is one of acquiescence in, and conformity to, some and perhaps all such varieties of order? Are they to be taught, rather, that they are potentially if not always actually its controllers and creators? Or is there some different answer still—one that does not merely strike an easy compromise yet manages to harmonize the first two contrasting attitudes?

The problem of human order stretches far beyond both of our examples. But even these should be sufficient for the single point that this opening discussion wishes to drive home. The problem of order is pertinent to every type and every level of educational experience. So pertinent is it, indeed, that educators can expect no success in solving it as educators merely. For it is a major problem of the culture. Thus they must turn *to* the culture for the causes and effects, the patterns and dynamics, of order itself.

THE PROBLEM OF HUMAN PROCESS

We are concerned here, again, with a cluster of problems. The nature of the cluster begins to be revealed by synonyms or near-synonyms of process—change, development, innovation, practice—all of them acquiring renewed importance to our own generation by virtue of the breathless speed with which the world moves.

The revolutions and counterrevolutions alluded to above; the daring social and economic experiments of many countries inside as well as outside totalitarian orbits; the awesome inventions of television, planetary radio, atomic energy, transcontinental air travel; the intermingling of peoples on an unprecedented scale; the control of disease, improvement of health, lengthening of the life-span; the weakening of supernaturally sanctioned moral standards and the correlative strengthening of scientific ethics; last but by no means least important, the magnificent beginnings of a world organization of nations—such is the range of dynamic processes that typify the cultures of the planet Earth.

The problems generated by these dynamic processes are problems of life and death. As innumerable observers have pointed out, the most terrible question facing the second half of our century is whether the human genius that has created new and powerful engines of change will result in uplifting world civilization to undreamed-of heights, or whether that same genius will cause the annihilation of the larger part of mankind. We know the horror that a single atomic bomb can produce. We can imagine, then, what agony of suffering and death lies stored within the vastly more lethal hydrogen bombs being piled higher and higher in arsenals of the most powerful nations.

Nor is it only fear of physical disintegration that hovers over the planet. George Orwell in the novel *Nineteen Eighty-Four*[1] has painted a grim picture of how totalitarianism could effect an even more dreadful disintegration—that of mind and emotion, of personality and character. Here, too, scientific genius is a double-edged sword. Habits can be molded and remolded, attitudes can be conditioned and recondtioned, even sense perception can be modified and re-modified. The crucial problem is not whether science *will* do any of these things; through the press, the movies, television, it is already doing them. The problem rather is: Who is to be finally responsible for doing them at all; and for what purposes, by what sanctions, shall they govern their responsibilities? Like order, the problem of process is in this context ultimately normative.

By the same token, the problem is educational as well. Consider again the normative component that justifies or not any practice, any method, that the school facilitates. To teach young citizens to exercise their voting franchise, say, but not to teach them how to discriminate between good and bad legislation, between good and bad leadership, is to provide them with but half an education in the sphere of political process—a half, moreover, that simply permits the other half (the value pattern beneath the surface) to work its effects haphazardly, often with damage to the common welfare.

But we must question whether education is deeply concerned with process at all. To be sure, the schools at least of America are attacked for being overweighted in skills, procedures, "tricks of the trade"— for training in techniques at the expense of subject matter. The attack is partly justified. Those who are most vociferous in leading it, however, are also most likely to suggest as a solution little more than a differently dressed reversion to traditional subject matters traditionally organized. This is unfortunate. The real weakness, I suggest, lies rather in too narrow a notion of what process in education means —a notion due mainly to the failure of educators to perceive that it is also and far more basically process in the culture. To understand process in the culture is to assure the single most rewarding opportunity not only to vitalize the methodology of learning, but to provide it with the richest sort of content. Such a content derives first of all from the struggles and victories, the regressions and progressions, of real people living in the real historical and contemporary world.

What, more directly, does this mean for the schools? In general, it means innumerable adventures in learning and teaching that are now either relegated to the fringe of the conventional curriculum or totally ignored. In particular, it means examination of, for example, the difficult question of how specific cultures undergo change, of how education shares in their changes, and of whether it can share more vigorously than it has hitherto. It means inquiry into causes—whether climate shapes the nature of cultures more than any other cause, or whether economic relations do, or supernatural power, or the instinctual drives of human beings, or perhaps none of these. It means investigation of the role of personality—its limitations and its potentialities—as a creative factor in the processes of culture. Finally, it means experimental ways for schools to test out these and other pressing questions by translating them into the specifics of their own communities—communities where cultural processes are ceaselessly at work and where, if anywhere, education should be able to discover opportunities for constructive achievement in behalf of desirable goals.

THE PROBLEM OF HUMAN GOALS

To speak of *desirable* goals without either determining which goals are desirable or the criteria of desirability is to raise questions but not to give answers. One result of this dispute is a widespread opinion that no common criteria are available—that each man and each group of men are the sovereign judges of their own goals, because each man and each group must in last analysis decide which among their desires are for them the most desirable.

Nor is this sort of belief confined to those who still swear allegiance to the Western tradition of private self-interest and anarchistic self-sufficiency. Curiously, some experts in culture help also to support it. True, a favorite axiom has been that the individual's primary values are fashioned not by himself but by custom alone—by what William Graham Sumner called the folkways— a view that at first glance seems just the opposite from the traditional individualistic view. At second glance, however, it is by no means opposite. If each culture alone determines its own values, then each alone is able to judge what to condemn or to condone. Hence no universal or trans-cultural criterion of desirable goals is possible at all. Every goal is relative—whether relative to the particular human being or group, as some traditionalists believe, or relative to the particular culture, as some culture-theorists believe.

But cultural relativism, as this view is called, is not the only problem arising from human goals. Another is: What goals do and ultimately should govern a "way of life"? Shall the democracies, for example, be satisfied to answer with such timeworn generalities as "Liberty, Equality, Fraternity"? If so, shall we not then admit that these generalities, since they are often reduced to the way that any individual or group chooses to interpret them, also help to demonstrate the relativity of values? If not, however, then what other more meaningful and more inclusive goals can we discover in our culture? Or, if none can be discovered, what justification might there be for the argument of various citizens that America ought then to fashion some—to chart its course more clearly, to set its sights more sharply, in brief to seek more precise normative commitments than hitherto known.

This last question becomes all the more distressing as we observe how many other cultures now answer in a strong affirmative. Not only have the Russian and Chinese nations recently expressed their goals more concretely than we; in addition, every devotee of communism fervently believes that his goals alone will be reached in the future. Nor are the communists unique in that conviction: peoples under the sway of the Roman Catholic Church (the Spanish and Irish are excellent examples) are equally convinced—not, of course, about the inevitability or desirability of communist goals!—but nonetheless in their fierce dedication to and faith in the goals of their own outlook upon life and salvation. At least in their hostility to the relative values more typical of democratic cultures, Russia, China, Spain, and Ireland are now strikingly alike.

The fanaticism and dogmatism that often accompany socio-political totalitarianism and theocratic authoritarianism are among the principal reasons, of course, why many a "liberal" American prefers relativistic approaches to desirable goals. Thus he often pleads that no clear-cut commitment to ends or purposes should even be attempted. For him, process—especially scientific process—is the all-important thing, in fact the best of all possible goals!

But many another thoughtful American is still dissatisfied. He does not agree that our choice is between the absolute goals of a Russia or Spain on the one side, and vague, innocuous, or simply no positive goals on the other side. Rather, he is likely to contend that here is one of the most impelling issues that confront not only our own but all remaining democratic cultures. Upon its resolution may depend their capacity to build such unmitigated confidence in their own purposes and promises as to enable them to prove their superiority over all non-democratic cultures.

Meanwhile, international relations become more complicated and more dangerous by virtue of this cleavage in human goals. World War II was fought, partly at least, because people deeply disagreed over what was most precious to them—a disagreement that has continued to haunt every effort of the United Nations to reduce explosive tensions. Is, then, some kind of normative consensus among nations really impossible? The United Nation's "Declaration of Human Rights" proves that it is not—that communication and acceptance of cultural values commonly shared and commonly respected can at least be verbalized. Whether they can also be translated soon enough into international policy enforced by mutual consent is the grimmest of anxieties.

The problem of human goals may be illustrated and dramatized by freedom, a goal to which every member of the United Nations professes to subscribe. Yet, ironically, few historians would care to argue that any time in history has experienced more painful disturbance than our own over the meaning and role of freedom. There are many reasons for this disturbance, but underlying most of them is the fact that in modern centuries freedom has itself for the first time become a powerful value in the self-conscious behavior of entire cultures. The development of political and economic systems that have stressed the necessity and worth of initiative, independence, and adventure; the English, French, American, Russian, and Chinese revolutions; the slow awakening of subject peoples in India, Africa, and the Orient—these are some of the events that have contributed to the magnetizing of freedom as a goal to be cherished both for its own sake and for what it is able, in turn, to generate by way of other goals.

In modern education, too, freedom assumes a prime position. Everywhere American schools, for example, teach that here is a noble ideal, and that American democracy is its noblest political expression. In some respects the schools are justified. The birth and growth of our democracy is a thrilling chapter in man's age-old struggle to liberate himself from the shackles of slavery, of authoritarianism, of ignorance, and of superstition. The greatest democracy in all history striding across the forests and plains, the rivers and lakes, the valleys and mountains, to embrace at last a whole new continent—here, surely, is a story that cannot be told too often or too well.

But it is a story with many blemishes, and one incessantly worried by half-expressed doubts. Gunnar Myrdal, the Swedish social scientist, who a few years ago was invited to America to study the life of our Negro citizens, epitomizes the problem in the title of his famous work: *An American Dilemma*.[2] This is the dilemma created by the glaring disparity between the democratic values we teach and the experience of these values. Thus, to say that freedom is a sacred right and then to deny any citizen the right to vote, the right to a job worthy of his capabilities, the right to health, even the right to equal education is only to say that the American people are cruelly hypocritical—if not always consciously, still by the test of consequences in the experience of millions of citizens.

It is not only America, of course, that suffers from the dilemma of verbal sanction and overt conduct. The Soviet Union has one of the most democratic constitutions in the world—on paper. Yet the disparities between professed and actual freedom have been, to say the least, wide. While we may still hope for improvement in the post-Stalinist period, the fact remains that illimitable power remains vested in a tiny fraction of the vast population—that freedom is still "freedom" to comply with the mandates of the Communist Party.

Many other areas could be chosen to exemplify the conflict over freedom as a goal of modern cultures. Thus sociologists have explored the effects of our technological age upon the average individual. They have shown how he may be swallowed up by mass-production, mass-consumption, mass-living—how he tends to submerge whatever uniqueness he possesses, to strive instead for maximum conformity and likeness, even at times to appear as though personal freedom were less precious to him than a kind of anonymous security.

Nor is education immune to this standardizing process. If mass-production and mass-consumption are still unknown to the schools of rural communities, the accelerating migration to urban centers has led in recent decades to the construction of huge factory-like schools and universities where thousands upon thousands of students are herded in and out of classrooms, kept track of by number, evaluated on statistical machines. "The lonely crowd" is too prevalent a phenomenon to permit complacency with regard to the vitality of freedom for any individual, in school or out.

Finally, some educators have begun to look at the control of education, and to express doubt as to how far freedom can be meaningful in the face of unrepresentative school boards, a monopoly of middle-class values, and pressures from powerful patriotic, religious, and economic groups that aim to model American schools after their own images. In the name of "national security," the rights guaranteed to a free press and free assembly, to free religion and free speech (and thus to free education in the widest, deepest sense) have recently been more sharply curtailed both by pressure and by law than at any other period except during war. They have been curtailed, moreover, with the sanction at crucial points of our highest courts.

Our zeal to prevent the spread of one form of totalitarianism comes perilously close at times to supporting another kind and thus, ironically, to endorsing less the goal of freedom in any genuine sense and more the goal of totalitarian order itself. This is, of course, identification with a dictatorial state—a mythical whole which, by semantic legerdemain, becomes the symbol of a "higher" freedom.

That educators have not attained agreement among themselves as to either the causes or cures of disturbances such as these is an understatement. If anything, they are probably more baffled and more buffeted about by conflicting interests than they have ever been. Nor does their insecurity arise solely from confusion over language. True, an appalling amount of discussion in educational circles is handicapped by fuzzy terminology and clichés. Yet, essential as precision of meaning undoubtedly is, we may question whether this can be attained by perfecting educational semantics. The "American dilemma" once more underscores the point: almost any adult Negro (or, for that matter, any American Indian or Mexican-American) could amply enough testify that the dilemma of freedom for members of his race is scarcely confined to the symbolic level. It is, first of all, a dilemma of human *events*—of deep-grooved discrimination, of segregation, of patterns of individual as well as social inequality on the plane of action.

If, accordingly, the educator hopes to clarify any issue involving human goals—and thus the goals of students, parents, teachers, or administrators—he, too, must move beyond mere verbalizing. In fact, he must move far beyond the domain of the school. He must look to the source from which all issues of education ultimately spring—where the sorrows and frustrations, the joys and satisfactions of real human life are in ceaseless flow. He must look, in short, to the culture.

GUIDING GENERALIZATIONS

Several guiding generalizations emerge from this introduction that should be summarized before exploring the three focalizing problems.

First, the array of tasks and opportunities that confront education in our time is not due primarily *to* education. Rather they are tasks and opportunities rooted in and emerging from that tremendous sphere (within the far greater sphere of nature) that man has fashioned by his own capabilities—that is to say, from the structures, the dynamics, and the directions of the human environment itself.

Second, one of the chief reasons, if not *the* chief reason, why educators become entangled in their own web of predicaments is a failure on their part to admit the full import of the first generalization. For, if they did admit it fully (or if so many did not admit it only to forget it), they would do a great deal more about that generalization than has been their common practice. They would first of all broaden the base of their operations: they would give prolonged attention to "that complex whole which includes knowledge, belief, art, morals, law, custom, and any other capabilities and habits acquired by man as a member of society." In consequence, they would face squarely and deal forthrightly with the encompassing problems that every culture, including their own, continually generates.

Third, it follows that a rapprochement between educational theory and practice on the one side and the several interweaving disciplines embraced by the term culture-theory on the other side is of utmost urgency. Among these disciplines, anthropology is the most productive. Yet the problems of culture are too multitudinous, too interdisciplinary, to become the franchise of even so inclusive a field, and especially so in view of its own widening cooperation with several other fields. Psychology, sociology, political science, history, economics, art, religion, philosophy—not to mention their subdivisions—all contribute because all are integral to understanding and controlling the total environment created and designed by man.

Fourth, the dominant problems of culture, particularly as they are crystallized in the problems of education, are normative. That is to say, they are colored and shaped by values that synthesize into standards of what is considered desirable either by the respective culture as a whole or by an influential sector of that culture. One of the reasons for the bewilderments of modern education lies in its failure to deal consciously enough with this normative dimension.

Fifth, although the problems of education might be approached in innumerable ways, I have chosen to draw them within three comprehensive categories. These categories—human order, human process, and human goals, in that sequence—will symbolize the constellations of primary problems considered by culture-theory today.

Sixth, all three categories of problems so overlap and interfuse that we cannot consider one without in some fashion considering both of the others. The most that we can hope to accomplish is to regard each category as one way to focus upon a wider, more diffused landscape of problems. Moreover, the three are not to be ranked in order of importance. The one way in which the arrangement might be considered logical is that (only roughly and with qualification) the problem of human order is the most venerable of the three in the history of culture-theory; the problem of human process has somewhat later received comparable attention (for example, in the culture-and-personality field); while the problem of human goals is only now beginning to receive the basic analysis and interpretation that has characterized the first two problems. But all three are imperative. And all three must be solved if any one is to be solved.

Seventh, in selecting these three problems, as much will be omitted as will be included. Here one may think of the study as proceeding from the more general to the more specific. The broadest concept is symbolized by "human" (reminding us, of course, of "human nature" or "humanity"). Next broadest are the three categories of order, process, and goals. But these, too, need more specificity. Thus we shall be concerned not with all their meanings (for example, with those meanings of special interest to the sociologist, such as "society") but rather with meanings of direct concern to students of culture. But even this is not enough specificity: our most focal concern will be with education as it exists and functions as an integral part of these more inclusive symbols. Humanity, order (equally, process and goals), culture, education—this is the intensifying sequence to which we shall pay attention.

Eighth, and finally, the significance of culture for the persistent problems of education can only be demonstrated by coming to grips with the problems themselves. Even at best, we cannot expect to provide answers to all the problems raised in this chapter; they are too comprehensive and involved for any single effort, or for a hundred of them. Yet, if we are to progress toward answers, one guiding principle must be laid down: just as we can hope to understand the meaning of culture not by a few definitions or sketchy observations but only by prolonged investigation and reflection, so we can hope to understand the problems of education not by hasty generalizations or glib illustrations but by patient appraisal of the most competent theory and research on the nature of man as the only animal with culture.

PART II

THE PROBLEM OF HUMAN ORDER

CHAPTER THREE

CULTURAL ORDER—PREVIEW OF THE PROBLEM

ORDER, NO LESS than food or shelter, is a necessity of life. Even animals—schools of fish in the sea, flocks of geese in the sky, herds of elephants in the jungle—typically carry on their struggle for existence in some kind of ordered, cooperative scheme without which successful struggle itself would be impossible. Nor is order invariably problematic on the level of human existence. Not only does man normally take for granted the order of day-and-night, the seasons, and many other regularities of nature; from the earliest, simplest human relationship (that of man, woman, and offspring) to the latest and most complex (a great industry, say, or a union of nations) the phenomenon of order as manifested in culture is accepted as an indubitable fact.

It becomes problematic to man when he begins to worry about the adequacy of whatever order he happens to experience at a specific place and time. When the prehistoric family joined with other families into larger orders, we may assume it did so at least partly because isolation was more hazardous than solidarity. When forty-some nations at last come together in deliberate effort to reduce the threat of war between their sovereign selves, we may assume they do so because they begin to realize the weaknesses and dangers in merely national order.

If, then, we are to face the meaning of order hopefully, we must first perceive that like other concepts of great scope it generates not one but many problems—problems ranging all the way from the simplest kind of face-to-face relations to those embracing the entire human race. All are generated, furthermore, by a sense of dissatisfaction, of difficulty, with one or more of the kinds of order that human beings experience as members of an ordered world. Among these kinds, man has made greatest strides in understanding one: the regularities of nonhuman nature. He has even learned to tame and harness its regularities—the energies of coal, water, uranium—so that, to an astonishing degree, he is now their master. To a lesser extent he has learned to understand and manage certain human regularities. He is by no means ignorant, for example, of the nature of disease and death—psychological and social as well as physiological.

The kind of order where he has made least headway is that which emerges from all other kinds yet which, curiously, is most indigenous and in a sense most important to him—the order which is culture. Cultural order is problematic for several good reasons. Let me now offer four propositions, and ask key questions about each. Thereafter I propose to examine these propositions at some length, the first three in successive chapters of this Part, the fourth in various places but primarily in Part IV.

1. Just because it does emerge from the physical, biological, and social orders, culture shares something with each, including their own problems, at the same time that it cannot be reduced to any one of them. (What, then, is similar and what is different in culture from other orders of nature? Still more crucially, what does it mean to assert that this emergent order is *real*—that it possesses a natural, in some ways autonomous, existence comparable to, say, that of the animal kingdom?)

2. Culture is the all-embracing human order. As Tylor said, it is the "complex whole" of man's beliefs and products, of his institutions and rules. (What can we say, then, of the relations among these parts? Is it plausible to contend that they possess some kind of patterned unity—or perhaps unities? Might an answer to these questions help to solve on a scientific plane the riddle of monistic versus pluralistic order that has fascinated thinkers on a speculative plane? Might we thus be provided with a new and stronger framework for politics, economics, morality, and even education?)

3. The order of culture is dynamic; it is never static. (Is there, then, a discernible sequence of stages or levels of historical development, in this dynamic order? And if the answer is affirmative, to what extent may men anticipate the future of cultures from knowledge of their past? To what extent, too, may they thereby direct the course of history toward desirable goals such as human freedom?)

4. The problem of order is epitomized by just this goal of freedom. (If we succeed in attaining freedom, what then becomes of order? If we succeed in attaining order, what becomes of freedom? Can the two be harmonized as complementary goals? Or must any such effort lead eventually to the subordination if not emasculation of one by the other?)

In this fourth group of questions we find the crux of the problem of order as education also ought to deal with it. Not only is order here intensely normative; not only does it reveal its implicit if not always explicit affinity with process and goals; more than this it demonstrates how order is a fine example of the *polaristic* significance of culture.

To say that order is polaristic is, for one thing, to reiterate that culture can never be characterized sufficiently by any one criterion. But it is to say more: culture is best perceived as a series of polarities— that is, of contrasting yet related and complementary criteria of meaning. Each of these criteria, while separately analyzable, is finally meaningful in whatever perspective may be afforded by all others.

As an illustration, consider again the goal of freedom. Suppose that you are an architect who wishes to build a house according to your own original design—a design that pleases you esthetically as much as it does practically. Are you free to do so? Clearly not, nor could you ever be. Financing arrangements, availability of materials, construction principles, zoning as well as other laws enacted by the community for its collective benefit—all of these set limits upon your activity, and thus create the problem of how much and what kinds of freedom you are able and entitled to have. At the same time, the freedom you equally require acts as a kind of regulator upon the demands imposed by order: if complete freedom would make it impossible for you to build at all, complete order would prevent you from choosing a suitable site, fitting plans to your particular requirements, or implementing your original ideas in designing the house. The fact is, of course, that the whole history of architecture down to and including Frank Lloyd Wright is a dramatization of the polarity of freedom and order—a continuous adventure of the esthetic imagination operating within the limitations of geography, available resources, and the knowledge, laws, customs, and needs of respective cultures.

Now the same bipolar relation appears everywhere in education.

As almost everyone knows, extraordinary concern has arisen in recent years over the problem of freedom, not only over academic freedom, though concern here is keen, but in everyday events of the ordinary classroom. The impact, for example, of the pragmatic, experimentalist philosophy of Dewey and his followers upon pseudo-military discipline, forced absorption of subject matters, and similar practices of the traditional school has been prodigious. Most conspicuously in primary education, the trend has been toward self-expression for children: toward freedom to learn according to personal interest and ability, toward freedom to criticize and question, toward freedom to feel as well as to think, toward freedom to move about, toward freedom to grow. Meanwhile, numerous critics of the trend, professional as well as lay, have contended that effective learning can occur only when the young are guided and restrained by definite standards, held firmly to tasks that are rewarded when successfully performed and punished when not—in short, made to adjust to the stern realities of cultural order which sooner rather than later they must adjust to in life.

Actually, of course, the problem in modern education is no more one of freedom *or* order than it is in constructing a house. Orderless freedom, on the one hand, would guarantee in both cases to produce not so much an educated person or a finished building as a state of chaos. Just as the builder must build with regard for the habits and rules of others living in his neighborhood, so the learner must learn with respect for the habits and rules of others belonging to his school. If, on the other hand, freedomless order became the exclusive goal, education would suffer as severely as would the art of architecture. To provide abundant opportunity for the child to develop his own distinctive personality, to encourage him to express his own talents, and even to feel free to be different from other children—this value, too, is supremely precious. How to achieve dynamic polarity of both values without jeopardizing either—here, as every prudent, conscientious teacher must surely be aware, is the heart of his problem.

If, indeed, there is anything astonishing about this daily problem, it is that it embraces centuries of cultural experience. For if, as I have contended, the polaristic relations of order and freedom are most universally expressed as relations of the culture, then it becomes at least as imperative to consider the whole of culture so that we may better understand a segment like education as it is to consider such a segment so that we may better understand the whole.

I do not belabor the polarity of order and freedom. Similar polarities operate everywhere in culture. They will be found, for example, in order and process: the spatio-temporal patterns of culture shape and delimit the ways that men attempt to modify or to reconstruct them; but these ways, in turn, alter the patterns too. Process and goals are likewise polaristic: educational and other means adopted by a culture to bring about change condition the ends that emerge, but the directions and purposes preferred by any culture serve as selectors of the actions utilized to reach them.

Yet, however interdependent each category is throughout actual cultural experience, it is also separable. Just as a physiologist removes an organ and dissects it to enable him better to grasp its service to the larger organism, just as a social scientist focuses upon the minutiae of a political party that he may better perceive its workings in a nation, so one may for logically comparable reasons isolate the categories of cultural order, process, and goals. More than this, however, one may find that even these categories should be subdivided—that when order, for example, is subdivided and then analyzed further it thereby emerges as more meaningful, more integral with other categories, than it was before. The fruitfulness of this approach to the great problems of education-and-culture will, I hope, become more apparent as we move forward.

CHAPTER FOUR

CULTURAL ORDER AS REALITY

THE SUPERORGANIC CONCEPTION OF CULTURE

WHAT IS SIMILAR and what is different in culture from other orders of nature? Even more pointedly, what does it mean to say that this kind of order is "real"? This, the first specific problem contained within the over-all problem of order, is by no means as simple to answer as might at first appear. Indeed, some culture-theorists contend that less agreement and consistency prevail today than, say, a quarter-century ago. Certainly it does strike one surveying the literature from the vantage point of another field that the question continues to be controversial—a testimonial partly to an inadequately refined vocabulary, partly to impatience with theoretical foundations and a correlative preoccupation with field research and practice, but mostly to the enthusiasm and vigor of a youthful discipline.

The problem of the differentiae of culture is anticipated, though far from crystallized, by two nineteenth-century philosophers, both major contributors to the early formulations of a science of society: the Frenchman, Auguste Comte, and the Englishman, Herbert Spencer. Comte, it will be remembered, draws a huge map of social development in terms of three successive stages called the theological, metaphysical, and positive. The last of these, which mankind is only now entering, is the stage of science: here we are able for the first time to study the life of humanity as a collection of facts and events that can be understood and controlled by logical, experimental principles no less precise than those which govern chemical or physiological facts and events. Comte's philosophy of positivism, as he called it, is a brilliant system, and its influence continues to our day. But it is primarily speculative, hence unverified, and open to doubts which we need not consider here. Of most significance for our interest, he lumps culture and society together, treating them not as two spheres but as one.

Spencer, the philosopher of evolution, does likewise. His own term for the level of social life is "superorganic"—a level that includes not only human but all animal phenomena distinguished by "the co-ordinated action of many individuals."[1] To be sure, the human superorganic is more complicated than the animal, and capable of evolving ever more novel forms. Also, the whole level of human and animal society rises above both the inorganic (the physical, chemical, geological, etc.) and the organic (the biological, physiological etc.). But the superorganic is no more to be separated from these lower levels of evolution than is human social life to be separated from that of animals.

While both Comte and Spencer thus helped, as did others also, in focusing attention upon humanity as a legitimate object of scientific study, further steps remained to be taken that would clarify the meaning of culture as such. Interestingly, one of the first and certainly widely influential efforts to analyze that meaning in detail borrowed Spencer's term for its own title: "The Superorganic," an essay published by Kroeber in 1917.[2] Of course fruitful definitions had been stated well before that time—Tylor's in particular. Moreover, anthropology was already hard at work demonstrating its right to be called a science, thereby providing research data which Comte, Spencer, and other philosophers lacked for their own formulations. But Kroeber, a practising anthropologist with strong theoretical interests, went further by carefully mapping out the territory of culture as a uniquely ordered domain.

Although since the paper was published he has modified and refined his interpretations in crucial respects to which I shall later refer, nevertheless several of his arguments deserve attention. Kroeber contends that culture is a genuinely new level of nature above that of the physical, biological, psychological, and social—a level therefore reducible to the characteristics of no other level. True, culture includes certain of those characteristics within its own bailiwick. For example, its material aspects—implements of the farmer, paintings of the artist, furniture of the dweller, medicine of the doctor, and millions of other objects—are derived from the nonorganic and organic levels of metals, pigments, fibers, plants, and animals. To say, however, that all material culture stems from lower levels of nature is not at all equivalent to saying that they are therefore reducible merely to those levels. To identify the conditions necessary to produce any culture with the products thereof is, indeed, to commit one of the oldest, most common of all logical fallacies—*the fallacy of reductionism,* of trying vainly to explain a phenomenon by reducing it to the sources from which it first emerged. What, in short, is essential if we are ever to interpret culture fruitfully is to regard it as a level which, though of course emerging from all lower levels of nature, at the same time can be examined and interpreted as not only existing by itself but perpetuating, modifying, and changing itself. The supreme task of anthropology, as Kroeber might express it, is to discover and specify the distinctive forms of the superorganic level of nature.

Several principles follow from this sketch. One is that culture is basically *deterministic*—that is to say, it determines the conduct, attitudes, customs, and other typical behavior of its constituent members. Kroeber does not deny that individuals have limited choice, at least in minor matters; he confesses that he himself goes about his daily business believing in a modest degree of his own efficacy. But in larger matters, it is our culture that settles what you or I shall do, and not you or I who settle what our culture does. Granting, as he later puts it, that man is the "efficient cause" of culture in the sense that it is the immediate effect of his activity, this is a different matter from asserting that any one of us—even if a genius—either can bring into being or do away with the traditions, folkways, institutions, or rituals of culture. Only culture can do either.

Another principle that Kroeber postulates is that culture functions without the mechanisms of heredity basic to the organic level. Contrary to the old doctrine that acquired characteristics can be inherited —a doctrine still maintained by Spencer, for example—there is nothing in the genetic structure of human beings that forces them to acquire certain habits from the culture and to pass them on to their offspring through that structure. Culture, in other words, is learned (learning itself having a biological basis, obviously), so that the one sense in which heredity might be legitimately applied to culture at all is that suggested by the familiar term, "social heritage." One generation "inherits" the customs of another generation only in the respect that they are taught to the former by the latter. There is here a break between the biological and cultural import of heredity. Failure to recognize this break is one important reason for the prevalence of false notions about racial heredity. Like other anthropologists, Kroeber is insistent that the characteristics differentiating Chinese from French, or Negro from Scandinavian, are only superficially determined by biological traits. Obviously there are differences—of skin pigmentation, most conspicuously, and these are inherited. What makes any racial stock different in behavior from another, however, is not these traits in any significant way (if at all) but the surrounding culture. That Kroeber is aware of the complicated problem of racial differences is indicated in the revised edition of his *Anthropology*. But that he would continue to subscribe to the position implied in his essay is also indicated when he says, "In short, it is a difficult task to establish any race as either superior or inferior to another, but relatively easy to prove that we entertain strong prejudice in favor of our own racial superiority"[3]—a prejudice which is itself, of course, culturally determined.

The self-perpetuating character of culture (Kroeber calls it "civilization" with almost equal frequency) is also demonstrated by the role of communication. He is not ready either here or later to say that language is *the* differentia of culture, although he agrees that without this feature no culture has ever been known to exist. Nor does he deny, of course, that the ability to communicate is rooted in physiologically inherited mechanisms. He does insist that there is nothing genetically hereditary about the kind of language that is learned, or the way in which it is used. For example, it is just as easy for a newborn Caucasian infant to learn Japanese as it is for the same infant to learn English. Language is but another instance—perhaps the most important—of the remarkable capacity of the human race to guarantee continuity to its beliefs and practices.

Still another principle, better clarified by Kroeber in other writings, is the difference between culture and society. Man alone, he contends, is possessed of culture, whereas other animals also have societies. What other animals do not have is the power to transmit learned experiences, and thus to assure that those experiences transcend the lifespan of any member or any group of members. Horses do not teach other horses to be beasts of burden; this cultural practice must be taught by man to each new generation both of men and of horses. Kroeber does not deny that intimate reciprocity exists between society and culture. In fact, he expresses liking for the term "sociocultural" as a substitute for both, since society is not only a prerequisite to culture, but the latter in turn influences the character and shape of every human society. Thus, the family is a society to be found in every culture (in many animal species, too); but the *way* the family lives, whether, say, it is polygamous or monogamous, is determined by customs and beliefs.

Although further implications could be drawn from "The Superorganic," there is one other of philosophic import that deserves mention because it encompasses all the others. David Bidney, an outstanding theoretician in the field of culture-theory, puts it this way: "Here we have the first statement, so far as I know, of the doctrine of emergent evolution as applied to the history of human civilization."[4] Now emergent evolution, as every student of recent philosophy is aware, is the influential theory of Samuel Alexander, C. Lloyd Morgan, and others who view the cosmos as evolving in a series of ascending levels—space-time, life, mind, and others—each rooted in earlier levels, yet each different in kind. Kroeber effectively views culture as still another such level, one at best vaguely apprehended by emergent evolutionists. Instead of allowing it to be confused with the animal level, as Spencer does, or with the psychological level, as various philosophers and even anthropologists have done, he is convinced that to study culture as scientists must study it is to treat this level of nature as possessed of its own distinctive qualities.

How far have other leading culture-theorists subscribed to Kroeber's original interpretation of the superorganic? This is difficult to answer. Tylor himself did much to prepare the way. Other anthropologists both in Europe and America have shown strong sympathy for it. But it was the French pioneer, Durkheim, probably more than any other social scientist besides Kroeber, who succeeded in formulating in different terminology the notion of cultural reality as an independent level of nature deserving independent treatment. While Durkheim in his writings does not use the term culture, he parallels Kroeber's meaning in such phrases as "collective ways of acting or thinking" that "exist in their own right" and that have "a reality outside the individuals who, at every moment of time, conform to it." His most characteristic terms are "collective representation," which refers to modes of thought produced by culture, and "social facts," which are treated as things alone, operating always as their own motivating force. Accordingly, he holds that "the determining cause of a social fact should be sought among the social facts preceding it" and not among the elements of individual consciousness.[5]

Today in America the most vehement exponent of the superorganic in its orthodox formulation is no longer Kroeber but Leslie A. White. He more than any other American has popularized the term "culturology" to define the "science of culture." White has unbounded admiration for Durkheim's formulation, as he does for Kroeber's earlier ones. For the most part, however, he is hostile to the trend that culture-theory has taken in recent years; he is convinced that it is now rapidly yielding its autonomy to other disciplines, particularly to the vaious divisions of psychology. As Durkheim and Kroeber insisted, it is also his conviction—not, as we shall see, always consistently maintained—that culture is *sui generis*, a genuinely unique level of existence which "generates itself." Therefore it is to be understood only in terms *of* itself, not reduced to anything else such as mental or biological processes and contents. He, too, readily admits that cultural experience is grounded in lower levels of nature, but his central thesis is that they are irrelevant to an explanation of such experience.

An ardent determinist, White holds that the study of culture can hope to become scientific only by repudiating the doctrine of free will, with its religious overtones of "soul" and other mystical notions, in the same way that the physical and biological sciences have repudiated it. "Any given cultural situation," he contends, "has been determined by other cultural events. If certain cultural factors are operative, a certain result will eventuate."[6]

THE OPERATIONAL APPROACH TO CULTURE

It is tempting for a lay observer to inquire whether White is correct in his generalization that the systematic study of culture has retreated from his position. Perhaps a case could be made for the contention that such study has rather become more sophisticated, more sensitive to its own complexities, and more conscious of the need to consider (if I may borrow a phrase from Harold J. Laski) its "inarticulate major premises."

For one thing, we ought not to forget that some experts in the field of culture have been consistently critical of the Durkheim-

Kroeber type of interpretation. Boas, for example, was never willing to accept so deterministic a view of the superorganic, although his rejection of the biological basis of race differences as well as other important views was in complete accord and much more influential. In England, the anthropologist, Radcliffe-Brown, while considered a follower of Durkheim, refused to accept an unqualifiedly *sui generis* interpretation of culture. Others who have been dubious include such famous experts as Ruth Benedict, Margaret Mead, Ralph Linton, Melville Herskovits, and two previously mentioned: Malinowski and Sapir.

For another thing, a growing interest in the relations of psychology to culture-theory might be appraised in more than one perspective. On the one hand, the argument of White that this should be construed as a "regression" is impressive, though not always for his reasons. Certainly it seems reasonable to suppose that the American penchant for psychological and psychiatric interpretations of human problems is partly due to our strong normative tradition of individualism rather than always to detached canons of research. Certainly, too, such interpretations are frequently "safer": not only do they tread less often on the toes of power groups that flourish in the social-political-economic spheres of culture, but sometimes, as White says, they disturb fewer of our deepest biases about the independence of man. But, on the other hand, is it not plausible also to expect some culture-theorists, simply because of the breadth of their field, to consider afresh how culture affects and is affected by the individual person without whom, after all, there would be no culture at all? Of all fields of human experience, culture is the most inclusive. To open wider the channels of communication between anthropology and other behavioral sciences is not therefore to be construed necessarily as corruption of the field, but rather as providing new ways of achieving much greater, and much needed, integrated knowledge about man.

It is thus a fair question whether Kroeber in qualifying his earlier views has not, in fact, strengthened rather than weakened his case for the superorganic. In discussing "White's View of Culture," for example, his candor is refreshing:

I take this opportunity of formally and publicly recanting any extravagances and over-statements of which I may have been guilty through over-ardor of conviction . . . As of 1948, it seems to me both unnecessary and productive of new difficulties if, in order to account for the phenomena of culture, one assumes any entity, substance, kind of being, or set of separate, autonomous, and wholly self-sufficient forces . . . I would now say that culture was *primarily* intelligible in terms of itself, not *only* in terms of itself.[7]

This restatement no longer places culture in a realm of nature walled off, so to speak, from the human personality. What it does is to distinguish between a legitimate focusing of attention for the purpose of experimental research, and an illegitimate *hypostatization* (the latter term meaning the common fallacy of objectifying or externalizing as a substantial reality what is actually a fruitful idea or hypothesis constructed by the scientific imagination for purposes of experimenting with some segment of nature).

In recent writings, especially in his "most mature and rounded" statement of the problem, Kroeber is so insistent upon this distinction that he would probably disagree with Bidney's interpretation of the superorganic as a new evolutionary emergent. To regard it in this way tends to place it within a grand-scale philosophic system based on the cosmic reality of evolution, and requires us to think of it in more organized relation to other levels of the system than is useful. The relations are not denied, any more than evolution is denied. But what is needed if we are to have *"an adequate operational method of science"* (where hypotheses, fruitful ideas, act as tools with which to operate on the phenomena of nature) is greater concentration upon areas that can be singled out for careful analysis and interpretation.

Apparently, true progress is made when every science is autonomous in its procedures, while also realizing its relation of dependence on the subjacent ones and of support to the independent overlying ones. It is an investigation on autonomous levels that is a precondition of most extensions of our understanding of the world . . . This does not mean that a new entity is hypostatized as the unique substance of each level. Life, mind, society, and culture are not outside matter and energy, not outside space and time and free of them . . . The levels represent empirically found segmentations of the total field of nature, in each of which somewhat distinctive intellectual procedures or operations seem to be most productive. The whole recognition of levels is, in one sense, an affair of scientific methodology . . .[8]

In a later work (prepared with Clyde Kluckhohn's collaboration) Kroeber is even more straightforward:

The danger in the construal of culture as an emergent level evidently lies in the consequent tendency to reify or hypostatize culture, to view it as a distinctive substance or actual superorganism . . . To put it differently, is the value of recognition of a cultural level essentially methodological and operational, or is it misleading because it must lead to substantification and stark autonomy? . . . the recognition of levels does not necessarily have ontological [i.e., the character of an objective, substantial reality] implication, but is essentially an operational view arising within empirical scientific practice.[9]

With this unequivocal commitment to an operational approach to culture, Kroeber considers a number of positive and negative characteristics which his earlier statements seem to subordinate or ignore. Several are especially pertinent to our subsequent interpretation. One is an interesting stress upon variability and plasticity which, in turn, make it difficult to reduce culture to any exact or systematic order. A second is that culture cannot be differentiated from other levels by any "invariable elemental units" in the way that physics can with its atom or biology with its gene. A third is that culture has no laws in the sense of the natural sciences, nor are any likely to be discovered for the good reason that anthropology is not purely a natural science. A fourth is that culture is "covert" as well as "overt"—that is to say, we are by no means always conscious of the way it affects us, how it changes, what its most potent motivations may be, and many other implicit aspects. A fifth is the power of the "nonrational" in culture—its lack of consistency and efficiency, for example. A sixth is the importance of values in every cultural experience, covert or overt, consistent or inconsistent, good or bad. And a seventh, which brings us back to the issue of the autonomy of culture, is Kroeber's recognition of the problems of personality as properly included within the field—problems which, though at the microscopic end of the cultural scale, are no less encompassed by it than are the more familiar ones of race and others at the telescopic end.[10] Here, if anywhere, we may hope the polaristic relations of order and freedom will appear more and more explicitly.

THE PHILOSOPHIC CRITIQUE OF CULTURE

Meanwhile, it is important to inquire further into the wider significance of the question we have been discussing. Why should culture-theorists be so concerned as to the distinctive properties of this pervasive level of nature? And what difference does it make, after all, to a practical institution like the school?

Part of the answer to both queries lies in the preceding quotation from Kroeber. The progress of science depends upon refinement of its procedures and, simultaneously, of the materials with which it copes. That a great step forward has been made with the delineation of culture as a level of human experience not reducible to any other level is now indisputable. It is a level with which, unfortunately, most curricula—certainly below the college level—are still only meagerly concerned.

There are, however, more fundamental reasons for the significance of the question—reasons in the nature of the culture out of which culture-theory is itself emerging. Let us look for a moment at its philosophic underpinnings, the assumptions and beliefs that always lie, visibly or not, at the base of men's endeavors to understand and control their world. Bidney, who has coined the apt term "metacultural" (beyond or below our experience with, or knowledge of, culture as such) to denote these underpinnings, tries to show that all culture-theory is governed by metacultural assumptions classified under such traditional categories of philosophy as "realist," "objective idealist," and "historical materialist." By a realist is meant here one who regards culture as real in the sense of organized behavior scientifically observable and manifested through tradition and similar human experience. Boas is an important example. By idealist is meant one who holds culture to be a stream of ideas and spiritual values that also have objective existence. The sociocultural theorist, Sorokin, has been so classified. Curiously, Bidney tries to prove that Kroeber, too, is an idealist by citing early passages where the superorganic seems to be interpreted in the manner of Plato, the greatest of all idealists. The historical materialist, who is like the objective idealist at least in believing culture to be transcendent (that is to say, it stands above individuals and societies as a reality subject to its own historical principles), is perhaps most closely represented in America by White. Bidney is himself dissatisfied with any of these positions, calling himself a "humanist," itself an ambiguous term.[11]

Now the relevance of these categories is that through them we come to realize that culture-theorists are by no means as immune to the influence of philosophy as some of them would like to contend. The issue of the superorganic—whether or not it is to be interpreted as a reality *sui generis* and, if so, what kind of reality—is itself reflective of a philosophic dispute extending at least as far back as ancient Greece. This, in brief, is the dispute over the "stuff" or substance of the universe and hence of the human realm as integral to the universe. In the modern world the success of the physical sciences in reducing nature to atomic and other energies, behaving in purely mechanical ways and explainable by purely quantitative and objective methods, has challenged the youthful social sciences to attempt a demarcation of their field: they would accomplish for the study of man what chemistry, say, has accomplished for the study of matter. Here, I suggest, is the philosophic import of Durkheim's effort to single out "social facts" and "collective representations" as wholly natural phenomena. Here too, at least partly, is the underlying significance of the superorganic as Kroeber's first conceived it. That he may have regarded it in traditional idealistic rather than materialistic terms is less important than that he wanted understandably to dignify it with complete metacultural self-sufficiency—a self-sufficiency which he now feels to be an unnecessary obstacle to scientific progress but which White, as something of a historical materialist, continues to defend.

Helpful as they are, we must be careful not to credit philosophic categories with more efficacy than they deserve. To assume, as Bidney often assumes, that we have clarified the issue of the superorganic when we have discovered its protagonists to be realists or idealists, for example, is to commit what I may call the *philosophic fallacy,* a fallacy more obtusely committed by another culture-theorist (whom, incidentally, Bidney himself criticizes): Northrop, in *The Meeting of East and West.*[12] In this stimulating work, Northrop seeks to demonstrate: (a) that the source of Western civilization is to be found chiefly in its "theoretic component," that is to say, the philosophy of science developed by Newton, Locke, Hume, and other giants of modern thought; and (b) that the source of Eastern civilization is to be found chiefly in the "esthetic component," by which he means the philosophy of intuitive art developed by Confucius, Lao-Tzu, and other immortals of Oriental history. Northrop almost never considers, however, whether these two philosophic constellations, assuming he is accurate in his formulations of them, are traceable to other forces within the great cultures where they are influential, or whether they are themselves largely sufficient sources of those cultures. The weight of his argument is always placed on the latter of these alternatives; the former he leaves largely unexamined.

The philosophic fallacy, to put the point in a different way, is a species of another discussed earlier: the fallacy of reductionism. To explain cultures either in theory or practice by reducing them to philosophic categories or systems is comparable to explaining their cultures by reducing them to their biological or psychological levels. This in no sense denies, of course, that philosophy like biology is important, in fact indispensable, to our understanding of cultures. Nor does it deny that culture-theorists are enmeshed in metacultural beliefs. On the contrary, philosophies are themselves symbolizations of culture from which no one, including culture-theorists, can hope to escape even when unversed in formal terminologies. It is one thing, however to recognize the influence of philosophies in Western and Eastern cultures; it is another thing to contend that we have thereby explained the meaning or development of those cultures by tracing them to their philosophies. If we may recall a logical distinction, philosophies, however necessary, are no more the sufficient conditions of culture or even of culture-theory than they are the sufficient conditions of education or even of philosophies of education.

THE MODERN DILEMMA OF CULTURAL REALITY

We return, then, to the question once more: Why is the meaning of a superorganic level of nature so significant? Granting that we are aided by more awareness of metacultural beliefs, the answer, I suggest, lies deeper in the nature of the culture within which efforts to delineate that level have so recently and painstakingly occurred. This culture, which with Northrop we may call Western or modern civilization, is not primarily the result of a certain philosophy (for example, the "theoretic component") nor, indeed, of any other single creation of human ingenuity. Like all cultures, but even more than most, it is an exceedingly "complex whole"—an interweaving of innumerable causes and effects, of conflicts, tensions, and unresolved problems.

Among all of these factors one seems to stand out, I believe, as worthy of careful attention as a hypothesis, and only as such. Modern civilization from the Renaissance onward has been haunted by a dilemma. In repudiating absolute, supernatural faith and theocratic rule in favor of secular, scientific beliefs and practices it has been compelled to seek new types of order and authority. At the same time it has often decried the grounds upon which, hitherto, such order and authority had been built. This dilemma is perhaps most widely manifested in the political institutions of modern culture, particularly in the ceaseless conflict between democracy and alternative systems of organized power. But it is manifested also in every other phase of culture—in moral life and in economic and religious institutions. In essence, it is the quest for adequate order in the midst of a multidimensional culture reluctant to restore the simple and comfortable order of a pre-scientific age.

And yet, while reluctant, Western culture is far from emancipated from this powerful heritage. The Roman Catholic Church with its medieval pattern of theocratic power has continued not only to flourish in the democratic nations; it exerts almost total control over the political, moral, and educational life of several other nations. Fascism, too, is in many ways a medieval system—one important reason why in Spain, for example, fascist leadership is able to co-operate so smoothly with the hierarchical authority of the Church. Even more alarming is the rise and spread of communist power—a program for the re-establishment of order which, while claiming with some justification to be antithetical to both fascist and theocratic order, nonetheless contains within itself much more of the same spirit and form of hierarchical, absolute faith than its devotees are able or willing to admit.

I do not say, of course, that these extreme solutions have been typical throughout modern history. Many have been more tempered, more concerned to reconcile the absolute order of earlier centuries with the adventurous spirit of individual as well as social creativity ushered in with such revolutions as that of 1688. American democracy, for example, rests upon assumptions that are partly in the spirit of the older approach (consider the doctrine of natural rights), partly in the newer (consider the self-correcting method of majority rule and minority dissent). Much of modern science, too, has sought to combine, as in Newtonian physics, a strong presumption of cosmic order ruled over by fixed axioms of nature, with an experimental method that continually forces revision of those axioms. In economics something of the same conciliatory effort is to be found in classical theorists of the competitive system later to be called capitalism—Adam Smith is the arch-advocate—while in early political science it is revealed by such audacious thinkers as Charles Montesquieu. At the threshold of contemporary social science, Spencer in England and Sumner in America may be considered striking representatives. In both, medieval assumptions about natural and human order seem at first glance to be abandoned. Yet in both one easily detects much of the same intransigent determinism, the same encouragement to conformity with hypostatized laws and forces as one finds in the Middle Ages, reigned over as it was by the eternal authority of God and His princes of the Church and state.

Granting that it is impossible, without ignoring various links in the intricate chain of historical events, to locate the exact problem of the superorganic on this great cultural map, still we ought to try. We ought to inquire whether the effort of Durkheim, Kroeber, and others to reify or objectify culture was not in the last analysis still another of the innumerable attempts of modern science, religion, politics, and other fields to resolve the dilemma that I have described. This effort too provided us, in other words, with a neo-medieval substitute for medieval order by subtly incorporating one of the main characteristics of that order—namely, the absolute self-sufficiency of culture as a level of reality *sui generis*.

This contention may become clearer if we turn for a moment to the theory of historical materialism. The geniuses of this theory and the fathers of communist theory and practice, Karl Marx and Friedrich Engels, emerged in the nineteenth century when struggles to throw off the shackles of inherited economic, political, and religious authoritarianism were at their height. As Charles Darwin wished to emancipate the biological sciences from that inheritance, so Marx and Engels wished to emancipate the social sciences. They did not succeed for their field nearly as completely as Darwin did for his, no doubt because in theirs the hoary tradition of cultural habits and values was still more encrusted. Nevertheless, they succeeded far enough to exert an influence that continues to be stupendous. Historical materialism draws a picture of the universe within which culture is interpreted according to laws of organization, conflict, and change that possess the same objective certainty as any other phenomena of nature. The individual too must therefore be understood according to these laws; his attitudes and actions are established by them. The system is developed in detail and with many qualifications that also anticipate the operational approach to culture and man. What is pertinent to our interest here, however, is that historical materialism exemplifies more influentially than any nineteenth-century doctrine how medieval or neo-medieval attitudes and habits can be incorporated at the same time that we are asked to suppose that they have been exorcised completely. While Marx and Engels reject the supernatural postulates of medieval order, they by no means reject its hypostatic character or tone. For them culture is conceived in some ways to be as much a dynamic but still absolute order as it is for the modern idealist, Hegel, from whom they learned so much, or indeed for the greatest of all medieval thinkers, Thomas Aquinas. It is this kind of order that provides the theoretical rationale for the Soviet type of authoritarian personality. No less than for members of a theocratic culture, the laws of history are cosmically grounded and man's role is accordingly ordained by their irrevocable mandates.

It is probably impossible to know how far historical materialism in its wider cultural significance has influenced the original formulation of the superorganic. There is no evidence that Kroeber has ever subscribed to its radical political or economic correlates, or to its methodology of cultural change. References to Marx and Engels are sparse in his writings, as they are in most contemporary writings of Western culture-theorists many of whom, one would suppose, have been at least tangentially affected by such potent philosophers of culture. The significant point in any case is that Kroeber, who now holds a clearcut operational interpretation, can no longer be charged with a position even broadly similar to historical materialism—a shift which for White may be regretted but which, nevertheless, impinges directly upon the question that we are now examining.

For the difference between Kroeber's earlier and later interpretations is the difference, ultimately, between a valiant but unsuccessful effort to emancipate the superorganic from medieval influence, on the one hand, and a successful effort to complete that emancipation, on the other hand. By hypostatizing the level of culture, man thereby is provided with an absolute metacultural and determined system which, however soothing to contemplate, however satisfying to man's longing for absolute security, has the practical effect of weakening if not wholly enervating the one facility that he needs before all others to protect and to improve. This is the facility (implied if not always appreciated or admitted even by Kroeber or by other advocates of the operational philosophy of science) whereby man learns painfully but more and more successfully to examine, to test, and perhaps gradually to refashion the order of nature-and-culture through intelligent, cooperative operations upon and with that order.

Such an approach is as inherently nonauthoritarian and non-absolutistic as it is potentially democratic and humanistic. But it is an approach which the culture-theorist, like other experts both in the physical and social sciences, has by no means entirely achieved because, like them, he participates in a culture which in turn has not entirely achieved it. The search for a theory of cultural order consistent with secular and scientific beliefs, habits, and practices is still, comparatively speaking, so novel and heretical that it would be surprising indeed if culture-theorists did not reflect many of the same vacillations, gropings, trials-and-errors to be found among, say, political thinkers and practitioners.

White is an excellent case. We have seen that his plea for the superorganic *sui generis* is induced by commendable concern that "the science of culture" become a mature discipline by liberating itself from the influence of arbitrary, capricious notions of man's independence of natural and social events. Under the spell, however, of a philosophy of science only partially emancipated from medieval influence he resorts to a solution which, like historical materialism, succeeds in replacing one form of hypostatized reality by another and more modern form—a solution which thereby reflects, again, the great cultural dilemma that has been discussed.

But White, too, is occasionally troubled by the fallacy of hypostatization (the "culturalistic fallacy," to use Bidney's term; the "fallacy of misplaced concreteness," to use Whitehead's). Therefore at numerous points he introduces a crucial qualification. Take as samples the following statements:

. . . although culture traits have no existence, and hence can do nothing without the agency of human beings, we can treat them scientifically as if they had an independent existence . . . the culturologist realizes that he can explain cultural phenomena *as cultural phenomena* only when he treats them as if they had a life of their own . . . we proceed as though culture . . . had an existence of its own independently of the human species . . . one may regard culture as if it were independent of man just as the physicist may consider vehicles as if they were independent of friction, or deal with bodies as if they were actually rigid.[13]

In each of these excerpts the key phrase is, of course, "as if." White would have his cake and eat it, too. To say that culture exists *sui generis* is *not* to say that we should merely imagine hypothetically that it does so for purposes of operational interpretation. To say that it is to be treated as a hypothetical construct for purposes of such interpretation is *not* to say that it exists *sui generis*. Bidney is right, therefore, in accusing White of a glaring inconsistency—an inconsistency to which Kroeber also calls attention despite large quotas of agreement with White. What neither Bidney nor Kroeber clarifies is that this inconsistency is the product of a dilemma implicit if not explicit in almost every facet of post-Renaissance culture. In sum, it purports to recognize the illegitimacy of hypostatized order in a scientific age, yet it seeks to circumvent that illegitimacy by all sorts of ingenious if not devious maneuvers that succeed only at the price of blurred logical distinctions or downright contradictions.

THE PROBLEM OF CULTURAL REALITY: ITS EDUCATIONAL IMPORT

We are readier in this perspective to look directly at education. The issue that we have been discussing permeates in various guises the efforts of theorists to develop a satisfactory framework for modern programs of teaching and learning. It could hardly be otherwise. If politics, economics, anthropology, even the physical sciences are involved in so pervasive a cultural dilemma, then education—itself inextricable from all of these—must also be involved. Of course it would be absurd to argue that practitioners or even all theorists would perceive or interpret the issue in the same way; certainly they would disagree sharply as to its solution. This is only to say again, however, that education always sooner or later acts as a barometer of the same basic fluctuations, the same agreements and disagreements, that prevail in the wider climate of culture.

The fact is underscored by the evolution of modern education from its ecclesiastic to a more completely secular orientation—an evolution that, even now, is far from complete. Medieval schools and universities were almost completely controlled by the Church, its first purpose being to train the young in obedience to its own absolute authority and thus to the supernatural order of reality upon which that authority ostensibly rests. To be sure, in the great Aquinas we find a more flexible view of education in that he frankly admits the need to live effectively on earth as well as the need to prepare for salvation. Yet in his philosophy, too, the former is always subordinate to the latter need—at best, a means to the end of destiny.

Renaissance education, heralded by such noble pioneers as Johann Comenius, was an attempt to resist such ecclesiastic domination by preparing citizens for the task of living in and serving a culture concerned more and more with the development of industry, huge cities, and new continents. John Locke, considered by Northrop and other interpretors as perhaps the most potent of all Western theorists in his influence upon modern political and social institutions, was deeply interested in the development of schools that would train the young in practical pursuits and in obedience to the rising class of entrepreneuers. Johann Pestalozzi, Johann Herbart, and Friedrich Froebel—mighty educational thinkers of the Enlightenment—also encouraged learning experiences that would free children from the strait jackets of authoritarian schooling and help them to grow into useful citizens.

Yet ecclesiastic traditions continued to press strongly upon these emancipators and upon education in general. All of them recognized in their respective ways the need to ground education in some kind of supreme reality—in what Froebel calls the "inner law of Divine Unity," or in what Herbart refers to as the "vision of the Absolute."[14] Meanwhile, both the Roman Catholic and Protestant faiths remained vastly influential in their control of education. Virtually all early modern schools and colleges were under their jurisdiction; many remain so today. True, their curricula now endeavor to incorporate science and other secular knowledge and skills. To contend, however, that their education has thereby broken from long-accustomed attitudes and habits would be incorrect. Not only do the Roman Catholic

Church and its educational affiliates continue to dominate the lives of millions; in addition (whether in public or private, elementary or higher, Protestant, Jewish, or secular schools), medieval if sometimes cloudy premises about objective and hypostatic order continue to affect the teaching and learning of young and old alike.

These premises are not, of course, exclusively ecclesiastic in form. Though it is reasonable on historical grounds to hold that they are traceable to pre-Renaissance culture with its axiomatic belief in divinely ruled order, it is also important to remember that modern culture has attempted over and over to supplant or at any rate to modify that kind of belief. This attempt, we have seen, has been difficult—so difficult that modern politics, economics, even natural science, have by no means succeeded as fully as their advocates often wishfully suppose. Little wonder then that education, too, has not succeeded. In addition to the persistence of ecclesiastic influence, exemplified in innumerable American public schools by a great variety of practices (Bible-reading is one), a secular variety of neo-medieval order is similarly influential. Economics, still taught in at least equal numbers of schools upon classical or pseudo-classical assumptions (the "inexorable" law of supply and demand is a glaring instance), inculcates in the young a devout faith in the unalterable reality, truth, and goodness of capitalist enterprise. Physics, chemistry, and other natural sciences are widely taught in the framework of a mechanically perfect universe governed by inviolable natural law. Frequently "character education" becomes indoctrination of moral precepts which if not explicitly called divine in origin are implicitly considered to be so. And in communist societies, the supremacy of historical materialism as the official philosophy underlying all forms of education guarantees that students of every age must learn "the one, true doctrine"—a doctrine which, despite its scientific aspects, claims for itself an inviolable certainty at least as arrogant as other hypostatic orders to which it is bitterly opposed.

Thus, viewed in long range, a fair question arises as to whether modern education does not on the whole epitomize the same dilemma which, if I am right about this hypothesis, pervades modern culture itself. The growth of anti-medieval attitudes and habits toward cultural order has been retarded and sometimes blocked by the continuing fascination of pro-medieval attitudes and habits. Neither kind, by and

large, has overwhelmed the other except in places where totalitarianism, political or otherwise, is now in control. In America, particularly,
the educational pendulum continues to swing—the potent experimental philosophy and practice of Dewey and his school being, for
the moment, on the defensive before the representatives of authoritarianism in school and community alike. Whether the present trend
will long continue, or whether the pendulum will soon again swing
in the direction of that philosophy and practice is a question that
culture-theorists might help us to answer.

In the light of our sketch of education's relation to the meaning
and fact of cultural order, it is apparent that the problem of the superorganic can be regarded as an apt symbol of that relation. For, just
as the superorganic is perceived in two fundamental ways—either as
an objectified reality of culture, or as a hypothetical construct uti-
lizable for scientific diagnosis and possible prognosis—so education
may be perceived in two equally fundamental ways. It is an institution
dedicated to the transmission of that objectified reality, and hence
primarily to teaching how and why the young must learn to accept
its mandates. It is an institution also concerned not merely with transmission but even more with teaching how and why the young may
through successive generations learn to operate upon and hence to
analyze, to modify, perhaps ultimately to redesign the culture of
which they and their fellow humans are, after all, its "efficient
causes."

We have seen that throughout the modern centuries, education
has wavered between these two ways, with the former oftener
dominant, with the latter struggling for a foothold, with both ways
more frequently than not combined in piecemeal, clumsy, even inconsistent fashion. As and if a crystallized operational interpretation
of the superorganic gains a more conspicuous position among culture-
theorists, it may be hoped that not only they but educators, too, will
more clearly discern the far-reaching implications of this alternative
for every sort of institution—and certainly the school.

CHAPTER FIVE

CULTURAL ORDER AS SPATIAL

THE HORIZONTAL-VERTICAL MODEL

RECALL NOW the second great problem posed by human order. What can we say of the *relations among* the infinite parts that constitute the "complex whole" of man's beliefs and products, his practices and habits? To what extent can we then assert that a culture reveals some sort of integrated structure—that it is perhaps organized, holistic, unified, rather than simply a huge grab-bag of disparate parts?

The problem is old but also new. Old, because it is inextricable from a question that has continued to puzzle human beings since before the earliest Greek philosophers: Is the universe really a *uni*-verse, a cosmic totality? New, because only within a few short decades has any substantial group of theorists of culture seemed ready to pay concentrated, scientifically controllable attention to the precise nature of the ordered relations that they begin to detect beneath the fluctuations of cultural experience.

It is to be expected that this readiness has also been typified, however, by a great deal of uncongealed language and of disputation. To begin with, the argument that has engaged our attention in the preceding chapter continues here: the issue over whether the super-organic is a reality *sui generis* or an operational construct applies inevitably to the system of relations, if any, possessed *by* the super-organic. It is far from clear that culture-theorists always distinguish between the two meanings. We have noted that Sorokin, for example, thinks of his cultural system as an objective although essentially spiritual reality. Some anthropologists, on the other hand, prefer to speak of various "models" by which culture may be symbolized—models which, somewhat like the chemist's molecule, may not purport to *be* reality so much as they purport to serve as intellectual devices for interpreting cultural order in graphic ways for purposes of explanation and possible control. Frequently the two approaches become entangled in the formulations of a single theorist, as in the earlier views of Kroeber and the present views of White. In terms of our educational interest the operational interpretation will be regarded as the more emancipated and the more fertile, although itself in need of further elaboration and qualification.

Another source of confusion and ambiguity derives from a tendency on the part of some culture-theorists to alternate without enough discrimination between what I shall call, metaphorically, *spatial* models of cultural order, on the one hand, and *temporal* models, on the other hand. By means of the former we are enabled, as it were, to observe and interpret any culture or subculture both on a horizontal plane and through a vertical cross-section; by means of the latter we can attempt to interpret any culture as a dynamic order evolving from its earliest to its latest stages. By combining both types of models into one, we might be able to view, say, the subculture of the American South both as a horizontal-vertical structure of human relations and as a historical continuum stretching across several centuries and into the future as well.

These two types of models are, of course, another instance of the principle of polarity. Just as the subculture of the South is spatial *and* temporal, and must eventually be seen in both perspectives if it is to be understood at all, so whatever relations may be discovered for cultural order must be seen in similar perspectives. But the anatomy of that order is dissectible, too—a process begun in the last chapter where the meaning of cultural reality was considered.

This chapter considers culture primarily as spatial models of relationship; the next will consider temporal models. The final aim is, of course, to provide a spatio-temporal synthesis in a fuller, richer conception of the human order called culture.

Among numerous questions, these may be selected for elaboration: (a) What are the general characteristics of cultural order viewed in its more or less "horizontal" relations? (b) To what extent can it be said that cultural order contains a series of layers, levels, strata—that is, of more or less "vertical" relations? (c) What is meant by the expression that culture is an ordered "way of life"? And (d) what possible significance do these questions have for education?

CULTURAL ORDER AS "HORIZONTAL"

A simple way to approach the first question is to proceed from the center outward—from the narrower to wider concentric cultural relations of human order. The narrowest, in a sense, and certainly the most central of all such relations may be called the culture-trait; the broadest and most embracing may be called the culture-configuration. Between these two may be considered the culture-complex, the culture-area, and the culture-pattern, in that order.

"Narrow" and "broad" are not used here in a geographical or otherwise literally spatial sense. Rather as a model the emphasis is upon the cultural structure in terms of ever greater inclusiveness at any given time. Spatiality is an operational and even then only roughly accurate symbol; its function is to suggest the *simultaneous relations of the parts of a culture.* In all cases, too, horizontal aspects of spatial order possess certain vertical aspects, and vice versa, so that this distinction like spatiality is metaphorical more than it is literal, to be utilized strictly as a device to refine further the gross character of cultural order.

The culture-trait, one of the familiar anthropological concepts, merely denotes an object, habit, or any single phenomenon common to cultures: house cats, tables, handshakes are examples. They indicate that culture-traits are by no means necessarily universal: thus, many cultures do not practice handshaking as a form of greeting. Equally obvious is the fact that the cuture-trait cannot be isolated completely; what it means to a respective culture depends upon its relations to other traits. Even in our culture, the housecat may be considered by one group only as a pet, or by another only as a useful substitute for mousetraps. As Herskovits puts it, "The form a trait assumes at a given time will thus be determined by its context, rather than by any quality inherent in it."[1]

The culture-complex is accordingly often a more practical concept, for it emphasizes the relational quality inherent in culture-traits. In common with many recent philosophies, culture-theory now increasingly assumes that the relations of experience on any level, inanimate or animate, are as integral and real as the parts that are related. Culture-complexes are analogous to the various integrations omnipresent in organisms: just as the physiologist may concentrate upon one organ, so the anthropologist may concentrate upon a culture-complex—that is to say, an integration within the larger whole of a culture. Thus in our culture we might single out ways of engaging in economic enterprise through profit-and-loss rather than, say, barter as characterizing our economic culture-complex. The concept is especially helpful in that it enables us to account for culture-traits that, taken out of context, appear meaningless or absurd: much of our advertising, although still absurd enough, nevertheless makes sense in terms of economic behavior centering in the goal of profit-making. Every culture, however simple, possesses a variety of such culture-complexes which can nevertheless be singled out for analysis and synthesis. The American economic complex shades into the political, for example, and it is also typical of numerous other countries; yet one may properly consider its distinctive characteristics as they converge in a cluster of relations.

Kinship is also a culture-complex, and the family in turn is the most important form of kinship. Obviously, certain vertical relations also pertain—for example, in the status relations of parent and child; we shall, therefore, mention kinship again in the next section. But familiar marriage forms can equally well be included here: monogamy, marriage between just two mates; polyandry, marriage between one female and two or more males; and polygyny, marriage between one male and two or more females.

The next wider concept, the culture-area, may be defined as a region within which groups of culture-complexes co-exist and achieve some degree of integration. Various maps of the world have been drawn in terms of culture-areas—maps which, needless to say, do not at all coincide with national boundaries. Like the other relational concepts thus far considered, culture areas are not to be thought of in a rigid sense; rather, there is likely to be a good deal of overlapping and fluidity among them. Also, the similarities which seem to mark off a culture-area are much more apparent to the expert than to its average inhabitants who, as in the case of members of two hostile African tribes, may consider themselves completely different at the same time that they appear to an anthropologist to possess many culture-traits and culture-complexes in common.

The concept of culture-pattern widens the circle still further. Here, however, we find less precision in culture theory, no doubt because of the magnitude of the idea. Although most if not all would agree that it, too, is to be utilized flexibly and provisionally, no two experts seem quite prepared to approach it in the same way. For example, a culture-pattern does not necessarily encompass the whole of one or more culture-areas: it may weave back and forth among the latter and yet not include all of any single culture-area; instead, it may include only culture-complexes or aspects of such complexes that are common to several areas. Julian H. Steward prefers the term "culture type" to characterize intra- and intercultural regularities that center in "culture cores" of "recurrent constellations of basic features."[2]

Kroeber illumines the concept of pattern with several fascinating examples. One is called "Hebrew-Christian-Mohammedan monotheism," which is characterized by "a single deity of illimitable power . . . and proclaimed by a particular human vessel inspired by the deity." Another is the alphabet as a method of writing, which is to be found in a large number of cultures with different languages, yet is not utilized by, for example, the Chinese. A third is "plow agriculture," which "comprises at least three essential features: the plow itself; animals to draw it . . . and food plants" that are grown in fields. His definition of their common character is also worth quoting: "basic patterns are nexuses of culture traits [what are called "culture-complexes" above] which have assumed a definite and coherent structure, which function successfully, and which acquire major historic weight and persistence."[3] Elsewhere he refers to them as "systemic" patterns in that they have the character of a system.[4]

Kroeber does not deny that it is possible also to think of culture-patterns in terms of whole cultures, and thus perhaps as dovetailing more closely with one or more culture-areas. Indeed, as we shall find in the next chapter, he has given careful attention to them in their temporal dimension. He is appreciative, too, of Benedict's remarkable effort to pattern certain cultures according to distinctive attitudes and habits.

Let us recall one or two of Benedict's contentions as presented in the book which has probably been read by more students in education than any other work by any anthropologist: *Patterns of Culture*. Her approach to the problem is directly influenced by gestalt psychology with its emphasis upon the forms of experience in which the "whole determines its parts, not only their relation but their very nature

. . ."[5]—a viewpoint which has recently become even more influential through the "vector psychology" of Kurt Lewin and other gestaltists in their approach to social life as "fields of forces."[6] Benedict insists that "patterning of culture cannot be ignored. . . . The whole, as modern science is insisting in many fields, is not merely the sum of all its parts, but the result of a unique arrangement and interrelation of the parts that has brought about a new entity."[7] The cultures she selects to amplify this viewpoint appear to express different temperaments: one is "Dionysian" in that it is self-asserting, out-reaching, after the manner of the god of wine; a second, the "Apollonian," is calm and restrained, after the manner of the god of healing; a third tends to be "paranoid" or violent, suspicious, treacherous, and tense; while a fourth is "megalomanic," impassioned by a will to power, by obsessive rivalry. She is not so much concerned to generalize from these characterizations as to show how particular cultures can and do acquire certain patterns of integrated attitudes.

It is revealing that Benedict pays tribute to Malinowski in the theoretical development of culture-patterns. One of the most influential if also controversial anthropologists of our time, Malinowski is important to the present problem because of his famous functional theory of culture.[8] According to this theory, as Benedict puts it, we must move away from the analysis of culture-traits treated largely in isolation, and move toward the study of "motives and emotions and values that are institutionalized in . . . culture." We must "study the living culture, to know its habits of thought and the functions of its institutions, and such knowledge cannot come out of post-mortem dissections and reconstructions."[9]

The relevance of this approach is that patterning is interpreted according to the organized functions or activities through which any culture carries on its daily life. This is by implication an operational view: it does not presuppose a pattern of order and then explain cultural functions in terms of that pattern; on the contrary, it explains whatever patterns may be discerned in terms of cultural functions. Moreover, the emphasis is always upon a plurality of patterns: Benedict does not think, as some traditional superorganicists might, that there is any monistic pattern that embraces all cultures. We shall see in Part IV that she is concerned rather with appraising each culture on its own merits, and doing so in terms of the variety of human values as these are attained through the instrumentality of institutions which are themselves, much more than culture-traits, the proper units of culture. One of Malinowski's definitions of culture epitomizes this view. It is, he says, "essentially an instrumental apparatus by which man is put in a position the better to cope with the concrete specific problems that face him in his environment in the course of the satisfaction of his needs." Certain similarities of this position to pragmatism and instrumentalism should be apparent to any student of American philosophy.[10]

But functionalism is only one of several ways to clarify the concept of culture-pattern. Robert Redfield tells us that more influential, thus far, is the "causal model" which attempts, with rather dubious results, to imitate mechanistic models of natural science. (With modifications, it is reflected in historical materialism.) A third is the "logical model" which, in degree, is exemplified by the expanding circumference of spatial order that we have been considering (with the aid of Herskovits, especially), but that is perhaps better represented by such philosophers of "systematic" culture as Sorokin. A fourth, the "esthetic model," is also adapted partly by Benedict, in so far as she approaches native cultures not only psychologically but through ceremonials and rites. And a fifth is the "symbolic model" which overlaps somewhat with the others but which attempts to organize cultures more sharply by means of the universal phenomenon of symbols—esthetic, scientific, religious, and others. None of these models, Redfield believes, has been as yet too successfully applied to the welter of cultural experience.[11]

That there are still further ways of patterning cultures is apparent from Bidney's discussion of "modes of cultural integration."[12] He finds nine such modes, some similar to Redfield's, others anticipating the temporal dimension of order. We need not enumerate them, for the main point is that they reinforce Redfield's opinion: although the entire problem of cultural patterning is far from approachable by any one set of agreed-upon categories, nevertheless patterning is itself an increasingly promising way to approach cultural order.

There is one additional concept in the widening series of cultural relations to which growing numbers of culture-theorists are now paying attention: culture-configuration. This concept is the most encompassing and perhaps most elusive of all. We shall return to it after we have considered the next in our series of questions about culture as spatial order.

CULTURAL ORDER AS "VERTICAL"

To what extent can it be said that cultures consist of a series of layers that may be perceived in a "vertical" perspective? The question logically precedes that concerning culture-configurations because it is in a sense narrower, and because conceivably it may be applied to the several concepts we have thus far considered: culture-traits, culture-complexes, culture-areas, and culture-patterns. In brief, we want to know whether it is reasonable to look at any or all of these spatial orders of culture in a kind of perpendicular cross-section. The answer is that it is reasonable, but that culture-theorists are no more agreed upon the best method of doing so than they are agreed upon the best categories with which to view cultural structures in the "horizontal" perspective considered thus far.

The earliest comprehensive research in vertical order seems to have been done in the field of kinship, to which I have referred as fitting also within the model of horizontal order. Here, however, let us think of kinship in terms of lines of descent. One of the first explorers in this field was Lewis H. Morgan, an American lawyer who lived in the nineteenth century. Although experts are now critical of his views in various respects, they are unanimous in their appreciation of his pioneering efforts to classify the numerous arrangements by which various cultures systematize human relations according to kin.[13]

It may be useful to record a few of the more familiar terms in kinship study: patrilineal descent, which follows the male side of the family; matrilineal descent, indicating the female side; exogamy, the practice of permitting marriage only outside one's group; endogamy, the opposite practice of permitting marriage only inside; clan, which among American anthropologists includes everyone within the broadest boundaries of a matrilineal descent group, and gens, of a patrilineal group. The many vertical orders that result from these and other kinship practices are often complex and at extreme variance with one another. They are obviously inseparable from sexual customs that are equally at variance. Also they may either cut across one or more culture-patterns, even culture-areas, or be limited to a very few subcultures.

Kinship is by no means, of course, the only type of vertical order. The broad category, *association,* may be used to designate all forms of "social units not based on the kinship factor."[14] Both literate and nonliterate cultures possess a great variety of clubs, lodges, secret societies, and other social units which, though they often function side by side, are characterized also by strata of authority and prestige.

A more fruitful way of viewing order in descending and ascending layers is Steward's theory of "levels of sociocultural integration." By this he means that cultures are to be interpreted, not by any one set of categories of integration (a mistake he thinks many anthropologists commit in trying to transfer familiar categories of tribal societies to complex societies), but by categories appropriate to the level being considered. He is especially critical of attempts to characterize "national character" by means of concepts that apply accurately only to subcultures. A nation is not the same as a family or a folk society; it is a level above any of these, and it has its own emergently distinctive qualities. Anthropology, Steward argues, has only begun to develop instruments that can explain such features of a nation as its "form of government, legal system, economic institutions, religious organizations, educational system, law enforcement, military organization, and others." His concept of levels is not to be considered substantively, however; it is "an analytic tool in the study of changes within any particular sociocultural system, for each system consists of parts which developed at different stages and through different processes . . ." As such, it may of course be utilized in a horizontal as well as vertical way of interpreting cultural order; instead of "levels" which suggest the vertical dimension we could also think of culture in terms of widening circles of integration. In any case, the main value of Steward's concept is its usefulness in avoiding oversimplified generalizations about whole cultures and about the individual's role on their various levels—family, factory, church, government, in each of which he is a somewhat different person because the level of integration is different. In short, it "is extremely important . . . that nationally shared features of socialization be distinguished from subcultural features which may differ on both the local and family levels."[15]

Probably the most influential recent development in the theory of vertical order, however, is that of the anthropologist-sociologist W. Lloyd Warner. With a number of collaborators, he has made elaborate studies in America of a type of cultural association which he calls "social classes."

The vertical arrangement of social classes, according to Warner, is six-fold: upper-upper, lower-upper, upper-middle, lower-middle, upper-lower, and lower-lower. We see here the time-honored division into the three classes of "aristocracy, bourgeoisie, and proletariat" subdivided once for more refined and modern purposes. For example, the "upper-upper" class consists of the "old families" of "ladies and gentlemen," while the "lower-uppers" share all the opulence and emulate all the dignity of the "upper-uppers" but are too "new" to be completely accepted by the latter. In "Yankee City," a New England town, Warner found the percentages of population concentrated in the six classes from top to bottom as follows: 1.5, 1.5, 10, 28, 33, 25 (1 per cent unaccounted for). All six are organized according to the judgments of people actually living in real communities. Therefore,

. . . a social class is to be thought of as the largest group of people whose members have intimate access to one another. A class is composed of families and social cliques . . . A person is a member of that social class with which most of his participation, of this intimate kind, occurs . . . Class is present in a community when people are placed by the values of the group itself at general levels of inferiority and superiority and when the highly and lowly valued symbols are unevenly distributed among the several levels.[16]

It follows that social classes are only partly affected by economic position. Prestige and other factors of status such as church and club membership, neighborhood and education, are equally important. Also, there is limited mobility up and down the cultural ladder: a person even in the lower-lower stratum may climb upward and conceivably attain status in a class several rungs higher; the reverse process may also occur; but neither process is as common or rapid as is generally believed.

These studies of Warner, who seems to have been motivated by early discernment of the vertical orders among Australian aborigines, have produced a lively reaction, both positive and negative. On the positive side has been noted, for example, the effectiveness of a functional approach to order discussed earlier in connection with

Malinowski (although Warner was reputedly much more directly influenced by another functionalist, Radcliffe-Brown). Warner's method has been to work with specific groups and specific communities, and thus with their observable present activities rather than with the formal historical approach of traditional anthropology. Also, he has punctured a balloon that has long diverted some Americans—the naive notion that our culture as distinguished from that of Europe is unstratified, equalitarian, and hence devoid of social classes.

On the negative side, the Warner group has been criticized for several reasons. Among them are: blurring of criteria, particularly for insufficiently distinguishing between "class" and "status"; encouraging generalizations about American culture from too limited data or without regard for the historical dimension of cultural order; and a strong inclination to assume that what "is" the case about social status may also be "right"—an inclination reminiscent of the conservatism implicit in such earlier students of cultural order as Spencer and Sumner.

At this point I shall consider a single reaction, since it bears directly upon our immediate interest in vertical order—namely, the distinction between class and status. The most potent theory of classes ever developed in the modern world is without question the Marxian—a theory which seeks as integral with its all-embracing system of historical materialism to define classes primarily according to their dual economic position as the exploiters and the exploited. Marx and Engels did not deny that their two great classes may be further subdivided according to particular time and place. Nevertheless, by and large, they held that civilized history may be dramatized as a contest generated by the fact of this duality—that is to say, as a "class struggle" which varies in intensity from surreptitious antagonism to open violence. Marx and Engels were, of course, chiefly interested in the coercive relations generated by capitalism between the owners of the profit-making instruments of production and the workers dependent upon these instruments for jobs.

Outside of communist countries, most culture-theorists today consider the Marxian doctrine, though by no means altogether false, grossly over-simplified. That it is they who sometimes do the over-simplifying rather than Marx and Engels is obvious to anyone who has ever taken the trouble to examine that doctrine. At the same time, serious questions may be raised, of which two are apropos here.

First, we have noted in the preceding chapter how historical materialism perpetuates, despite protests to the contrary, a good deal of the spirit if not the substance of neomedieval absolutism by committing the fallacy of hypostatization. This fallacy is epitomized by the proposition that economic classes not only exist *sui generis* but that they act according to inviolable laws of the material world—laws that inevitably if sometimes belatedly force most human beings into one of the two hostile camps of "proletariat" and "bourgeoisie." Made over a century ago, this prediction has so far proved erroneous: particularly in the greatest of all capitalist nations—our own—the large and diffuse "middle classes" have not only maintained themselves but often held the balance of political power. At present, moreover, the middle classes are growing rather than shrinking; they even include astonishing numbers of trade unionists who buy their homes, own automobiles and costly electric appliances, send their children to college, sometimes make modest investments in the huge enterprises that employ them, and therefore become allies of the profit-making economy. Also included are a substantial percentage of owner-farmers and millions of "white-collar" people such as service employees, many professionals, and echelons of managers.

The second question with regard to the Marxian dogma, only slightly qualified by its creators, is that the cause of class structure and class conflict is economic. Culture-theorists, influenced by such careful empiricists as Boas, are leary of any such single-track theory. They do not deny that economic factors are influential but, as Chapter Eight will show further, their research convinces them not only that these factors demand precise analysis but that numerous other influences, such as those revealed by Benedict in her study of culture-patterns, deserve more consideration. Religious, esthetic, or psychological influences may in fact overshadow the economic in specific cultural situations. This pluralistic viewpoint is reflected in the Warner studies.

It is one thing, however, to expose oversimplifications in the theory of economic classes and another to reject its central contention that such classes, operationally interpreted, clarify our understanding of cultural order. Granting that the duality postulated by Marx does not seem to be crystallizing as he predicted, granting too that motivations other than economic are often powerful, one may still hypothesize that at least in some cultures, including the American, economic classes (much more analytically treated, to be sure, than Marx treated them) help significantly to fix the positions of human beings within the vertical strata of culture. True, many of us may not be aware of how crucial or powerful these classes are—in Marxian terminology, we may have developed no "class consciousness." Yet it is possible for such astute sociologists and culture-theorists as Robert S. Lynd and C. Wright Mills[18] to demonstrate that we have failed thereby to perceive our true situation—that a bank clerk with middle-stratum attitudes and ambitions, for example, may have been lured into a false assessment of his actual class position, and that his potential power and his deeper, long-range interests are in fact much closer to the wage-earning people than to those of any other class.

To put the difficulty in another way, Warner's approach may oversimplify in one direction as severely as Marxism does in a second. While Marx and Engels may underestimate the influence of status and other factors, Warner may underestimate economic classes and the power structure associated with them. By defining classes primarily according to how people on various levels evaluate one another as to status, he fails to consider clearly enough whether, by more objective and refined criteria, such evaluations might often prove deceptive. The status that certain groups cherish for themselves is by no means always synonymous with their economic class, the teaching profession being an obvious example. One problem of vertical order is therefore that of distinguishing both kinds of levels, as well as of observing the degree to which they may be juxtaposed.

That they are often juxtaposed would not be denied, of course, either by Marxian theory or by the Warner group. Particularly at the top and bottom layers one is likely to find a large degree of identification between social status and economic class. It is in the middle groups, to which Marx and Engels paid less careful attention but which have become so important in cultures such as our own, where the greatest difficulty of interpretation is likely to occur. Thus a family that is lower-upper in social status may be lower-middle in economic class—a phenomenon which the culture-theorist Thorstein Veblen has dissected with precision.[19]

Perhaps one reason that the relations of status and class deserve further investigation is that they do not appear to have been given the painstaking attention by anthropologists that has been given to those of horizontal order. Not only do Marxian ideas receive much more of the "silent treatment" than they deserve in view of their explosive impact; the writings of Veblen in America, of Mannheim and Max Weber in Europe,[20] each of whom has examined the class problem with great perspicacity, are often paid only passing notice if they are not ignored. Even Warner's work does not seem to have been assimilated fully by some of his fellow anthropologists. A fertile interdisciplinary opportunity may lie in this area, since it is one which sociologists, economists, political scientists, and social philosophers have already explored with fruitful results.

Another type of vertical order, however, has received close attention from some anthropologists—namely, that of *caste*. Many cultures erect caste systems which ordinarily are both more readily discernible and less controversial in meaning than are classes. In one of the most fascinating studies supervised by Warner (entitled *Deep South*) caste is defined, after Kroeber, as "an endogamous and hereditary subdivision of an ethnic unit occupying a position of superior or inferior rank or social esteem in comparison with other sub-divisions."[21] In the deep South, castes are of course two in number, Negro and white, within each of which may be found the several levels of "social classes" as Warner interprets them. The custom of endogamy is considered to be of special importance, although there is a good deal of surreptitious sexual practice between the two races. Also, the upper-upper level of the Negro race is not as high in status as the upper-upper level of the white race, nor is the lower-lower of the latter as low as that of the former. Nevertheless, the stratifications within each caste are quite as observable as they are in communities of only one race. The research of John Dollard tends to corroborate the Warner conclusions at numerous points, although his techniques and hypotheses are often dissimilar.[22]

The fact that studies mentioned in this discussion of vertical order are largely American should not mislead us. Kinship, status, class, and caste are more or less prevalent, more or less sharply demarcated, in all culture-areas and in all cultures, even subcultures, within these areas. The caste system, as everyone knows, has operated relentlessly for many centuries in a country like India—only very recently beginning to show signs of weakening. Classes based on economic divisions are treated in the works of Plato and Aristotle and were typical of their times, as they were throughout medieval history and continue to be in the modern world. Status levels were equally typical, and still prevail throughout the Occidental and Oriental worlds, including Soviet Russia and Communist China. That still other operational ways are available for arranging vertical orders is obvious. Interested students would benefit by examining one of the most exacting treatments of this and other problems of culture-theory: *The Foundations of Social Anthropology*, by S. F. Nadel.[23]

CULTURE-CONFIGURATIONS AS "WAYS OF LIFE"

The last form of spatial order to be considered—culture-configuration—encompasses, in one sense, all of the narrower forms of horizontal order and the vertical levels as well. It varies from these not so much in its magnitude, however, as in its qualitative inclusiveness. It is concerned, in other words, with the meaning of any culture as a "way of life"—an integration of the infinity of material and nonmaterial factors which enfuse it with a unique character and thus enable us to differentiate one culture from another in somewhat the same way that we differentiate between two personalities.

The magnitude and subtlety of the idea encourages a more varied terminology than in the case of other concepts of spatial order. Pattern is sometimes interchanged with configuration—as it is by Benedict, among others. Other terms used by culture-theorists that give us clues to the sought-for meaning are "theme," "sanction," and "ethos."

The most exciting approach to configuration that I have found appears to stem from a penetrating essay by Sapir: "The Unconscious Patterning of Behavior in Society." He argues that every culture is characterized by "deep-seated culture patterns" that "are not so much known as felt, not so much capable of conscious description as of naive practice . . ." These patterns consist "merely in a typical unawareness on the part of the individual of outlines . . . of conduct which he is all the time implicitly following." Moreover, "the relations between the elements of experience which serve to give them their form and significance are more powerfully 'felt' or 'intuited' than consciously perceived." For this reason it becomes difficult for an average person to identify himself with the beliefs and practices of cultures other than his own. What he does, rather, is to project into them his own familiar experiences. "In other words, one is always unconsciously finding what one is in unconscious subjection to."[24]

An authority on linguistics, Sapir supports his thesis by numerous examples from grammar, numbers, and music. The grammatical structures of, say, Chinese and English are extremely unlike and complicated; yet in the cultures where these languages are native they not only are ordinarily learned without any conscious awareness as to how they differ from each other in structure, but they are learned with equal ease by children of either culture. Again, economic patterns differ enormously, although again usually unconsciously.

"Thus, the acquirement of wealth is not to be lightly taken for granted as one of the basic drives of human beings . . . Many primitive societies are quite innocent of an understanding of the accumulation of wealth in our sense of the phrase."[25] The effort to universalize from Western experience is simply a case of illicitly projecting a special pattern into areas where it does not belong.

Sapir himself stresses the term pattern rather than configuration (although he mentions the latter). In Kluckhohn's development of Sapir's thesis, however, we find the two clearly distinguished. Following the semanticist, Alfred Korzybski, he speaks of $Pattern_1$ and $Pattern_2$—the former designating the conscious level of cultural structure, the latter the unconscious. $Pattern_2$ is then the type of which Sapir is speaking, and it is this that may best be called a culture-configuration:

$Pattern_1$ is a determinate relationship of various highly concrete pattern-parts. It is inevitably tied to a particular culture content . . . Of phenomena of $Pattern_2$ there is minimal *articulate* awareness on the part of the culture carriers. These are the "patterns" of the *covert* culture and, to avoid confusion, we shall call them *configurations*. Patterns are specifically oriented; *configurations* have a more generalized orientation . . . Any *cultural* conception is an abstraction . . . But the point I wish to make here is that a configuration is a conception at a much higher level of abstraction than a pattern. Likewise, inference predominates much more in the operations of deriving configurations. To a considerable extent patterns are arrived at by simple abstraction from trends toward uniformity in statement and deed . . . Configurations, on the other hand tend to be purely inferential constructs.[26]

Kluckhohn argues that it is these about which Benedict is really talking most of the time, and that her habit of intermingling Pattern$_1$ and Pattern$_2$ is one of the chief reasons why her adventurous study has generated so much diverse interpretation.

Another way of approaching this view of configuration is to say that it is concerned primarily with the *implicit* or covert culture, whereas patterns are more strictly *explicit* and overt. Being implicit, configurations are ordinarily unconscious in the sense discussed by Sapir. They constitute the deepest of all premises, the esthetic designs, the philosophic themes, the ultimate "Why's" of both nonliterate and literate cultures. Sometimes, as in a culture undergoing rapid change, a configuration suffers from strain and inconsistency both within itself and with regard to the practices that rest upon it. Yet no one, not even in an unusually articulate culture such as our own, can possibly be aware of all the premises in that configuration, or even how it exerts an effect as overpowering as in cultures that have attained much less in the way of systematic formally expressed philosophies.

To be sure, even in the latter cultures one may discover "intellectuals" and "thinkers" who have succeeded in developing "inferential constructs" that meet the definition of configuration. Paul Radin's *Primitive Man as Philosopher* contains rich evidence of their remarkable profundity.[27] But, as Kluckhohn is careful to point out in his essay, "The Philosophy of the Navaho Indians," the fact is that in addition to any articulate formulations,

. . . many distinctively Navaho doings and sayings make sense only if they are related to certain implicit convictions about the nature of human life and experience . . . These unstated assumptions are so completely taken for granted that the Navaho (like all peoples) take these views of life as an ineradicable part of human nature and find it hard to understand that normal persons could possibly conceive life in other terms.[28]

Among such implicit beliefs, with their consequences for every sort of daily behavior, are the following: the universe is orderly, tends to be personalized, and is full of dangers; evil and good are complementary, and both are present; morality is traditionalistic and specific rather than abstract; human relations are centered in interpersonal family experiences.

We are now better able to understand why the idea of culture-configuration becomes a kind of climax to the forms of order already considered. It is so pervasive that it affects not only the meaning and use of culture-traits and other varieties of horizontal order, but all varieties of vertical order as well. In America, for example, the values and habits correlated with class and status relations are probably as symptomatic of our implicit, covert culture—that is, of Pattern$_2$—as any that could be discovered. It would be as painful if not incomprehensible to, say, a lawyer of an upper-middle status to imagine himself accepting the configurations of a Navaho Indian as it would to the latter to accept the lawyer's.

We are also better able to see why the concept of configuration is apropos of culture as a "way of life." It is the long-emerging, all-embracing but elusive spirit of a people for which we are searching, and which enables us to speak of a whole culture—the French, the Japanese, the Eskimo, or the Dubuo—as possessing a certain binding quality that distinguishes it from every other at the same time that it possesses many qualities in common with others. Here we begin to anticipate not only the next chapter, where culture-configurations are considered in historical perspective, but even more the final problem of our entire study: human goals. For when cultures are viewed as "ways of life" they are necessarily viewed also in terms of their purposes, their ends, and highest values—indeed, in terms of the whole normative component of cultural order.

This is why terms like sanction and ethos become helpful. The former, because a way of life is after all a way of sanctioning or approving fundamental if unconscious attitudes and practices. The latter, because a way of life is also, as Kroeber says, the "total quality" of a culture, the "system of ideals and values that dominate the culture and so tend to control the type of behavior of its members."[29]

SPATIAL ORDER IN EDUCATION-AND-CULTURE

The three concepts of horizontal order, vertical order, and culture-configuration that we have considered as components of spatial order are also concepts important to contemporary education. They exemplify as well as any that might be selected how beneath every educational issue one may discover, if one looks, a cultural fountainhead from which flow the vital sources of that issue. I shall attempt to support this assertion by reconsidering the three concepts in turn.

1. The recognition that culture is characterized by widening circles of horizontal order is invaluable to the educator's present attention to the problem of integrated learning. One may even wonder whether it is coincidental that concern with patterns and configurations, which has developed so intensively within two decades among culture-theorists, roughly parallels among educational leaders a similar span of concern with such relatively new devices as the "core curriculum," "common learnings," interdepartmental syntheses, and other ways of combatting the traditional pigeonholing of courses and contents. These devices are symptomatic of wide dissatisfaction with curricular over-specialization and atomization.

As a matter of fact, we should be surprised if no common cultural influences pressed upon both groups. Perhaps the single most revolutionary event of our century is the accelerating interdependence of the world's cultures. This event, in turn, is due immediately to technology, and thus to incredible new means of communication and transportation—all of which combine to weaken, sometimes even to abolish, the traditional divisiveness and isolation of organized human life.

It is unnecessary to prove, however, that the causes of common interest in the problem of integration are exactly the same for educators as for culture-theorists. Surely they are not, though search for a satisfactory theory and practice of integration properly and seriously occupies the attention of both groups. And yet, any inspection of typical proposals on either lower or higher echelons of educational leadership reveals anything but agreement as to how such integration is to be effected. Survey courses, "great-books" programs, the "social-problems" approach, "general education," "life-adjustment" programs, integration through the natural sciences—these are among the current schemes that are frequently tried. None of them, however, seems to have carefully considered one of the most promising of all hypotheses, namely, that a design for general education based firmly and directly upon the kinds of order revealed by the study of culture would provide the principle of integration for which they have been searching.

I am not maintaining that culture-theorists could possibly provide ready-made formulae to implement this principle. We have seen, on the contrary, how they have failed thus far to develop even a refined terminology, much less to hammer out an acceptable conception of cultural order. Redfield's survey of half a dozen models, Bidney's numerous modes, the confusions in works like Benedict's—these are sufficient evidence of much unfinished business. Yet, amid the welter of views and concepts, certain leads do emerge that should help in the task of integrating education—leads about which one finds the beginnings of consensus among culture-theorists themselves.

One lead is the growing documentation of cross-cultural experiences. It is now more legitimate than earlier to speak of these experiences with assurance of empirical support. Culture-traits and culture-complexes can be grouped and classified, not merely within one but among many cultures. Thus, when education searches for some ground besides romantic sentiment upon which to build appreciation among young personalities of their relations with personalities in other cultures, science is able to give them impressive reinforcement. As, moreover, the student's provincialism ebbs, a more cosmopolitan outlook is likely to emerge, and with it that wider perspective upon modern life which is a central aim of general education.

And when such evidence of cross-cultural commonalties is fused into related meanings, then we have a second lead. We discover a provocative new way to satisfy the need for integrated learning—the way of patterns, *gestalten*, and "organic" wholes. Benedict's early recognition of this approach is enlightening. She reminds us that in natural science "field" hypotheses are revolutionizing older mechanistic theories. By means of them the phenomena of, say, electromagnetism are now examined in terms of interplaying forces, of constellations of energy, rather than in terms of discrete particles of matter. Similar events are at work in the relations of men so that here, too, constellations modelled in spatial or esthetic forms are better able to account for the interactions of human behavior than the older static models.

Here, I think, is an educational principle of immense potentiality. Once it is grasped, the organization of education into "discrete particles" of subject matter, and thus the whole traditional system of courses and units, becomes less and less defensible. Likewise, organismic and gestalt psychologies (the influence of which, we shall see, grows in almost inverse ratio to the decline of atomistic, stimulus-response psychologies) become much more than methodologies of learning: they provide a master principle of curriculum design.

Yet to approach the problem of integration as a "field of forces" is not enough. Were it enough, we might expect the best designs to be provided by physics and related natural sciences. Much as we may learn from the philosophy of science and necessary as all the natural sciences are to modern man, they are neither as compelling nor in fundamental ways as crucial to the majority of those for whom general education is intended as are the problems of the human being in his relations to other human beings. It is these relations, first of all, in which each one of us continues throughout life to be directly, deeply, and inescapably involved.

One way, then, to provide a pattern for integrated education is to adapt to it the spatial models of order, and to remold these models into a single great *sphere* of human-relations problems rather than to treat them either on a horizontal plane or as a vertical slice of culture. At the core of this sphere, and closest to the individual, are those problems generated by interpersonal relations—by family, sex, and all face-to-face associations. The next wider sphere is the complex of relations typified by racial, religious, class, caste, and status groups. The outermost sphere, enclosing the others, includes the relations of regions, areas, nations, systemic and whole cultures. All three spheres interpenetrate of course: problems of interpersonal relations are ultimately separable from intergroup and even international relations only for purposes of logical and critical dissection. At a time like the present, especially, the strain between nations across the globe affects almost every person at home in some direct or subtle way.[30]

In proposing that human relations, guided by culture-theory, provide the experimental framework for a reconstructed pattern of integrated education, it would be necessary, of course, to include additional aspects. Some of these will be included as we adventure further.

2. Here we return to spatial order in its vertical dimension. What do concepts of kinship descent, of class, status, and other strata suggest to education?

They suggest a good deal. Steward's concept of levels of socio-cultural integration, to take one example, provides an instrument by which education should be considered, not only as a whole, but as a cultural agency functioning on different levels in quite different ways.

Its role in the family or folk society is by no means identical with its role in such economic institutions as the labor union; certainly it is different when viewed as a national institution. To consider education as a single phenomenon without distinguishing between its respective roles on various levels is illegitimate, whether we move from simple to complex types of cultural experience (as anthropologists traditionally do) or in the opposite direction. Similarly, we can hypothesize that even the roles of formal education in different subcultures will differ markedly both among themselves and from the national culture. Thus the role of the public school in the Southern subculture of the United States is far from identical with that of the Northern subculture; it is different not only in its racial patterns but in its approach to fields such as science and religion. The concept of levels is, in short, of value to education both as a safeguard against simplified generalizations and as an instrument of scientific precision.

Problems of class and status, too, are of great value. It is to the credit of Warner and his associates that, more than most culture-theorists, they have tried to come to grips with the bearings of their work upon the public schools. Moreover, they have succeeded in generating healthy debate over their contention that education must re-analyze itself in the light of their distressing evidence that ours is a culture stratified into status levels. Out of the voluminous literature dealing with this contention, certain areas of both agreement and disagreement between the Warner group and various educational authorities emerge.

On the one side, there is wide agreement that the public school system, or at least a considerable part of it, is stratified into status levels that fairly well approximate the six levels all the way from upper-upper to lower-lower. Teachers, however, are predominantly from both sub-levels of the "middle class" (according to the Warner criteria), and they tend not only to bias their teaching in the direction of their own status values or those above them, but to reveal a bias against lower-class values. Since by far the largest group of students comes from the three lowest levels, the result is a great deal of conflict and waste in learning. William H. Burton offers a sharp summary of the situation:

The school generally attempts to impose middle class values upon huge numbers of lower class children. Problems, assignments, projects set by the school are, therefore, not at all the same problems when tackled simultaneously by upper and lower class children. The motivations are not at all alike. Many lower class children simply do not value the objectives and processes of the school, hence do not try. The school immediately dubs these children "unintelligent," "uncooperative," or "stubborn." The old class clichés may enter; the children are lazy, shiftless, irresponsible. The facts are that the school often simply does not meet their needs or ambitions, does not operate within their framework of values and motivations.[31]

Moreover, measurements of intelligence, as the anthropologist-educator Allison Davis has shown, have been geared too narrowly to the verbal facilities of middle and upper strata—another bias that works to the serious detriment of the lower strata. As a matter of fact, "in making the linguistic factor the chief basis for judging mental capacity, the test-makers have chosen one of the poorest indicators of basic differences in problem-solving capacity."[32] Finally, opportunities for lower and middle groups to move upward toward higher levels appear to be decreasing: room at the top is insufficient to accommodate great numbers of young people who, nevertheless, are encouraged by teachers and curricula to consider membership in the upper strata as synonymous with success and in the lower strata with failure.

On the other side, sharp disagreement prevails as to the adequacy and interpretation of the research thus far conducted, as to the models of vertical order employed, and as to the solutions offered for correcting the present situation. Not only do various critics question whether the educational samples taken in such communities as "Yankee City," "Jonesville," "Old City," "Elmtown," and others are sufficiently typical of the country; they also raise doubts, for example, about the degree to which the undisputed monopoly of school-board and administrative posts by upper-level citizens is consistently reflected by upper-level educational policies. And they urge additional research on such questions as the correlation between status biases of the teacher and the kinds of learning that result from them.[33]

As to constructive proposals, agreement largely ceases after two preliminary points have been made: one, that the present status structure of the schools disturbs the traditional American creed of equality of educational opportunity; two, that something should be done about the inequalities that result from that structure. Even in the field of intelligence testing, disagreements are almost violent. Meanwhile, most students both in the lower and higher learning continue to be measured largely by verbalized techniques that mitigate against lower-class capacities.

Perhaps the most widely known educational diagnosis and prognosis thus far made of the social-status problem is in *Who Shall Be Educated?* by Warner and two collaborators: Robert J. Havighurst and Martin B. Loeb. Based directly on anthropological studies of vertical order discussed earlier, the book makes the following recommendations: that the schools help young people to appreciate more clearly that there are other kinds of success than those associated with upper-level status, therefore "that it is not necessary for everyone to shoot for the top"; that there should be a program of general education open to all, based upon common democratic values and appreciation of a common cultural heritage; that vocational training and work experience be made available to all; that college preparatory requirements be tightened and generous scholarships be provided for the competent minority qualified to train for top-level positions; and that teachers "be selected from a somewhat wider range in the social scale and not bunched so much in the middle."[34]

Although some of these recommendations are commendable, dangers lurk in others. The most serious, I believe, is the implication that the inherited status structure must be accepted not only as a fact but as an irremediable fact. At moments, indeed, one senses a strong temptation in the authors to hypostatize that structure, and to consider education chiefly if not wholly a passive reflector of a fixed cultural order. Theory and practice that conceive of education as an instrument of social change are condemned with such undefined and emotionally charged terms as "propaganda" and "indoctrination."

The question is never carefully examined as to whether, granting that some kind of status system will continue to operate in American no less than in other cultures, we need necessarily acquiesce in the present one. As Foster McMurray points out in a devastating critique, an educational program that even by indirection encourages "passive adaptation to circumstance" may well produce more psychological and social maladjustment than one that deliberately encourages critical dissatisfaction and therapeutic action to improve conditions perpetuating the *status quo*.[35] Moreover, the proposal that college training be more strictly confined to the most "able" reveals an aristocratic bias that is again not only conservative but smacks of upper-stratum values. Possibly, on the contrary, sounder testing of abilities such as Davis advocates, plus more generous opportunities, would show that the majority of young people are competent to receive a type of college training suited to much wider ranges of talents and interests than present colleges provide. Such training might, in turn, radically modify the vertical order itself.

Among many further educational issues that arise from the Warner studies, a final one cannot be overlooked. This is the issue earlier touched upon as to the operational distinction between class and status, and the current tendency to blur them. It is legitimate to inquire whether educators are entitled to use the Warner definitions and criteria as uncritically as many have done.

The teacher himself is one example. His middle status, whether lower or higher, may in fact serve as a kind of drug addicting him to dreams that becloud perception of his actual position as a wage-earner rigidly restricted by the economic and political structure. Confronted by economic obstacles and opportunities more similar to than different from those of other wage-earners, teachers who have affiliated and worked with organized labor are often astonished to discover not only that their class level is different from what they had supposed, but that their status also deserves to be sharply modified in the light of that discovery.

Thus to propose that teachers experience direct cooperation with working sections of the population is to propose one antidote for the frustrations and confusions induced by conflicting loyalties and interests. It is an antidote that might persuade teachers, as no amount of preachment could persuade them, not only to recognize their actual position in the strata of vertical order, but to enter more sympathetically, more understandingly, into the lives of the majority of children who are themselves from families of wage-earners. When a work such as *Who Shall Be Educated?* fails even to mention a proposal of this kind, it is difficult to avoid the suspicion of an unconscious preference for the middle status now prized by the bulk of American teachers—a status that assuages them for their lack either of social power or of rewards commensurate with their services.

I do not, of course, suggest that clearer awareness on the part of teachers as to their class and status relations would solve all problems created by disparities in these relations. Nor would it correct them even if the teaching profession acted concertedly. Similar disparities, far more serious in terms of sheer numbers, may be discovered among students of all ages. How to construct an educational program that would gradually aim to correct the inequities and hypocrisies induced both by status *and* class stratifications (caste, too, in some areas)— here is a task which has not been discerned by most educators much less undertaken.

Are we readier to define that task? Perhaps not fully, but ready enough so that it now should be attempted. Unfortunately, it can only be attempted if it is viewed in the perspective of still other relationships—in short, in terms not merely of order but of process and goals as well.

At this point, however, our obligation is a single one—to perceive that the educational model needed for an integrated policy and program can no longer be regarded as a pattern on a single plane. Just as such a model must cut across cultural boundaries to provide the breadth of outlook and experience needed for an intercultural and international age, so it must equally encompass all levels of organized human life viewed in perpendicular cross-section. It can no more legitimately disregard or belittle the interests, abilities, and hopes of lower-status people than it can those of upper-status people. It can no more properly conceal the function and power of economic classes than it can conceal those of color or religious castes. It can no more assume in advance that the values of certain strata of the population are alone worthy of emulation than that those of certain others are unworthy. Later we shall find that educational preferences *can* be justified and goals redefined. But certainly not before such examination, not from the fact that middle-status or any other customary biases happen currently to dominate the schools. In short, our first necessity as we search for a new educational design is to make sure that we have been sufficiently inclusive, that we have safeguarded ourselves not only from a "horizontal" provincialism, as it were, but from a "vertical" provincialism as well.

3. The concept of culture-configuration which, we remember, is a helpful way of conveying the notion of a "way of life" is equally

helpful in conveying one of the most serious but elusive needs in education itself. This is the need for greater sensitivity to implicit and covert premises which, just because they do operate unconsciously, invisibly, beneath the surface of culture, likewise operate in every school and college.

To develop such sensitivity is not easy. Indeed, it is an objective no more capable of complete accomplishment than it is in the culture at large. At the same time it is one which, at least as much as any other, education cannot responsibly ignore. In our own time, men are wondering with anxiety about their "ways of life." They are questioning the meaning and consistency of the premises to which they have been accustomed. And they are asking what changes in those premises may be imperative in view of the changes taking place everywhere in cultural experience. One instance of this situation we have just met in the schisms among American beliefs and practices regarding status, class, and caste—schisms that are found to have repercussions also in education. Between cultures, too, discrepancies in "ways of life" are now so acute as to contribute markedly to the sense of strain and suspicion, to the fear of another global war, and thus again to educational perplexities. How can our own schools continue, for example, to teach the supremacy of the "American way of life"—whatever that may mean—yet at the same time expect children to develop international-mindedness, appreciation of other cultures, and genuine support of world cooperation via the United Nations?

The question then arises: (a) Since these discrepancies are on the level of implicit culture, can education do anything fundamental to alleviate them; and (b) assuming that it can, should it really try? The former half of this question was faced in the previous chapter. If one holds a *sui generis* view of the reality of culture, then one is likely also to hold that education can accomplish little except to conform with and endorse already given culture-configurations. If, however, one holds an operational view, then one may more plausibly contend that education can articulate and even act upon the problems generated by these configurations.

The latter half of the question brings us back to the essay by Sapir which opened our discussion of configurations. After delineating the meaning of "the unconscious patterning of behavior" in culture, he concludes with the following passage:

No matter where we turn in the field of social behavior, men and women do what they do, and cannot help but do, not merely because they are built thus and so, or possess such and such differences of personality . . . but very largely because they have found it easiest and aesthetically most satisfactory to pattern their conduct in accordance with more or less clearly organized forms of behavior which . . . one might almost say are as self-evidently imputed to the nature of things as the three dimensions are imputed to space. It is sometimes necessary to become conscious of the forms of social behavior in order to bring about a more serviceable adaptation to changed conditions, but I believe it can be laid down as a principle of far-reaching application that in the normal business of life it is useless and even mischievous for the individual to carry the conscious analysis of his cultural patterns around with him. That should be left to the student whose business it is to understand these patterns. A healthy unconsciousness of the forms of socialized behavior to which we are subject is as necessary to society as is the mind's ignorance, or better unawareness, of the workings of the viscera to the health of the body . . . We must learn to take joy in the larger freedom of loyalty to thousands of subtle patterns of behavior that we can never hope to understand in explicit terms . . .[36]

This is a disturbing statement to anyone who takes an operational view of culture and of education as an instrument of culture. It can be construed as an invitation to relegate efforts to examine and express the premises of any implicit culture solely to an intellectual elite. It can be construed as an invitation, also, to leave the rest of us blissfully ignorant of what our culture deeply means, and therefore insensitive to its disparities, its lags, and its obsolescences. If Sapir were merely to mean that we cannot and should not always, at every moment, be conscious of culture-configurations he would, of course, be right. Cultural like individual experience is, in Dewey's terms, immediate as well as mediate or reflective, just as it is for Henri Bergson and several other eminent philosophers of modern man. But Sapir does not mean this merely. Rather, he implies a dualistic thesis: on the one side, there are the few who alone are competent to delve into the mysterious depths of unconscious culture; on the other side, there are the many who are incompetent.

Such a position, the motivations of which might themselves reflect the implicit premises of an upper-status bias, is untenable in a democratic culture—or even in one that might become democratic. However great the task, however frequent the failures, such a culture is one that must be understood, genuinely understood, by the largest possible proportion of those who carry its burdens, who hold ultimate responsibility for its failures or successes, its ends, and its means. Hence utmost consciousness of configurational order is likewise their responsibility.

There are, I suggest, at least five steps that education must take if it is to be seriously concerned with this kind of order. The first is for the schools and colleges of each culture to enunciate as clearly and explicitly as possible their implicit premises—premises that are, of course, more or less precisely those of their respective cultures. The second is to consider wherein their resultant formulations appear outworn, inconsistent, or otherwise wanting in view of transformations occurring in the economic, moral, religious, and other spheres of life. The third is to experiment with restatements that more honestly enunciate their actual as against traditionally professed configurations, and of course to implement these restatements through integrated policies and programs. The fourth is to provide for comparative studies of the results, and by many educational agencies of many cultures. The final aim is to achieve not only a whole array of educational formulations that have profited by critical interaction, but also a unified international formulation that accepts common principles, common tasks, and common objectives for education everywhere on earth.

These five steps, difficult and huge though they may be, are not as idealistic as at first they seem. Actually, sporadic and fumbling efforts along similar lines are already under way in schools of local communities, on the state level, occasionally by national groups (the White House Conference was a beginning), and above all in the United Nations Educational, Scientific, and Cultural Organization. One trouble with many of these efforts has been, not that they have not been well-intentioned or motivated by cultural disturbances, but that they have often been superficial because of unwillingness or inability to penetrate to the covert level where the real problem of configuration lies. Moreover, there has been a failure to perceive that any effort to reformulate a unified conception of education for our age must consider it in relation to what we have called three "spatial" dimensions of culture. These dimensions (to which we shall add a fourth, the temporal, in the next chapter) are: the horizontal dimension of culture-patterns, the vertical dimension of culture-strata, and the qualitative dimension of culture-configuration which compounds the first two and permeates them with the esthetic character of a "way of life."

What we require, in short, is a design—a modern philosophy of education-and-culture sufficient both to integrate its parts and to enfuse its whole with meaning and purpose. Here educators need help not merely from culture-theorists but from others deeply concerned with culture—from various psychologists, religionists, artists, historians, and certainly philosophers. We shall rely heavily upon some of these experts as we continue our search for the meaning of cultural order.

CHAPTER SIX

CULTURAL ORDER AS TEMPORAL

TIME AND HISTORY IN CULTURE-THEORY

THE PROBLEM of cultural order must be viewed not merely in its horizontal-vertical dimensions but as a developing reality out of the past, through the present, and toward the future. The indispensability of time to any adequate theory of culture is as certain as it is to the theory of relativity in contemporary physics. One could make a case for the contention that culture is a species of what physicists sometimes call the four-dimensional continuum of nature: it always possesses width, length, depth, *and* time. None can be omitted from any full interpretation. In the technical language of some anthropologists, culture is both "synchronic" and "diachronic."

And yet, while few if any authorities would deny this assertion, unanimity by no means prevails among them as to the role that time plays. Probably even more than in their approaches to spatial order, differences are often so sharp as to dramatize again the growing, exploratory character of culture-theory itself. This is particularly true with regard to the place of history considered as the study of past cultural events. Not only do experts disagree as to how important such events are to our grasp of cultural order; they disagree also as to what history itself means and how it shall be used.

One influential group of anthropologists, for example, holds the view that the historical sources of a particular living culture may be, if not irrelevant, then nonessential to scientific efforts to understand it. This view is often associated with Malinowski. His position centers in the effort to interpret cultural experiences by the way they try to satisfy human needs. Thus, if we wish to explain such a simple culture-trait as a table fork, we shall waste our time if we search for the historical "first causes" of the fork. "Since its form, its function, and its general context . . . can be shown to be substantially the same wherever we find it, the only intelligent hypothesis . . . is that the origins of the fork are the performance of the minimum tasks which this instrument can perform." We do not, in short, explain the uses of a belief or tool by discovering its origins; we explain its origins by discovering its uses. The same rule holds with regard to so-called cultural "survivals": things, attitudes, habits survive from the past because they continue to have meaning and function in the present. "Antiquated types of automobile are never used simply because they have survived, but because people can not afford to buy a newer model." The only exception is their preservation for purposes of "retrospective sentiment."[1]

As Bidney has demonstrated, Malinowski is far from consistent in his theoretical statements. Moreover, his polemical style tends toward overstatements which sometimes, in turn, cause his interpreters to misjudge his "scientific theory of culture."[2] Herskovits, for example, exaggerates in asserting that for functionalism "time depth has no relevance."[3] Nevertheless, it does seem fair to assert that in its widest intent Malinowski's outlook is nonhistorical, and hence concerned with cultural order primarily in its "spatial" aspects. During his life he was a philosopher and scientist of culture who wished to break away from the study of culture as antedeluvian lore in order to develop a discipline concerned, first of all, with the problems of living human beings.

An interesting dispute has waged over whether Boas was also nonhistorical. He left no systematic treatise on the question. If there is any consensus at all, it would seem to be that he was by no means so in the manner of Malinowski; indeed, he engaged in considerable historical work in particular culture-areas of North America. But he did look with skepticism upon attempts to produce any grand scheme of temporal development by means of pat formulae. His own standards of research were meticulous in their respect for evidence, for detail, for conclusions cautiously restricted by warranted findings. The ultimate goal of a total history of culture is proper enough, but now premature: "We refrain," he says, "from the attempt to solve the fundamental problem of the general development of civilization until we have been able to unravel the processes that are going on under our eyes."[4] Like Malinowski, Boas inclined toward a pluralistic position, but he went further in regarding history also pluralistically: not only are there many recognizable cultures, but as many histories of those cultures.

The prodigious influence that Boas exercised results in a similar attitude among many of his disciples. The anthropologist, William Duncan Strong, summarizes the situation thus: "I can only say that the first quarter of the twentieth century in the United States saw . . . relatively little historical . . . generalization."[5] The historical-temporal pole of cultural order is not ignored, but neither is it paramount. The research of Mead is representative: her *Coming of Age in Samoa*, like her other studies of South Pacific cultures, is not primarily an attempt to trace the history of these people; rather its chief aim is to examine and interpret a specific cross-section of their way of life from direct observation of values, practices, and habits.[6]

One may inquire as to the cultural reasons for this prevalent empirical pluralism among culture-theorists. Kroeber suggests that American anthropologists (he would no doubt add American social scientists generally)

. . . belong to a nation which in virtue of recent migration has an unusually brief history of its own, prides itself on the fact, and mostly assumes that the way to surpass other nations in civilization is to develop more present energy through having shallower historical roots . . . Probably most important, however, is the current high prestige of science, which has attained fetishistic proportions in contemporary civilization, with a corresponding depression of history . . .[7]

The point impinges, I believe, upon education as well. Although history is taught in practically all American schools and colleges, it is too seldom regarded in any challenging way as the temporal dimension of the culture within which the young are immersed. Rather, it becomes for most students simply another course, separated from others and tolerated as a body of self-contained subject matters that must be absorbed for reasons concealed from the absorbers. By comparison, the sciences rank much higher; here the stress is again more on the definite rule and the precise technique than on their integrative or normative significance for our contemporary culture.

But just as education may, as proposed in the last chapter, construct new ways cf integration with the aid of "horizontal" and "vertical" models of the spatial order of culture, so it may move further in that construction with the aid of temporal order. The criticism from Kroeber implies, indeed, that not all scientists of culture are content with the subordination of the historical dimension. And philosophers of culture, understandably enough, are even less likely to be satisfied.

As a matter of fact, the recent de-emphasis of time and history is not typical of culture-theory viewed in retrospect. It would be profitable to look briefly at the record and then to turn again to contemporary interest in the problem—an interest that we shall find is as sure to be stirred by the swift cultural currents rising in the second half of our century as was the Boasian viewpoint stirred by those of the first half.

CLASSICAL EVOLUTIONISM

Like all modern fields of knowledge, culture-theory is rooted deep in the history of philosophy—that is to say, in fundamental beliefs about such age-old problems as the relations, sources, forms, and directions of life and nature. Philosophers of the West have been fascinated by culture in terms of these beliefs: Plato, Aristotle, Augustine, Vico, Diderot, Kant, Hegel, Herder, Schopenhauer, Fichte, Bradley, Royce, Dewey, Whitehead, Russell—to name the contributors is to call the roll of history's mighty thinkers. Nor is the fertility of their ideas exhausted: Kantians or neo-Kantians, for example, are still conspicuous, and all of them are concerned with the place of time in nature and culture.

I limit myself, however, to the period when culture-theory was struggling to become more strictly a systematic and scientific discipline: the second half of the nineteenth century. It was in the year 1859 that what is universally regarded as the single most explosive idea in the career of the biological sciences was proposed by Charles Darwin: evolution, or the theory of the origin and selection of organic species in the course of time by purely natural means. But the impact of the idea was by no means confined to the biological sciences. It spread to the social sciences as well, including those dealing with the development of culture.

Not that such pioneers as Tylor, Morgan, and Spencer merely transferred Darwinism to their own theories. Tylor, for example, states specifically that his own work was already well mapped out before coming into contact with either Darwin or Spencer[8]—a significant instance of a hypothesis that we shall have occasion to examine further, namely, that like ideas and inventions tend to originate in clusters within relatively narrow segments of time. What should be emphasized here, meanwhile, is that Darwinism served to reinforce the key postulate of these and other pioneers: no less than every plant or animal, culture evolves entirely by natural, orderly means.

Thus the nineteenth-century culture-theorists also challenged a central dogma of Christian theology. As Darwin found it superfluous to introduce divine creation in accounting for new biological species, so Tylor and his peers found it superfluous in accounting for new cultural species. Also, they denied that man has fallen from grace— from the original idyllic Garden of Eden; on the contrary, man's lot is slowly but steadily improving. Tylor, always cautious and qualified in his formulations, admits that some degeneration always occurs. Yet, on the whole:

> An inspection of the geographical distribution of art and knowledge among mankind, seems to give some grounds for the belief that the history of the lower races, as of the higher, is not the history of a course of degeneration . . . but of a movement which, in spite of frequent stops and relapses, has on the whole been forward; that there has been from age to age a growth of Man's power over Nature, which no degrading influences have been able permanently to check.[9]

Back of this belief is another: that "similar stages of development" —more or less *parallel and independent of one another*—occur in different cultures because everywhere human beings possess a "similarity of mind." Or, in a phrase still more familiar, there is a psychic unity of mankind. Here, then, the widespread belief in hereditary psychological differences according to race is already tacitly rejected.[10]

We have observed something of Spencer's evolutionism in his theory of the superorganic as that level of social life rising from lower levels of inanimate and animate nature. We have not observed his effort to show how cultures, too, everywhere evolve in orderly sequence from custom-ruled, through militaristically-governed, to industrially-ordered patterns of society. Tylor and Morgan also agree in general on a unilinear evolution of mankind, but their sequence is different from Spencer's. Thus Morgan posits three chief periods: savagery, barbarism, and civilization proper. They do not insist that every culture must pass through this sequence, and they are chary of attempts to establish inviolable laws of cultural development. They do usually insist that comparative investigation of the history of peoples reveals an evolutionary trend from lower to higher stages without reference to racial or biological changes in those peoples. In brief, says Bidney, ". . . the theory of cultural evolution . . . was essentially a philosophy of the culture history of mankind from prehistoric to modern times."[11]

It is hardly necessary at this juncture to examine further the qualifications, contradictions, and distinctions that pervade this theory. That there are many will be apparent to anyone who takes the trouble to examine them. The important point for our purpose is that it is easy to understand why there should have been a reaction against them by Malinowski, Boas, and other empiricists. For one thing, cultural evolutionism is much too simple—much too given to schematic generalizations on the basis of limited facts. For another thing, it tends to be melioristic, that is, to assume uncritically and often under the influence of optimistic philosophers of the Enlightenment that cultures are not only evolving but evolving in a progressive direction, from a worse to a better state—the "better" sometimes being equated ethnocentrically with modern European culture. For still another thing, and related to all these other doubts, one detects more than a little of the familiar fallacy of hypostatization in cultural evolutionism—perhaps least in Tylor's theory and most in Spencer's.

At the same time this kind of approach to temporal order cannot be dismissed. The assumption that cultures do evolve by natural and temporal processes of change and selection, even though not necessarily either progressively or in a straight line, is an assumption that few if any culture-theorists today would care to reject.[12]

CONTEMPORARY EVOLUTIONISM AND THE CULTURE-HISTORY SCHOOL

As we come to the twentieth century, it is worthwhile first to bolster the preceding statement by pointing to two or three current examples of cultural evolution as a theory of temporal order.

By far the most influential, if measured by the vast numbers who continue to be indoctrinated by it, is the incorporation of Morgan's theory in *The Origin of the Family* by Engels[13]—a classic of historical materialism. He and Marx had read Morgan's *Ancient Society*,[14] and had found in it support for their own melioristic doctrine that history is inevitably evolving from savagery, where primitive communism was practised, to civilization, where technological communism will be practised. That this is a doctrine unacceptable to non-Marxian culture-theorists goes without saying.

In America, the most vigorous exponent of an evolutionary viewpoint is White. For him, the superorganic, which is culture, moves through temporal stages reminiscent of, though not identical with, Tylor's and Morgan's. But White attempts to distinguish between the purely historical and evolutionary dimensions of culture in a way that they did not consider. Each is temporal, but whereas the historical is limited to the unique and singular event, the evolutionary also includes "forms" (in our terminology, horizontal and vertical order) and is a continuum of time *and* space, a "temporal-sequence-of-forms." For purposes of research, it is often practicable to consider culture either in time or space: thus we can study culture as a non-repetitive sequence of events, that is, as "cultural history"; or we can analyze it scientifically in such repetitive or spatial "slices" as, say, a social-status structure in the way that Warner does. Actually, however, cultural evolution for White is alway both at once; and it is only as both that we can understand it as a *sui generis* reality.[15]

The English archaeologist, V. Gordon Childe, likewise holds a theory of cultural evolution, but it appears to be less vulnerable if only because it better avoids hypostatization. For example, in his *Man Makes Himself* Childe attributes creative power to the human species in a way that his American colleague shuns for fear that we shall revert to "free will." Both scholars distinguish between while recognizing common factors in biological and cultural evolution. But Childe goes further than White in that he does not hesitate to imply what I have called the operational viewpoint:

Man's equipment and defences are external to his body; he can lay them aside and don them at will. Their use is not inherited, but learned, rather slowly, from the social group to which each individual belongs. Man's social heritage is not transmitted in the germ-cells from which he springs, but in a tradition which he begins to acquire only after he has emerged from his mother's womb. Changes in culture and tradition can be initiated, controlled, or delayed by the conscious and deliberate choice of their human authors and executors. An invention is not an accidental mutation of the germ-plasm, but a new synthesis of the accumulated experience to which the inventor is heir by tradition only.[16]

But having made this and other qualifications, Childe is prepared to defend the hypothesis that the Tylor-Morgan postulate of man's evolution from savagery through barbarism to civilization is still a fertile one substantially supported by archaeological evidence.

In sum, an evolutionary approach to the temporal order of culture is by no means obsolete, despite the weaknesses of its early proponents and the strictures of later critics. Strong properly expresses appreciation of White as well as Childe: . . . "I still welcome scholars who attempt to put interpretation and synthesis into that vast array of . . . materials so assiduously gathered by many timely, but often uninterpretative, anthropological fact-finders of the first half of the twentieth century."[17]

But this approach has received perhaps less attention in recent years than another equally concerned with time—the theory sometimes designated as the "culture-history school." No less than the evolutionary, this theory too has been severely criticized by Malinowski and by others dubious of the fruitfulness of history for anthropological research. Yet it seems reasonable to argue, as Kluckhohn does at length, that particularly one wing of the culture-history school—namely, the Austrian—has not been rightfully appreciated, certainly by American experts. At the present time its influence seems to be growing, at least in South America.[18]

What is the Austrian position? The key to it is provided by the concept, *kreise*—translated as circles, spheres, zones, cycles, and still other terms. According to its two outstanding exponents, Fritz Graebner and Father W. Schmidt (they by no means agree at all points), clusters of culture-traits radiate outward from a few simple centers or circles of culture. Thus the problem is to reconstruct cultural history by tracing out the evidence for the temporal as well as spatial connections and interminglings of these radiations. Borrowing and imitation are the most powerful psychological habits to facilitate the process, so that original and independent beliefs, arts, or inventions prove to be relatively rare. In largest part, the great cultures of the world did not develop autonomously or in parallel at all, as the evolutionists have held. Rather they are related to one another in a myriad of ways.

How are we able to demonstrate that a radiation has actually occurred? Graebner's criteria are two: the quantity of comparable traits that are found in two or more cultures, and the complexity of those traits. Consider a hypothetical case: if great numbers of people in two islands remote from one another are found to speak a similar even though not identical tongue, it seems proper to infer either that contact and borrowing must have occurred between their ancestors, or that members of one culture or the other originally migrated to an uninhabited island and established a new colony. If, in addition, both cultures have a number of the same culture-complexes—religious rituals, say—the likelihood of a radiation having occurred increases accordingly. We need not prove *why* radiation took place, or even how. The important judgment is that at some time in history it did take place.

The Austrian culture-history school strengthens and qualifies its *kreise* theory much more than I am able to suggest. For example, it does not deny that similar inventions or arts may occasionally be created and developed independently, hence without any culture contact. Also, we should remember that Schmidt and some of his followers, being Roman Catholic priests, inescapably grounded their theory in the philosophy of the Church—a philosophy which, in its ultimate postulates, is much more hostile to naturalistic, pluralistic neo-Darwinian theories of cultural evolution than most American and English interpreters (if we may judge by the brevity of their comments on this fact) seem to have appreciated. These interpreters do agree on three general points of evaluation: first, that the *kultur-kreislehre*—as it is also called—is frequently fuzzy in its conceptual formulations; second, that many of its conclusions as to the occurrence of *kreise* are less substantiated than some of its proponents claim; third, that it has made a genuine contribution by persistently hammering at the importance and complexity of plural radiations as a historical fact.[19]

I pass over another culture-history school—the English, which developed from the German—because it is now repudiated for its oversimplifications and hasty generalizations. An additional word, however, should be said regarding the importance of history in the culture-theory of Boas and his followers. While they are certainly not antihistorical, they insist upon scrupulous techniques of investigation limited to manageable areas and data. With these qualifications they are ready to recognize the legitimacy of historical reconstruction up to the point of varying degrees of probability. Indeed, Boas goes so far as to declare that it is impossible any longer to deny the great importance of history in effecting such reconstruction—an importance that will receive further attention when we consider the concept of diffusion in the next chapter.[20]

In terms of our immediate interest—that of temporal order—a few main impressions emerge from this rapid review of evolutionary and culture-historical theories. One is that the arguments between them sometimes seem forced: actually, culture properly understood is both evolutionary *and* historical; each approach is needed in order to understand the other as integral to the temporal dimension. Another impression is that the ablest exponents on both sides concede much more to the other than hasty summaries are likely to disclose: just as Schmidt, for example, admits that cultures or at least parts of cultures may develop parallel to and independently of others (as the evolutionary school likes to contend), so Tylor admits that more or less parallel and independent developments from a single fountainhead may at times be interspersed by contacts between cultures (as the *kulturkreislehre* likes to contend). A final impression is that the sometimes bewildering disputes generated by both groups may again be due in considerable part to the still youthful spirit of culture-theory itself —a spirit that has been too excited by the fertility of the field to consider with patience either the common denominators of a mature temporal outlook, or its philosophic underpinnings.

CULTURAL ORDER AS HISTORY-AND-SCIENCE

There is already evidence of exceptions to this youthful exuberance, however. A close rapprochement between scientists, philosophers, and historians of culture is much nearer than it was in the first decades of our century. The demand for more and better theory among experts in culture is heard with increasing persistence. And in one anthropologist—Kroeber—an amalgam of science, philosophy, and history is already profoundly attained.

His philosophy of history as integral to his theory of culture may be considered in two parts—his formal conception of historical knowledge and his substantive application of that conception to the development of historically known civilizations. I reserve the second part for a later section.

In articles[21] in which he struggles with increasing precision to clarify his problem, Kroeber argues the thesis that history and science are two different but interrelated ways of knowing culture. Much of the theoretical confusion that has arisen over the historical approach has been due to failure to recognize this truth. Science, he contends, is primarily a method of reducing any kind of phenomena to quantitative and generalized processes and laws "not attached to particular time or place."[22] Physics and chemistry are the most mature examples. History, on the other hand, is primarily a method of harmonizing phenomena into forms or patterns so as to include their particularities in all their qualitative richness. It has been a grave error, however, to assume that the two methods have nothing in common. Just as paleantology, geology, and astronomy are historical (they study such problems as the age of organisms, the earth, and stars), so anthropology is scientific (physical anthropology measures anatomical racial structures, for example).

One is reminded of a sliding-scale—the natural sciences and especially physics tending to be least historical, the social sciences and especially anthropology tending to be most so, but each group always in degree being both. Kroeber does not, of course, deny that the study of culture must be scientifically conducted, or that eventually a genuine science of culture may develop with the aid of such tools as statistics. Even so, he believes that the historical approach aided by scientific method is now the more fruitful, and that many of the difficulties in anthropological research have been due to too rigid imitation of the exact sciences. Thus the effort of classical evolutionists of culture, such as Morgan, was doomed to failure because it tried to reduce cultural history to scientific laws comparable to those of biology.

One of Kroeber's many insights is that it is not the temporal dimension which demarcates cultural history but rather the fact that phenomena are described in terms of their integration—that is, relationally or in context. Instead of dissolving phenomena into abstractions of process, as in chemistry, "the historical approach preserves its phenomena, on whatever level it happens to be operating" (on the level of fossil remains, say, or on the level of artifact remains) and puts "each preserved phenomenon into a relation of ever-widening context with the phenomenal cosmos."[23] Problems of causality, so basic to the exact sciences, are not paramount to such historical interpretation. Time is always implicit in every event of history, certainly, but often it is impossible, even unimportant, to know what the temporal sequence happened to be in dealing with the effects of a given historical stratum or period. In such a case, and here is the significant point, one may depict a "cross-sectional moment"— that is, one may delineate "more clearly the significant structural relations of his phenomena by now and then abstracting from their time relations."[24]

Although it would be rewarding if he would develop further his theory of culture as history-and-science, I venture to infer two or three corollaries only partially treated by Kroeber himself. The first is the implication of an operational viewpoint toward history as well as toward science. Kroeber's original conception of the superorganic, we remember, has been redefined in operational terms—that is, as a fruitful construct that operates by analyzing, interpreting, and controlling phenomena on the emergent level of nature symbolized as "culture." Once this position is taken, as against a purely *sui generis* position, it is plausible to approach cultural history in the same way— that is, to operate upon past cultures by reconstructing them either sequentially in which spatial factors are subordinated, or in "cross-sectional moments" in which temporal factors are subordinated, or with due regard for both.[25] Such reconstructions are, of course, only *probably* true; they cannot possess the certainty of findings in the exact sciences because, for one thing, they deal with phenomena no longer directly observable. But here again, the difference is one of degree rather than of kind. In both domains, whether of physical or of cultural nature, we always reconstruct in the sense that we build richer and more adequate meanings as we operate upon them. It is unnecessary to keep the two domains separate so long as we regard science and history on a sliding-scale.

A second implication is the synthesis achieved by Kroeber between what were called spatial patterns and configurations of cultural order in the preceding chapter and historical reconstructions in this chapter. We find here, indeed, another rich example of the polaristic relations of cultural concepts: what was earlier defined as order in spatial terms was only a partial definition, for it lacked the historical component. For Kroeber this component, let us reiterate, is not determined by spatial relations alone, nor merely by temporal, nor even by both together, but by the forms, styles, and patterns of culture which enfold *both* space and time within them. These forms are the reconstructions of cultural history. Each one "attains the most harmonious fit possible of all its parts . . . it aims to preserve as much as possible of the complexity of individual events, which vary endlessly, while also constructing them into a design which possesses a certain coherence of meaning."²⁶

The third and last implication is the most comprehensive. Kroeber, I believe, has gone further than anyone else in developing the outlines of what might be called a gestalt philosophy of cultural order. It is the nearest approximation of the statement by the historian, Eduard Meyer, whom Kroeber himself quotes as saying that anthropology, properly understood, is "the study of the general . . . forms of human life and human development—often miscalled the philosophy of history."²⁷ I am not clear as to why Meyer says "miscalled," unless he is thinking of speculative systems of history such as Hegel's. But philosophies of history are now emerging that are not of this character: these utilize scientific method, they respect the evidence of science, but they also recognize the relations of science to other phases of nature and life. Anthropology when classified as science is likewise miscalled for, as Kroeber has shown, science (at least when traditionally defined as a quantitative, abstract methodology) is not sufficient to understand or interpret cultures. Yet as integral to a gestalt philosophy of culture, science emerges as a major partner of the larger operating whole.

To what extent is this theory congenial to other culture-theorists? An often cited article by Boas, "History and Science in Anthropology: A Reply"²⁸ reveals strong disagreement but also, as Kroeber points out, a remarkable lack of comprehension of the intended meaning. This is no doubt traceable to the premises from which Boas worked: for him, history must be used primarily to locate specific temporal processes, not to reconstruct cultural styles or patterns. It is to be expected that White also would take issue with Kroeber's view since, we have seen, history for White is entirely concerned with the unique and discrete rather than with reconstructed forms. Extreme functionalists, meanwhile, would simply deny the primary importance of history to cultural research. Indeed, it seems to be unfortunately true that, in largest part, Kroeber's refreshing theory has as yet been assimilated by few culture-theorists of any school. One Englishman,

E. E. Evans-Pritchard, has shown as much sympathy for it as any American—if anything, he has gone much further than Kroeber by repudiating the notion that cultural anthropology is essentially a science at all, and by regarding it primarily as the theory and practice of history.[29]

Bidney is perhaps as close to Kroeber's position as any American theorist who has examined it with care, although his interpretation is marred by the habit already mentioned of sticking philosophic labels upon authorities who, in broader context, may not always deserve them. To say, for example, that Kroeber in earlier years may have been influenced by neo-Kantian philosophers in their separation of science from history, and that he tended therefore to assume an idealistic position, is possibly correct. But it is hardly correct to attach any such interpretation to Kroeber's later formulations or to his present operational approach. Such an approach toward history, science, and culture is no more "idealistic" than it is "realistic"; it considers both philosophic symbols to be largely outworn. Of course, it recognizes the constructive role of intellectual constructs (that is, of hypotheses or creative ideas) but equally it recognizes the physical, biological, and human environment (that is, the real, objective world) upon which these constructs operate in order to build clearer meanings about and closer relations with that environment.

And this is the point of view which, at least part of the time, Bidney himself seems to support. Thus his definition of history as "our human description and interpretation of any natural process or sequence of events in the context of space and time . . ." and comprising "a study of both patterns, or forms, and processes"[30] is essentially in accord with Kroeber's conception. Bidney has, if anything, sharpened that conception by calling emphatic attention to the temporal factor always present in history—a factor which Kroeber, because he does not consider it the earmark of history in cultural interpretation, sometimes suppresses more than he may intend. But with this helpful addendum, the two views are more similar than not.

Steward also seems to be close to Kroeber in various respects. While he has less fully developed his own theory, and while his terminology is different, Steward is as unequivocally operational as he is completely inductive and empirical. The over-all term he prefers for his theory is "multilinear evolution," which he contrasts with the "unilinear evolution" of the Tylor tradition and the "universal evolution" of White and Childe. With Kroeber he seeks for recurrent forms and patterns in culture, but he rejects "world-embracing schemes and universal laws." His contention that one may discover both functional relationships in culture (suggesting Kroeber's "cross-sectional moments") and sequential or developmental relationships that are therefore historical is also Kroeberian, although there is less concern with how the two types may be related. But he is equally insistent upon parallel regularities of function and form in the evolution of cultures, and in this insistence he, too, departs from the often extreme pluralism of the Boasian school. "For . . . the greatest promise lies in analysis and comparison of limited similarities and parallels, that is, in multilinear evolution . . ." The task is to "formulate the interrelationships of particular phenomena which may recur cross-culturally but are not necessarily universal."[31]

RECENT PHILOSOPHIES OF CULTURAL HISTORY: METHODOLOGICAL

At this stage it is profitable to sample, briefly, recent philosophies of history with a view to asking how far a meeting-ground between the philosophy of culture and the philosophy of history is already being cleared. I shall first consider three different examples of what may be called formal or methodological theories of history.

One of the most influential theories of the past twenty years is without doubt that of R. G. Collingwood, an English philosopher. Influenced by such idealists as Kant, and a great admirer of Croce whose views are often similar, his basic approach stems from the now familiar distinction between science as the objective analysis of abstract processes of nature and history as reconstruction of human experience by interpretation. A few excerpts from *The Idea of History* bring out the point sharply:

The . . . right way of investigating nature is by the method called scientific, the right way of investigating mind [and human nature] is by the methods of history . . . The processes of nature can therefore be properly described as sequences of mere events, but those of history cannot. They are not processes of mere events but processes of actions, which have an inner side, consisting of processes of thought; and what the historian is looking for is these processes of thought. All history is the history of thought . . . and therefore all history, is the re-enactment of past thought in the historian's own mind . . . [The] past, so far as it is historically known, survives in the present . . . a living past, kept alive by the act of historical thinking itself . . . Thus the historical process is a process in which man creates for himself this or that kind of human nature by re-creating in his own thought the past to which he is heir.[32]

Collingwood denies that this conception means that historical understanding is arbitrary or subjective. It must have a locale in space and time, for example; it must be consistent; and it must rest upon evidence (a term that he carefully defines). Enough, however, has been suggested for our purpose. Despite deviations, his central argument offers support for Kroeber's later position—namely, that the history of culture, and hence spatio-temporal order, is by no means the mere reproduction of sequences that theorists, bound by a mechanistic or positivistic philosophy of science, want us to believe it is. Rather it demands reconstruction by the creative interpreter if it is to be history at all.

The next position, that of Morris R. Cohen, the American philosopher, is still closer to the view toward which Kroeber, Evans-Pritchard, and Bidney seem to be moving as culture-theorists. Although Cohen does not mention Collingwood, he does discuss Croce sufficiently to assure us that both the latter should be regarded as altogether too much in the idealistic tradition to give us a satisfactory theory of history for our time. What is needed is a theory that combines the power of imagination to reconstruct past events with the natural reality of those events.

While obviously only a conscious being can understand history and it would be absurd to eliminate thought from the human scene . . . [the] physical or purely organic phase of life cannot be read out of human affairs . . . It is because human beings are part of physical and organic nature that they build homes, or move about with the changes of weather or the presence or absence of food and drink . . . Only as we realize that the events of human history include both mind and matter as polar components can we escape the grosser errors of those who would spin the world out of ideas . . .[33]

Cohen's constructive theory, as developed in *The Meaning of Human History,* is best grasped through his concept of "multidimensionality." No one factor can account for history. Scientific knowledge is, of course, essential to our interpretation of it, but so too are art, religion, and other human achievements. The concept of "institutions" as human arrangements through which learning can occur and be passed on seems to attract him most in his search for a pluralistic approach—a view that anticipates our later discussion of Malinowski. Cohen is not as explicit as Malinowski, however, in utilizing the concept of culture as temporal order, though what he says is often helpful to our understanding of that concept in its historical perspective.

Herbert J. Muller, an American professor of English with strong theoretical interests, provides a helpful third example in *The Uses of the Past*. As against the anti-historical bias of some culture-theorists, Muller argues that understanding of the past is indispensable to understanding the present and future:

It not only constitutes all the "experience" by which we have learned: it is the source of our major interests, our claims, our rights and our duties. It is the source of our very identity . . . [As] the present is forever slipping back, it reminds us that we too shall in time belong wholly to the past.[34]

Moreover, says Muller, as students of the past share their findings and subject them to public scrutiny, the abundant opportunity for error diminishes. There has not been "a steady advance toward absolute truth." But there "has been a progressive clarification, a fuller consciousness of what has happened, and how and why."[35] Indeed, the increasing sensitivity of able historians to the impossibility of pure objectivity tends, paradoxically, to increase the degree of objectivity. For, with the aid of such students of the problem as Marx, Freud, Sumner, and Boas, students of history are now able to become more self-conscious of and thereby to exercise greater control over their own biases.

Like Kroeber, Muller does not believe that history is reducible to a single causal explanation. Perhaps more than Kroeber, however, and certainly more than White, he stresses the importance of men's creative power—i.e., their freedom to direct history even minus the capacity to predict it very far. Also, he anticipates another problem with which we must grapple: the normative factor in history, itself a symptom of the growing concern of students of culture with the whole problem of values and of human goals. In this latter emphasis, Muller points toward an aspect of temporal order that has not thus far been stressed—the aspect of the future, the realization that it is no more possible to dissever the yet-to-be from the present moment than to dissever the already-was. Any mature theory of order will accordingly have to reckon as carefully with expectations, hopes, ambitions, plans, and other future-centered, normative influences upon cultural habits, customs, and beliefs as with past-centered influences. The future is an essential component of what Muller aptly pleads for: "an anthropological view of our history."[36]

As anyone familiar with the literature in the philosophy of history will recognize, these three samples far from adequately represent the contemporary field. Nor do they begin to specify its array of problems. The one that has been most touched upon is historical knowledge, but other problems such as historical causation, to be considered later, have thus far only been mentioned. Perhaps the single most influential type of current theory not exemplified by Collingwood, Cohen, or Muller is the Marxian or neo-Marxian. The influence of this theory upon many non-Marxian historians continues to be powerful but, so far as I know, it is not now expounded systematically by any outstanding philosopher of history outside of communist-dominated countries. This fact certainly does not alone justify disregarding it here. But it does lead us to suspect that, for the immediate future at any rate, opportunities for cooperation between theorists of culture such as anthropologists and philosophers of history are likelier to occur among such representative thinkers as are considered above.

RECENT PHILOSOPHIES OF CULTURAL HISTORY: SUBSTANTIVE

One other important opportunity for cooperation is relevant to our problem. I refer to those philosophies of history-and-culture concerned primarily with a content or substantive approach. What have they to offer that may enrich our understanding of culture as temporal order?

Even more strikingly than in his formal or methodological contributions to that kind of order, Kroeber among anthropologists today stands virtually alone in providing a liaison with philosophers of culture. It is hardly surprising that the sociologist-philosopher, Sorokin, should include him among the half-dozen or so important theorists who in recent decades have coped fundamentally with the

vast problem of historical order and sought to demonstrate its substantive as well as formal character.

The work in which this is attempted, *Configurations of Culture
Growth,* rests upon ideas with which we are already acquainted—particularly Kroeber's theory of patterns or themes as the index to spatio-
temporal order in cultures. The hypothesis he wishes to examine is
whether the great civilizations of history reveal curves of patterned
growth and decline as marked primarily by levels of relatively brief
productivity in the fields of philosophy, science, and the fine arts.
Among the cultures chosen for such description are the Egyptian,
Greek, Norman, Arab-Muslim, Western, Indian, Chinese, and Japanese. These, however, are frequently subdivided; for example, he pays
extended attention to such Western countries as Germany, France,
Spain, England, Poland, and the Netherlands.

Although Kroeber is satisfied that his hypothesis is on the whole
proved, he is guarded in his conclusions—more so than any other
philosopher of culture with whom we shall deal below. Thus:

> In reviewing the ground covered, I wish to say at the outset that I see no
> evidence of any true law in the phenomena dealt with; nothing cyclical,
> regularly repetitive, or necessary. There is nothing to show either that every
> culture must develop patterns within which a florescence of quality is
> possible, or that, having once so flowered, it must wither without chance
> of revival. After all, cultures merge into one another, and so cannot have
> the individual entity of higher organisms.[37]

Let us consider several highlights of Kroeber's elaborate investigation. Using recognized geniuses as the mark of creative productivity,
he is insistent that they are not to be regarded as the cause of such
productivity but rather as "indicators of the realization of coherent
pattern growths of cultural value."[38] This contention, which he deals
with at length also in other writings, is another way of opposing the
doctrine of "free will"—in this case, the belief that great men of
extraordinary talent and power are the makers of history. It is his
view, on the contrary, that able human beings are potentially available in every culture, but that conditions must be ripe for their ideas
or plans if they are to be recognized. One of his favorite examples is
the theory of evolution earlier discussed—a theory which, although
developed concurrently by a group of thinkers, became by more or

less fortuitous circumstance primarily associated with the admitted genius of Darwin.

With such "indicators" as his measuring-stick, Kroeber sees no evidence either of unilinear progress in history or of the inevitable death of every culture. He does see a good deal of evidence for the tendency of cultures to reach peaks of creativity followed by periods of imitation and sterility. Perhaps the nearest he comes to an explanation of this phenomenon is here:

. . . any notable cultural achievement presupposes adherence to a certain set of patterns; . . . these patterns, to be effective, must exclude other possibilities, and are therefore limited; . . . with successful development they accordingly become exhausted; and . . . there must be a breakdown or abandonment and reformulation of patterns before the culture can go on to new high achievement.[39]

An example is the present situation in the arts of Western culture. Since about 1880, Kroeber contends, they have shown more and more symptoms of pattern disintegration—a repudiation of the creative harmonies and forms developed by Beethoven, Goethe, Rubens, and other geniuses. This situation, as typified by dissonance in music, by surrealism in sculpture and painting, is not necessarily undesirable. Older forms have been exhausted, and new ones have not yet emerged. Certainly it is true that other cultures have often experienced a series of "pulses and lulls in growth."[40] Revolution *may* be succeeded by new growth; but "whether this is to be greater or less, no one can foretell."[41]

Kroeber is careful to deny at least as many generalizations as he affirms. No proof is available, for example, that creative fields always develop either together or in a certain sequence. Some cultures have been exceedingly weak in one or more fields—Egypt in philosophy, Rome in painting, Arabic civilization in sculpture. Others have produced brilliant interrelations in such fields as painting and sculpture (as in Italy and France), or in science and philosophy (as in Greece). Again, there is no symmetry to the curves of growth and decline either between fields or within any one. A duration of growth may be limited to less than half a century or it may continue for a millenium, while its period of decline may be slower or faster than the incline. Yet one may also contend that the larger civilizations, again granting variations, experience patterns of growth that roughly extend from a thousand to fifteen hundred years. Finally, while Kroeber denies any strict correlation between national achievement and high esthetic or intellectual productivity, he does admit that oftener than not some correlation occurs. He is much less sure whether any correlation is discoverable between (a) wealth and population growth and (b) growth in creativity—an interesting commentary on historical materialism.

This bare outline indicates that Sorokin is justified in comparing Kroeber's contribution with a number of more famous philosophies of cultural history—for example, Spengler's, Toynbee's, and Sorokin's own philosophy.

Kroeber himself has recognized an affinity between his views and theirs. Thus in his study of cultural configurations he is careful to note that Spengler (to whom we now turn as another remarkable interpreter of temporal order) is similar in using individual persons as measures of cultural patterns rather than as ends in themselves or as causes of history. Still more apparent is the common opposition of both theorists to a melioristic philosophy of culture; both regard inevitable progress as a wishful sentiment. But Kroeber is also critical of Spengler's intuitive, subjective, and dogmatic approach to complex cultural problems; of his "discovery" of a single master key to unlock the secret of each great culture; of the artificiality of any attempt to show that all cultures rise and fall through parallel stages; of his insistence that all cultures eventually die; and of other serious flaws.

Kroeber might have considered more critically than he does another central postulate of Spengler's grandiloquent plan. Cultural order, Spengler says, is fundamentally "organic." It must be viewed as an example of *morphology* (defined as that branch of biology dealing with the form and structure of animals and plants), with the consequence that, exactly like every organism, every culture has the same life-cycle: germination, birth, infancy, youth, maturity, senility, and death. (Sometimes Spengler changes to the metaphor of seasons: spring, summer, fall, and winter.) But the comparison between biological and cultural phenomena, while helpful up to a point, is finally false: as Kroeber and other anthropologists have made entirely clear, the power of "branches" and "leaves" of the "tree of culture" to grow together in many places radically differs from the tree of botany. On this point alone the "organic" autonomy of cultures, central to Spengler's theme, breaks down.

The Decline of the West[42] limits the great cultures of history to a few in number—the Egyptian, Babylonian, Indian, Chinese, Mexican, Graeco-Roman, Arabian, and Western. Though Spengler deals in detail only with the last three of these, each great culture nevertheless is said to have its own type of art as well as its own religion, philosophy, even mathematics and science; each can be characterized by a "prime symbol" duplicated nowhere else. In Western civilization such a symbol is "pure and limitless space," exemplified by the conception of an infinite God in religion, by mathematical physics in science, by abstractionism in art, by mechanization in economics.

The "civilization" of each great culture is Spengler's term for its period of winter or old age. To select the West again, we can only accept the fate that is in store for us—the fate of an irrevocable decline that is signalized early by democracy and later by the "Caesarism" of dictatorship, the product of democracy's own weaknesses.

Just why the cultural cycle of birth, maturation, and death presumably occurs is never really explained. The best that Spengler offers as a cause is the mysterious force of "Destiny"—omnipresent in history. To believe in the capacity of reason to control or modify Destiny is an illusion carried over from the Enlightenment and similar tender-minded movements. In his anti-intellectualism, Spengler thus reveals more than a little of a mood common to such disparate figures as Machiavelli, Nietzsche, and Pareto.[43]

Although his influence waned markedly only a few years after his study was published in Germany in 1918, Spengler's able American interpreter, H. Stuart Hughes, is probably right in asserting that today, due to two factors, the theory is once more in ascendency. The first factor is that some of Spengler's most pessimistic and disturbing predictions, his emphasis too upon irrational forces in man and history, can no longer be dismissed—for example, his prediction that Caesarism would grow rapidly in power and threaten to submerge the democracies. Thus, while also recognizing the errors and exaggerations in Spengler's major work, Hughes goes so far as to assert that it "offers the nearest thing we have to a key to our times. It formulates more comprehensively than any other single book the modern *malaise* that so many feel and so few can express."[44] Hughes' second factor, however, is still more immediately relevant: the growing impact of theories of culture that reflect the influence of Spengler's own theory. Of these, by far the most widely known is Toynbee's gigantic *A Study of History*.[45]

Like Kroeber and Spengler, Toynbee rejects historical meliorism as a legitimate assumption of temporal order. Also like them, he looks upon this order not only in grand perspective but in terms of configurations of origin, growth, stagnation, and collapse. But he is as critical of Spengler's dogmatisms and colored judgments as Kroeber is. The latter's evaluation of Toynbee's work is revealing by comparison:

It is a careful, voluminous intelligent endeavor to find a recurrent pattern enabling a better understanding of the whole range of human history. Its focus of interest lies in civilizations, of which events and personalities are regarded as expressions or indices . . . As a solution of an endlessly intricate Gordian knot, his formula, like any other, is . . . inadequate . . . It is in the imaginative, often unconventional, recognition of . . . patternings, which express themselves recurrently in variety, that Toynbee shows himself to be not only a penetrating historian, but, what is rarer, a fruitfully comparative one.[46]

Toynbee's importance is thus considered to be his treatment of the same theme that intrigues Kroeber himself—the theme of cultures as historically patterned—rather than such special Toynbeean concepts of historical causation and change as challenge-and-response or withdrawal-and-return.

Toynbee's systematic study embraces twenty-six civilizations ranging across much of the recorded time and space of human experience. Their growth, except for certain arrested civilizations such as the Eskimo, is traced through a number of major stages. For example, a civilization arises under two indispensable conditions: the emergence of a "creative minority," and the presence of an environment neither too favorable nor too unfavorable to permit vigorous development of natural and human resources. Breakdown results when the creative minority becomes sterile and repetitive, when the majority no longer finds inspiration in or respect for the leadership of that minority (which has meanwhile become oppressive), and when conflict and class-war are accordingly generated by an "internal and external proletariat" who destroy the unity that the culture displayed in its earlier dynamic stage.

Only a few more of Toynbee's provocative contentions can be mentioned here. Sixteen of his civilizations are dead, and of the remaining ten all but one (our own) have already broken down. Some of these developed independently but, contrary to Spengler, the majority were affiliated with previous civilizations (a viewpoint consistent thus far at least with the culture-history school). Toynbee also refuses to regard cultures either as morphological or cyclical: with Kroeber, he finds no inevitability about the curves of history, hence no inevitability about the collapse of our own culture.

The single sharpest distinction from both Kroeber and Spengler, and one source of severe criticism by numerous scholars, is the intrusion of Christian tenets. Toynbee's religious faith so deeply permeates his thought and becomes so impassioned in some of his latest writings that, although admitting that we, too, are "already far advanced in our time of troubles," he believes it is possible that we can still be saved from the fate of other civilizations. Certainly, we "must pray that a reprieve which God has granted to our society once [the period of comparative peace before the French Revolution] will not be refused if we ask for it again in a humble spirit and with a contrite heart."[47]

The final philosopher of culture-in-time to whom we shall pay attention—Sorokin—has made careful comparisons between his theory of order and Kroeber's, Spengler's, and Toynbee's, among others. Both he and Kroeber, for example, agree that it is characteristic of a culture to enjoy more than one spurt or peak of creativity; that all great cultures are pre-eminent in several fields such as art, but none in all the major ones; that the curves of upswing and downswing are irregular; and that it is impossible to attribute the development of any cultural pattern to a single causal factor, and certainly not to material or economic forces.[48]

Although Sorokin's own position is developed systematically in his tour de force, *Social and Cultural Dynamics*,[49] the assumptions and intent of that position are more openly revealed in briefer works. His chief postulate is that the temporal order of cultures may be grouped into three major types of meaningful systems or unities—the sensate, ideational, and idealistic—each of which is subdivided in various ways. His claim that all three are to be appraised neutrally and objectively is not borne out; in his *The Crisis of Our Age*,[50] particularly, he radiates as passionate a hostility to the sensate type of culture as he does a sympathy for the ideational.

What does he mean by these key terms? Sensate refers to a culture characterized by the dominance of sensory experience in all aspects of culture—science, art, philosophy, and politics. It is a "this-worldly" culture, secular and empirical. Ideational is at the opposite pole in that it considers the "ultimate, true reality-value" to be "a supersensory and superrational God"; thus the attitude it encourages is one of indifference or negativity toward sensory experience with its wealth, its pleasures, its mundane preoccupations. Lastly, the term "idealistic" harmonizes qualities of both the others: it creates a "Manifold Infinity" of the sensory and superrational, combined with the logical or rational.

The temporal sequence in which these "supersystems" develop is from ideational to idealistic to sensate, out of which a new cycle typically begins. Though he is not insistent upon the universality of any such sequence, Sorokin is able to say that "during some thirty-five centuries . . . in all observed cases, after the decline of the Sensate supersystem, a new Ideational (religious) supersystem becomes dominant."[51]

The greatest ideational culture in Western history was, of course, the medieval. But beginning in the twelfth century it began to decline, says Sorokin, and during the thirteenth and fourteenth it became idealistic. By the sixteenth century the emerging sensate culture had become dominant; it is itself now fading. Thus the present crisis in Western culture is due both to disintegration of sensory, utilitarian, materialistic beliefs and practices, and to fresh surgings of the idealistic and ideational. As Sorokin puts it:

. . . the sensate form of Western culture and society . . . wrote one of the most brilliant pages in human history. However, no finite form, either ideational or sensate, is eternal. Sooner or later it is bound to exhaust its creative abilities. When this moment comes, it begins to disintegrate and decline . . . and so it is happening now with our sensate form, which has apparently entered its decadent stage. Hence the magnitude of the crisis of our time. Even if it does not mean the extinction of Western culture and society, it nevertheless signifies one of the greatest possible revolutions in our culture and social life. As such, it is infinitely deeper and more significant than the partisans of the "ordinary crisis" imagine. A change . . . from capitalism to communism is utterly insignificant in comparison with the substitution of one fundamental form of culture and society for another . . . We have the rare privilege of living, observing, thinking, and acting in the conflagration of such an ordeal. If we cannot stop it, we can at least try to understand . . . and . . . we may be able, to some extent, to shorten its tragic period and to mitigate its ravages.[52]

No less than the other theories considered above, Sorokin's is documented by abundant data from numerous fields. In addition, his sociological interest enables him to deal with areas such as the family and criminality to a degree not found in comparable works, and even to utilize statistical methods. Nevertheless, his own strongly ideational and idealistic preferences become even more obvious than they do in Toynbee. For example, he contends, on the one hand, that no single type of supersystem has a monopoly on truth or value; yet, on the other, he asserts that the "ultimate intuitional verities" (of ideational culture) are "the basic foundations of the beautiful, of moral norms, and of religious values." Sensate truth becomes a "norm of mere convenience" in the hands of pragmatists and instrumentalists. For Sorokin, "an adequate theory of true reality and value" requires "the unfolding of the Absolute in the relative empirical world, to the greater nobility of Man and the greater glory of God."[53]

The four philosophies of history-and-culture sketched above as influential examples of a substantive approach to temporal order are not, of course, any more exhaustive of the field than are the three earlier examples of a methodological approach. Were it feasible to consider still others—Ortega y Gasset's is one—we should discover further similarities. But we should also find such marked differences as to permit few additional generalizations other than the one which for us is most significant: however vulnerable all recent attempts may be, cultures both within themselves and in relation to other cultures can legitimately be characterized as temporal forms of order. They reveal dynamic, patterned regularities that it should now become the serious business of education to examine and incorporate within its own theoretical and practical endeavors.

THE TEMPORAL ORDER OF CULTURE: OPPORTUNITIES FOR EDUCATION

1. In the preceding chapter a plea was made for fresh approaches to the problem of integrated education—approaches that would amply utilize the concepts and research of culture-theory gathered together under the rubric of human order. As was already apparent from this discussion, however, horizontal-vertical models of order, while necessary, are not enough: to them must be added the models of temporal order that have now been examined.

Insistence upon the importance of time and history in culture differentiates the needed theory of educational integration from some of those now popular. The functionalist tendency in anthropology to de-emphasize history, for example, is likewise discernible in types of general education based on the belief that the imperative task of education is not so much to become familiar with the past as to help young people to achieve "life-adjustment," or at any rate to deal intelligently with problems in the present. The deadliness of many conventional courses in history has encouraged this kind of reaction, with the result that attention to the temporal order of culture sometimes receives less sustained attention than it deserves.

Actually the issue is not whether history is desirable and important; it is both. Rather the issue is the kind of history, where it belongs in the curriculum, and how it shall be organized and taught. Here, I believe, culture-theory may render great assistance.

One necessity is to distinguish between approaches to temporal order among culture-theorists themselves. Particularly is it essential to be critical of the classical evolutionary viewpoint that we now familiarly associate with Tylor, Morgan, and Spencer. It is a viewpoint, we recall, that finds the history of culture to be a unilinear, progressive development toward "civilizations" such as our own.

Yet there is little doubt that, indirectly perhaps more than directly, classical evolutionism continues to influence the teaching of cultural history today. The assumption, for example, that other cultures are to be judged by the extent to which they approach and emulate the attainments of American culture is one of the commonest of all assumptions in the public schools. Indeed, an interesting hypothesis would be that a characteristic belief of teachers holding middle-status values (and we recall that, if Warner is right, a large majority do) is the belief in the inevitability of progress toward more and more of these values, especially values as defined by service clubs and other middle-status groups that often dominate school policies.

If this kind of naiveté is to be avoided, one priority in building and implementing an adequate theory of integrated education is to re-examine the premises from which time is related to space in the study of cultures. The fact that the classical evolutionary position is now strongly criticized by experts would indicate that, in so far as curriculum-makers continue to view history from an analogous position, they are deficient and outdated. At the same time, if Childe is at all right, the traditional approach need not be repudiated in every respect; rather the need is to reappraise that approach in terms both of recent research by such sciences as archaeology and of sharper awareness of value judgments that, like those of the implicit culture, unconsciously permeate the teacher's view of history.

Equally needed is more stress upon the role of power and other forces in cultural dynamics, as well as upon the pluralism and empiricism always insisted upon by two such different interpreters of history as Boas and Cohen. Avoidance of hasty conclusions from limited evidence, especially of dogmatic pronouncements about "laws" of cultural change that have not actually been established, should be just as much an unbreakable rule in teaching about cultures in history as it is in teaching about organisms in biology.

The Austrian culture-history school is a useful example both of what education should avoid and what it should include. That the theory has been misused and oversimplified seems now well agreed upon. The errors of the English branch might, indeed, be cited by teachers to reveal the hazards in too incautious an adaptation of any single dogma of cultural origin and development. At the same time, hypotheses of historical reconstruction, operationally applied, provide a fascinating way to appreciate the interrelatedness of the human race, the dependence of cultures upon one another, the incredible fortitude and ingenuity of early man in navigating oceans, and his equally incredible capacity to learn and to transmit his learning from group to group, from race to race, and from nation to nation.

I suggest a series of experimental units and projects on the elementary and secondary levels that could be constructed on the basis both of Childe's concepts of evolutionary culture and of Schmidt's *kulturkreise*. Utilizing these as contrasting models, such a series could highlight the affinity of Western young people today with past peoples, both nonliterate and literate. And it could dramatize the fact that the temporal order of culture may be viewed through more than one set of historical lenses—lenses that reveal different perspectives as they focus upon different meanings inherent in the development of cultures.

2. Education can extend the time-dimension of cultural order still further by incorporating some of the recent philosophers of history into the modern curriculum. I refer not only to those whom I have described as the formal or methodological contributors, like Collingwood, but also to substantive contributors like Spengler.

Such incorporation is certainly not easy. The first reaction of curriculum experts is likely to be that philosophies of cultural history are much too sophisticated and technical for any purpose except graduate study; hence they are unsuitable for programs of integrated education. I submit that a response of this kind is not tenable: granting the difficulties of translating and transfusing these interpretations, the task nonetheless is imperative if temporal order is to be given the place in these programs that it should be given.

The thinkers selected to illustrate the philosophy of history offer numerous concepts that are not only not difficult to understand, but —educationwise—are exceedingly provocative. One example is the contention of Collingwood that historical thought is an enterprise of creative imagination by which man works (always with respect for evidence) upon events of "the past to which he is heir." This position, maintained in varying respects also by Cohen and Muller, would if fully grasped undoubtedly alter the implicit attitudes of innumerable teachers and students toward the meaning of history. The notion that the past is unalterably fixed leads in turn to an attitude already encountered—that history, like culture, is a hypostatized reality above or beyond human efficacy to modify or change it. The creative spirit of Collingwood's philosophy not only discourages this sort of attitude; it leads plausibly to the view of Muller that just as man as historian constantly reinterprets his past, so he may also reinterpret his present and future. Moreover, through such reinterpretation, man guided by future purposes may learn in degree to redirect and control cultural events—an attitude clearly of significance for education's role in temporal human order.

Philosophers who provide us with substantive philosophies of cultural history are equally rewarding. Admitting that those we have considered—Toynbee, for example—are highly controversial both in their treatment of evidence and in their frames of reference,[54] the fact still remains that each provides us with stimulating as well as comprehensive judgments about cultures in time.

Perhaps the most important of these judgments is their repudiation of the unilinear theory of historical development. The contention that modern Western culture is part of a longer and larger pattern— a pattern resembling in various ways those of a remarkably limited number of other great cultures—may come as a shock to the typical young citizen. But it could be a therapeutic shock. It could serve, for example, to purge some of his softness and provincial smugness toward, say, the American culture. It could force him to consider, probably for the first time, whether it is possible that we are approaching a state of cultural "exhaustion" because we are too rapidly consuming our creative (not to mention natural) resources. It could disturb the dogma, still prevalently held, that "great men" are the main cause of cultural growth and achievement, hence that what we need today is another "great man" to lead us toward the light.

These philosophies of cultural history should, of course, be approached critically and circumspectly. The sparse attention that all four selected theories give to education as an institution of culture is itself an instance of their deficiency. Also, twentieth-century systems could be supplemented by earlier ones—that of Hegel, say, or of Marx and Vico. Yet, granting the limitations that all such systems possess, they do satisfy a demand for grand-scale, audacious temporal designs in a way that ordinary history courses very seldom satisfy. And while no single cultural synthesis ever accounts for the multiplicity of historical facts, this does not at all justify disregarding attempts that have been made by substantive philosophies of history to interpret and harmonize what for them are the most significant among these facts.

Here again the operational outlook is indispensable. The question is not whether Spengler, for example, has accurately included and appraised all or even most of what is relevant to culture as temporal order. Clearly he has not. The question is whether, despite his glaring faults, he has thrown new light upon and drawn fresh meanings from the cultures of the West that can widen the student's vista and toughen his historical opinions. Evaluated along with other substantive philosophies of history, *The Decline of the West* is both a challenge to complacency and a daring adventure of historical and cultural imagination.

3. The concluding generalization is not so much an addition to as a reaffirmation of the first generalization to the effect that spatial and temporal order must be considered always as polaristic. Primary concern in this chapter with the temporal dimension should not, therefore, cause us to lose sight of the principle that in actual cultural experience time can no more be dissevered from space than space can be from time.

The corollary of this principle is that the integrated curricula now required by education should be governed by deepened appreciation of and experimentation with interdisciplinary learning. In terms of cultural order, this is only to assert that spatial aspects such as, say, culture-complexes and social strata need to be synthesized with temporal aspects such as, say, peaks and valleys of historical florescence and decay.

This sort of interdisciplinary learning is invited especially by Kroeber's theory of culture as science-and-history. Each side, we recall, bolsters the other—science stressing the quantitative and exact, history the qualitative and patterned, with both functioning on a single "sliding-scale." Earlier I termed Kroeber's position a "gestalt philosophy of cultural order." Its importance for an educational theory of order is that by implication it undermines the atomistic if not chaotic "system" of courses, credits, and units, and substitutes for them a continuous "field" of interacting experiences between nature and man. A curriculum built from a theory of science-and-history could, in short, provide an organic design by which all the major disciplines, however specialized at points, eventually flow into and enrich one another exactly as do the *gestalten* of culture itself.

Such an interdisciplinary conception vitalizes still further the educational import of culture as temporal order. In cultural no less than in other problems of nature, diagnosis is always necessary to prognosis, and diagnosis demands analysis and interpretation of those past events leading up to present and future problematic situations. Functioning thus as a cultural resource, history must be regarded less as an isolated discipline and much more as a cooperating partner in the enterprise of learning to cope effectively, actively, with these situations.

Finally, the interdisciplinary conception of spatio-temporal order reinforces and further explicates the meaning (discussed at the close of Chapter Five) of culture-configuration as a "way of life." Actually, to view this important concept as we did within spatial order was, to say the least, a truncated way of viewing it. A "way of life" is never a static cross-section; it is always dynamic for it always builds out of past cultural experiences, encompasses the flowing present, and moves forward into a future. In this sense, culture-configuration serves as the main principle of unity between space *and* time in culture.

The task of operating with the significance of this principle in its full polaristic meaning is one of the most adventurous that education could undertake. For such a task is nothing less than the construction of a philosophy of life and culture that penetrates to the covert and implicit stratum of cultural reality; that gradually expurgates obsolete, even hypocritical modes of expression and behavior; and that aims to replace these by modes both as honest and as adequate as human integrity can fashion. Here the closest possible cooperation among all fields concerned with the nature of culture and man as its creator is thus an imperative requirement. The concept of culture-configuration is the key to an emerging interdisciplinary discipline that alone will be able to provide the foundations for a fully integrated educational policy and program.[55]

PART III

THE PROBLEM OF HUMAN PROCESS

CHAPTER SEVEN

CULTURAL PROCESS—PREVIEW OF THE PROBLEM

PERHAPS THE most threadbare of all truisms reiterated by American educators in recent years is that we live in "a changing world." Addresses before teachers' conventions on this theme have been literally endless, and rarely does an introductory textbook in education fail to have the phrase somewhere in the first chapter. Occasionally textbooks of a somewhat more substantial nature—*Change and Process in American Education*[1] is one—document the contention convincingly. Yet even these rarely examine their own premises, with the result that oftener than not they beg many questions.

Chapter Two recalled some of the events that should bring the problem of human process to the forefront of educational concern: the great technological and political revolutions, for example, that have shaken the world of the past half-century. Even these events, however, receive but passing attention by many leaders in the field of education. There seems to be almost chronic reluctance to face the realities of their age at the same time that they continue to pay lip-service to the alleged importance of economic, social, moral, and other forms of change.

In this Part, I shall try to overcome some of this reluctance, first by dissecting the main components of cultural process, and then by applying them to educational tasks. Many of these tasks raise such questions as the following: What kinds of learning experience that implement concepts of cultural process can be provided by the modern school and college? How can students and teachers become more conscious of and involved in the rapid changes taking place within and among cultures?

And what are some of the relations between individual human beings and cultural process that might assist education, in turn, to interfuse personal experiences with cultural events? For after all if education is concerned with the living person, not merely with impersonal and objective forces, then we must ask: What is his role in the complicated processes so swiftly and so hazardously taking place on every level and in every area of the culture of our time? Here the interrelations between the psychological sciences and culture-theory, especially anthropology, become of central concern. Is it even possible that educational psychology could itself contribute to culture-theory in strengthening such interrelations? And, if so, how might the resulting partnership affect the training of teachers?

As anyone must recognize who has followed this study from the beginning, we have already been hovering close to these and comparable questions. Particularly have we been close throughout the preceding chapter, for to speak of the temporal dimension of culture at all is to speak also of the processes—the changing and stabilizing of culture—by which that dimension is experienced. Every important concept of temporal order is, indeed, one of process as well: evolution and culture-history are only two of the more conspicuous.

To recapitulate briefly, we have found that culture can be viewed as a species of spatio-temporal order in nature within which, accordingly, change takes place continually and inevitably. We have also found, however, that authorities in anthropology and allied disciplines are far from agreed as to the nature or meaning of such change. Traditionally, culture has been approached as an orderly development that can be structured in terms of great patterns, stages, levels, circles —an approach today perhaps most influentially expressed in world-wide perspective by the theory of historical materialism, but also more or less consistently expressed by *kulturkreislehre,* by classical evolutionism as adapted by White and Childe, say, and by non-Marxian substantive philosophies of history like Toynbee's. This approach has been challenged by two interrelated and extremely influential viewpoints—the empirical and pluralistic methodology represented in anthropology by the Boasian school and by the operational philosophy of science and history that detects a *sui generis* absolutism lurking in most or all of the traditional positions.

Kroeber, more than any other recent culture-theorist, has made a valiant effort to reconcile the older and newer approaches without yielding to compromise. While continuing to insist upon the primacy of spatio-temporal patterns and configurations, he now increasingly interprets them in operational terms which, I believe, point in turn toward explosive consequences for the meaning of cultural process in general, and for educational process in particular. His formulations, we have seen, have undergone so much amendment over the years that one cannot be sure how far he would agree with all the implications that I find in them. Nevertheless, whether intentionally or not, Kroeber forces us to re-examine one of the most pivotal of all problems in the theory of culture—that of the actual functioning of the human being in the processes of culture. Or, in terms pertinent to education in a universal rather than merely formal sense, it is the problem of the ways that teaching and learning operate upon the patterns of any given culture, and thus of the ways that they help to fix or to alter these patterns.

Theoretically, the expectation that education's role is at least latently powerful and not another case of wishful thinking derives in large degree from the operational viewpoint—itself inherently transformative and creative. Not that this viewpoint denies for a moment that nature, including culture, possesses a multitude of regular or irregular resistances to individual and collective actions upon them. On the contrary, the more man learns to operate effectively, the more he learns also how to estimate and to behave intelligently in accordance with these resistances. But, as Anatol Rapoport argues, once we absorb the full implications of the "operational philosophy," our relation to the world radically alters. Instead of attitudes of acquiescence or even of fatalism that are often correlative with traditional conceptions, we are incited to develop "the disciplined imagination of the mature, creative, self-critical mind, the sort of mind that cannot feel free without a self-imposed discipline."[2] This "self-imposed discipline" may well be regarded as the *process* of culture operationally analyzed, synthesized, and directed within and through the *order* of culture.

To consider the same point in a different way, the problem of process is another instance of the polaristic approach to culture-and-education. Just as the space and time of cultural order are reciprocal, so both of these are reciprocal with process. True, spatio-temporal order radically conditions the ways that process can and does occur. But the principle may be equally true that process radically conditions the form and substance of order. Thus, if educators expect to learn anything from the study of culture as to how they and their institutions can help to change and/or stabilize the course of events in the world of our time, they first must consider this polaristic principle. To operate with any success whatever upon the order of cultures so as to modify their character, the order must of course be understood with maximum precision. But operations are indigenous to, not separate from, such understanding. Moreover, they exert a direct influence upon the character of order itself. In the present Part, then, we shall be concerned with the nature of this influence—with special regard for the educational process as an instrument of cultural "permanence and change."

As before, it is necessary to limit investigation to concepts most central to our interest—all of them likewise interrelated, all of them involving ramifications and subdivisions[3] that we shall have to disregard. In contemporary anthropology, the cluster of processes known as discovery, invention, diffusion, acculturation, and assimilation are frequently stressed. Innovation, focus, and crisis, while less often stressed, are also fertile concepts. Threading through all of these are such disturbing issues as causation and prediction: Who or what causes cultures to change? How far, if at all, can we predict the outcome or at least the direction of changes that do occur? Finally, if it is the human individual and he alone who "carries" the traits of culture, then may there not be a sense in which personality causes culture to change or stabilize when it is changed or stabilized at all?

The next two chapters aim to determine what culture-theory can contribute by way of answering these and related questions. The first considers the clusters of concepts mentioned above. The second deals with the import of personality in the context of cultural process.

Meanwhile, two assumptions about process deserve explication. The first assumption is that no culture is so static or homogeneous as to permit no change whatever. There appears to be strong agreement among culture-theorists that (a) on the whole, cultures are "conservative" in the sense that they tend to support processes that encourage permanence rather than those that encourage change with its threat of impermanence; (b) nevertheless, cultures of different types, in different spaces and times, differ widely in their practices and attitudes toward innovation in customs and beliefs, institutions and habits; (c) our own period of history is distinguished by the speed with which such attributes of culture are being modified and often altered; (d) the American culture, probably more than any other unless we except the Russian, regards deliberate change to be a regular and proper attribute of its own configuration; and yet (e) even remote and nonliterate cultures are by no means impervious to change.

Thus the distinction often made between the static homogeneity of the latter kind of cultures and the dynamic heterogeneity of sophisticated, literate cultures becomes more and more dubious in the light of extensive research and, in our own day, of accelerating contacts between both kinds. Change is a ubiquitous fact of *any and all* cultures.

The second assumption is that process occurs in two logically divisible domains: one, within cultures and/or subcultures; and two, between cultures. But it would be artificial if not impossible to keep internal and external processes strictly apart. All the concepts that we shall review may refer to processes both within and between cultures, although some, such as focus, operate most meaningfully within one culture, while others, such as diffusion, operate most meaningfully upon cross-cultural experience.

CHAPTER EIGHT

SOME MAJOR CONCEPTS OF CULTURAL PROCESS

DISCOVERY AND INVENTION

REGARDED BY EXPERTS as key processes, discovery and invention are important to our problem because they dramatize the remarkable ingenuity and creativity of human groups. The tendency has been to think of these processes in relation primarily to material, utilitarian objects and techniques, although they just as properly apply to "immaterial" manifestations of culture such as ideas, political constitutions, and musical compositions.

Dispute seems to have arisen over the relation of the two terms to each other. True, invention often connotes a more deliberative kind of achievement, discovery a more spontaneous one. Yet a moment's reflection reveals that discovery may involve a great deal of prior deliberation (the location, say, of a metal deposit beneath the earth's surface) while an invention may involve considerable spontaneity and accident (vulcanized rubber and penicillin are two of countless instances). The most we can safely assert is that the former is perhaps less often premeditated than the latter; also, it is more often close to the raw materials of nature which invention then refines, modifies, and combines. Thus the discovery of aluminum has led to the invention of a great number of artifacts that are increasing today at a more rapid rate than ever before. The discovery that a hollow reed produces sounds of different pitches has evolved into a variety of musical inventions all the way from flute to pipe-organ.

The problem of *why* these complementary processes occur with such universality is by no means as easy to clarify as the fact *that* they occur. Since I deal with the question of causality more thoroughly below, it is necessary to make but two brief observations here. One is that we do not have the answer in any complete sense. That men are motivated to discover and invent both because of the way they are constituted psychologically and the way they learn from the cultures in which they live is really to say little; we still need to know, of course, precisely how men are constituted and why they learn as they do. This much seems sure: men discover and invent, at least partly, to satisfy prior needs and wants; but these in turn are affected by new modes of living, by new discoveries and inventions, that thereby serve to generate new needs and wants. Circular or reciprocal causality is the rule rather than the exception in this process of culture.

The other observation is that discovery and invention, while properly regarded as occurring within cultures, also occur even more widely through the meeting of different cultures. Here again we do not thereby provide anything like a satisfactory explanation of these processes: contact, in any of its manifestations, is at most a necessary and not a sufficient cause, for it tells us little if anything of why or how people respond *to* contact. Nevertheless, contact is an important factor in such explanation. Granting that independent and even parallel inventions and discoveries are now generally conceded to occur—increasingly conceded, indeed, as investigation more and more fully proves the resourcefulness of people of all races and environments—the fact remains that borrowing from one culture by another is common. No culture ever studied has been either completely original or completely imitative, although some are more one than the other. Thus, Western culture in modern times is extraordinarily fertile in technological inventiveness; yet we may doubt whether it compares with, say, ancient Greece either in esthetic or philosophic inventiveness.

DIFFUSION

Reference to contact and borrowing has already drawn us toward the problem of human process between cultures, and thereby to one of the major concepts concerned with that problem—namely, *diffusion*. One of its important adaptations has already been described in the discussion of *kulturkreise*. Because, however, the concern of that discussion was primarily with the order of culture rather than its process, the term "diffusion" was avoided in favor of the term "culture-history"—a particular theory of historical reconstruction with metaphysical overtones in which diffusion, regarded in broadest terms as the spreading of culture-traits and complexes from one culture to another, has taken place in the past through a limited set of radiating circles that are inferred rather than observed.

A majority of contemporary experts would probably quarrel with the special theory of the Austrian school of culture-history. They would scarcely quarrel, however, with the definition of diffusion just given; certainly they would not challenge the fact of its ubiquity among cultural processes. Also, reflecting again the strong empiricism of recent anthropology, they would prefer to consider diffusion in its specific manifestations, and thus attempt to demonstrate how elements of one culture become diffused into another by a process of spreading.

Different anthropologists tend as usual to highlight different aspects of the inclusive meaning. Thus John Gillin stresses the fact that diffusion typically occurs "without direct or long-continued primary contact between the cultures involved." Contact often occurs between individual members to be sure, but "the societies as wholes are usually not in direct contact . . ."[1] He gives the example, among others, of the transfer of the habit of smoking tobacco to the Japanese via Europeans who, in turn, learned it from aboriginal American Indians. Herskovits finds it more helpful to think of diffusion as "achieved cultural transmission," where the accent is on historical reconstruction by inference rather than by direct observation of concrete experience[2]—a notion consistent with *kulturkreise* theory, though not limited to it. Kroeber probably would not be satisfied with either demarcation: for him, rather, diffusion is more largely the spatial or geographical, as against the historical, process of transfer of particular culture traits or complexes from culture to culture.[3] The emphasis is on the part rather than the whole—an emphasis exemplified by his concept of "stimulus diffusion."

This concept attempts to single out the sort of transfer that occurs when one culture stimulates another through ideas by which the latter constructs new objects, techniques, or other cultural phenomena. "In this case it is the idea of the complex or system which is accepted, but it remains for the receiving culture to develop a new content."[4] Perhaps the simplest example of many offered is that of porcelain. Europeans in the eighteenth century learned to produce their own porcelain from models obtained in China—a need induced by the difficulties of transporting porcelain thousands of miles. Here both discovery and invention were also involved: the former in the discovery of deposits of suitable raw materials in various parts of Europe, the latter in prolonged experimentation with the material leading to the eventual manufacture of porcelain itself. The stimulus of China thus produced a diffusion dependent on the original source of the idea. There was independence of invention only in a qualified sense.

ACCULTURATION

While other special types of diffusion could be noted, it is more profitable to turn now to acculturation. The relation of this widely utilized concept to diffusion is by no means as yet satisfactorily delineated.[5] Diffusion often appears to be the more encompassing term, with acculturation considered one important aspect, but even this much agreement does not seem clearly established.

Here is the single most frequently quoted definition: "Acculturation comprehends those phenomena which result when groups of individuals having different cultures come into continuous first-hand contact, with subsequent changes in the original cultural patterns of either or both groups."[6] This definition is now criticized by various authorities, including its own formulators. It does nevertheless emphasize what I find to be a helpful operational distinction from diffusion—namely, the emphasis upon continuity, upon the active, on-going process of cultural contact as against achieved or completed transmission. Associated with this distinction is the importance Herskovits attaches to the empirical, documentary character of acculturation studies by comparison with his assumption, noted a moment ago, that diffusion studies are more properly concerned with inferential reconstruction of past cultures.[7] There seems also to be considerable fruitfulness in the idea that acculturation tends more strongly to involve a mutuality of influence between cultures in contact, even though the influence is often much heavier in one direction than another. Again, as viewed at least by some anthropologists, greater stress is placed upon holistic processes of transfer in the case of acculturation than in that of diffusion where we have found the stress placed more often on the transfer of particular elements.

Finally, a few anthropologists are now paying attention to the disturbing notion that "force" is an index to the meaning of acculturation as compared with diffusion. As Ralph Beals puts it:

In such discussions, force is broadly treated to include not only overt or naked force but pressures resulting from deprivations, introduction of compelling new goals, or psychological pressures arising from sentiments of inferiority and superiority. A corollary type of approach is the suggestion that acculturation be confined to situations in which one of the groups in contact, for whatever reason, loses complete freedom of choice or freedom to accept or reject new cultural elements.[8]

The most graphic example of recent acculturation of this kind that would occur to many of us is the forceful superimposition of the Soviet pattern in countries like Poland. But Africa, India, and many other parts of the world have also experienced it. Nor can we forget our own record of treatment of the American Indian, which surely suggests the meaning given by Beals. We may also raise the question of whether recent American foreign-aid programs do not have more than a little of this quality.

However unrefined conceptualization may still be, there is no dearth of interest in the process itself. In the twentieth century, acculturation, surveyed on a planetary scale, is more widespread than at any time in history. That earlier periods have also been deeply affected by culture contact of this general kind is indubitable. Never before, however, have so many peoples in so many parts of the world been changed so rapidly by mutual and large-scale contact— a phenomenon immediately due to the revolution in transportation and communication, as well as to such overwhelming events related to these revolutions as World Wars I and II.

But anthropologists who have examined the process agree that the mere fact of direct contact between cultures is in itself no guarantee that acculturation occurs. In fact, antagonisms resulting from contact may widen the cultural distance between two groups rather than narrow it. "Nativism," a movement to preserve traditional habits and institutions against outside encroachments, is one such reaction. In some respects Gandhi symbolized another in his "passive resistence" to British imperialism. Likewise, the record of opposition of nonliterate cultures to missionary invasions is a long one, despite the fact that missionaries have exerted tremendous acculturative influence. More familiar to Americans of recent generations are the psychological, economic, and other barriers between immigrant groups (Chinese, Mexicans, Puerto Ricans, Irish, and others) and already established groups who look with suspicion upon all newcomers. Xenophobia, the fear of strangers, is an ailment that continues to afflict millions of us, immigrant and "native" alike. Clearly the therapeutic and hence educational problem here alone is of gigantic scope.

Mention of the immigrant problem requires that we pay more careful notice to the fact that acculturation occurs within as well as between cultures. Actually, as should now be evident, differentiation of the two processes is by no means always clearcut. In important respects the Southern Negro possesses his own subculture; so too does the upper-upper group of an urban community. Redfield has explored rural-urban "subacculturation" in Latin America[9]—a field for anthropological research in the United States that remains largely untouched. Indeed, the whole problem of subcultural interaction in this country alone is so many-sided that no one could list all of its potentialities.

In largest part, rather, anthropologists thus far have concentrated upon acculturation as the active process of impact by so-called literate upon nonliterate cultures, with due consideration of reciprocal effects. Malinowski, for example, gave prolonged attention to the problem in Africa. (We know that under racist political regimes it has reached a stage of violence and hatred since his death in 1943.) His methodological studies are as strongly against the forcing of European patterns upon African culture as they are strongly for a gradual program of adaptation in which native traits, habits, and values are given utmost consideration and appreciation. His preferred term for both the descriptive and normative process (incidentally, in the last article he ever wrote) is "transculturation"[10]—a process equally applicable, in his opinion, to the Southern Negro in America. Not dissimilar to Malinowski's are numerous interpretations of Indian cultures in their relations to the dominant white culture in the United States.

ASSIMILATION

The next major concept of process—assimilation—is operationally close to acculturation and diffusion, so close that experts have as much trouble with its delineation as they do with either of the others.

The stress by some writers seems to be upon the process whereby one culture has absorbed another to a fairly complete extent; by others, upon the mutuality of such absorption by two or more cultures. Actually, as in the case of acculturation, one cannot generalize: it depends upon the particular cultures or subcultures one is discussing, and upon the aspects that are assimilated. The culture-theorist and sociologist, Robert E. Park, defines the concept as "the process or processes by which peoples of diverse racial origins and different cultural heritages, occupying a common territory, achieve a cultural solidarity sufficient at least to achieve a national unity."[11] Beals defines it "possibly" as "that form of acculturation which results in groups of individuals wholly replacing their original culture by another . . ."[12]

Acculturation may occur without leading to the extreme consequence of assimilation (where the original character of a culture, or some part of it, is no longer clearly distinguishable). Kroeber gives numerous examples of the former without the latter: the subcultures on the common frontier of Mexico and the United States are one example, the Jewish subculture is another. Both examples also show, however, that no sharp line can usually be drawn between these processes. Rather, diffusion and acculturation are on a continuum with assimilation—a fact repeatedly dramatized in our own country where some Mexican-Americans are being increasingly assimilated, and where some Jews have so completely lost their religious and cultural traditions as to be no longer strictly classifiable as Jewish at all.

The question of how much and what kinds of assimilation are good is obviously different from that of the extent to which it is occurring. Here we have the old but lively issue of cultural pluralism versus the so-called "melting pot" theory; the former maintains that diversity of cultural and subcultural attitudes and practices is far more conducive to long-range human welfare; the latter that maximum assimilation of races, nationalities, creeds, and habits is the ideal now required by cultures increasingly cosmopolitanized. Since the issue is primarily one of relative and universal values—to be considered later—I merely note that, whether we like the fact or not, assimilation is now taking place perhaps as rapidly and widely as acculturation itself. Whether it can and should be directed toward desirable goals by deliberate, organized planning is a problem which education should surely help to solve.

INNOVATION

Although innovation has been utilized intermittently for years, it is still largely ignored as an explicit concept by some leading theorists —Bidney being one—while it is treated by most others loosely or incidentally. The publication of H. G. Barnett's *Innovation: The Basis of Cultural Change*[13] should help to elevate innovation to major rank in the theory of cultural process. There is even considerable merit in considering it logically as the genus of which other major concepts of process, including those just studied, are the species. That is to say, every invention and discovery is an innovation, as is every instance of diffusion, acculturation, and assimilation: this is their common denominator.

Barnett, an anthropologist, seems to proceed from idealistic metacultural assumptions. Fortunately, his interpretation of the chief characteristics of innovation is not necessarily vitiated by such assumptions, certainly by no means all of it. I am reasonably certain, on the contrary, that a pragmatist, realist, or even historical materialist would still find much of value in what another anthropologist, Felix M. Keesing, calls the "definitive work" on innovation and "the first modern book-length study of culture-change theory."[14]

Innovation is defined at the outset "as any thought, behavior, or thing that is new because it is qualitatively different from existing forms." The emphasis is "upon reorganization rather than upon quantitative variation . . . Innovation does not result from the addition or subtraction of parts. It takes place only when there is a recombination of them."[15] Of course innovation varies tremendously in scope and effect, but, far from being an unusual phenomenon, it is universal. Barnett insists that whether "primitive" or "civilized," whether black, yellow, red, or white, people innovate abundantly and constantly. The old issue of whether parallel inventions often occur independently or through borrowing and other concomitants of diffusion is resolved by the persuasive contention that of course they occur both ways. But even when artifacts or complexes are borrowed they are never merely duplicated. Typically, there is an element of novelty and creativity in the transferred idea, object, or institution that results in a revision of the original. For this reason, doubt is expressed toward the concept of stimulus-diffusion according to which, we remember, the idea (of, say, porcelain) is not altered in such a transfer but only the applications of it. Barnett insists that the idea too is altered, for acceptance always involves modifications of the whole relationship.

I by-pass his complex interpretation of the psychological and logical bases of innovation in order to illustrate how the central concept is dissected. One of Barnett's major categories is the process of "acceptance"—a process involving advocates of innovation who attempt to win acceptance for their ideas. They are of various kinds. Among them are professional inventors, advertisers, politicians, public-relations experts, migrants or repatriated individuals, and conservatives who wish changes to occur in the direction of the status quo. Prestige and personality are important factors that help these advocates. Always, however, if the innovation is to be accepted, the acceptor must associate it with some experience familiar and desirable to him—a principle that the advocate also needs to appreciate if he is to be successful in his methods of effecting change.

Barnett does not believe it possible for a culture to classify people as purely acceptors or rejectors. All of us are partly one, partly the other. He does insist that amenability to any innovation depends upon three overlapping generalizations: that it offers to satisfy some want better than previous means; that it fits the personality or biographical pattern of the potential acceptor; and that it motivates some people who are dissatisfied with the way things are. Several types of acceptors emerge: the dissidents, who are nonconformists perhaps for personality reasons, perhaps for others; the indifferent, who are not bound by any one pattern (children are the most numerous); the disaffected, who have repudiated an earlier pattern because of frustration, hardship, or some other condition; and the resentful, exemplified by underprivileged groups who view with envy and perhaps anger the greater wealth or status of other groups.

It is surprising that nowhere in Barnett's exacting study does he develop by analogy the biological concept of "mutation." Linton has contended that there have been three mutations in the history of culture: the earliest, "the development of tools and the use of fire"; next, "the invention of food raising"; and most recently, the combination made possible by "two fundamental inventions, that of how to produce power and that of the scientific method." Of particular significance to us is Linton's belief that

The forces which the third mutation has unleashed are so vast that they cannot be left to work themselves out without conscious direction. If they are so left the most probable result will be a collapse of the cultures which have experienced their first impact—those of western Europe and America . . . [There] are a larger number of individuals in all Western societies who recognize the need for conscious planning and direction in the development of a new social order and know that there must be a new social order, planned or otherwise.[16]

It is also surprising as well as disappointing that a book designed to encompass so wide a scope of relevant issues bearing upon innovation should make so little effort to gather together practical techniques of application in the face of pressing contemporary need. In this respect, Gillin's much briefer treatment of innovation (though yet the longest I have found in a survey of anthropology) is more helpful. Speaking of the problem of acceptance, for example, he summarizes his recommendations in terms which, while not markedly different from Barnett's principles, seem closer to the level of workable strategy:

One must know what people want. One must be able to show them that the suggested innovation is more satisfying than anything they know. One must be able to present the innovation so that it can be clearly comprehended as a stimulus. And one must induce people to try it out. If the innovation is not designed to satisfy current wants or drives, it may be necessary to develop new acquired drives which it will serve.[17]

FOCUS

The concept of focus developed by Herskovits is a further contribution to the problem of process. He designates it as "the tendency of every culture to exhibit greater complexity, greater variation in the institutions of some of its aspects than in others."[18] This being so, certain characteristics tend to remain in the background, others to loom in the foreground.

Foreground characteristics, because they are less taken for granted and hence more conscious to more members of a culture, are typically more pliable, more subject to discussion, experimentation, and modification. Technology is regarded by Herskovits as the focus of our American culture, although we might note also our relatively great awareness of democracy as a political institution, and of science as a method of thinking and control—both of these phenomena related in diverse ways, of course, to technology itself. Other cultures, both literate and nonliterate, have different foci from ours: the Todas of India (ceremonialism involving their buffalo dairies); the Ponape of the Eastern Carolines (yam-growing), and so on.

Herskovits believes that we shall learn how to utilize the concept of focus to direct change only as we obtain more psychological knowledge of the process by which individuals themselves come to accept or reject innovations. But the point is well taken that one of the most fertile fields for innovation is that within which the most conspicuous pattern of cultural activity steadily recurs.

Cultural focus makes "for the dynamic drives which bring about greater ease in change, and consequently greater diversity of manifestation in some aspects of culture than in others."[19]

CRISIS

The concept of crisis in cultural process, to which we turn next, is selected because of its timeliness rather than because anthropologists have generously enriched its meaning. True, a few of them have done so. For the most part, however, crisis as a major concept enters into the thinking of philosophers of culture oftener than that of other culture-theorists—an immediate reason being the stricter research interests of many of the latter. Another more fundamental reason, perhaps, is the status of American anthropologists who may unconsciously reflect the attitudes of a culture that thus far has tended to consider itself beyond the pale of the revolutions and counterrevolutions that have been erupting elsewhere.

Whether this contention is valid or not, the fact remains that crisis as an *explicit* concept receives neither analytic nor comprehensive attention in the huge symposium *Anthropology Today,* nor does it do so even in the collaborative volume titled, a bit ironically, *The Science of Man in the World Crisis.* Also, for the most part it is at best implicit in Keesing's survey of anthropological studies of "culture change—present and future," even though he skirts the problem under such headings as "tensions and change" and "cultural disorganization."[20] Equally disconcerting is a perusal of the tables of contents of the *American Anthropologist;* beginning in 1940 and running beyond the second World War exactly one article, by Bidney, is systematically concerned with the concept of cultural crisis.

Bidney distinguishes between natural and cultural crises by regarding the former as due to forces (such as hurricanes) largely beyond human control and the latter as humanly created (such as civil war). He therefore defines cultural crisis as "a state of emergency brought about by the suspension of normal, or previously prevailing, technological, social, or ideological conditions." Moreover, he points out that the outcome of any particular crisis of this kind is never preordained: it may move toward a radical reorganization or toward the *status quo,* but the tendency is always toward resolution of some kind "since man abhors living in a state of cultural suspension . . . and no society can maintain itself for long in a condition of cultural suspension or chaos."[21]

Crises may be theoretical or practical, Bidney continues, but it is important to note that the two kinds always sooner or later influence each other—above all, that "one's theory as to the nature and origin of cultural crises is itself a major factor in the resolution of such crises."[22] Thus a *sui generis* or transcendent theory of culture—whether materialistic or idealistic—encourages attitudes of acquiescence toward crisis which are less likely to be found in a "humanistic" theory such as his own.

It is Bidney's position that our own age suffers from acute crisis—crisis induced partly by acculturation of unprecedented scope, partly by conflict in basic values, partly by the threat of wholesale destruction, partly by the struggle for power, and partly by still other interrelated factors. Even so, man as the carrier of culture will not ordinarily resolve a crisis at the cost of sacrificing in exchange for survival alone all that he has learned to cherish. Herein lies the ultimate expectation that man will be able to cope successfully with the world crisis today. Notwithstanding all obstacles and setbacks, the fact is that

Man . . . is not content with mere self-preservation in the biological sense, since the self he is most concerned to preserve is his cultural and spiritual self, the one expressed in his moral, religious, and scientific aspirations . . . In a sense, cultural man reverses the natural biological order and determines for himself the conditions and standards of a tolerable and desirable existence.[23]

Another brief anthropological treatment of crisis as a cultural concept is Barnett's effort to weave it into his larger theory. The concept is not so much analyzed as such, however, as it is viewed in relation to the incentive to innovation termed "the deprivation of essentials."[24] Since here alone the term "crisis" is consistently used, Barnett would apparently contend that it is most likely to arise when cultural groups are denied such essentials as land, health, food, or life itself, though it is hazardous to generalize even about these. In any case, a condition of crisis is also opportunity for innovation. Implements of war—atomic energy is easily the most dramatic in our time—are an example if we bear in mind that most of them were already in the making before a crisis precipitated demand for them. But it is equally important to bear in mind that crises do not inevitably produce novel ideas or things. Instead they are frequently restrictive—upon academic freedom, say—for if they do not throttle creativity by force they frequently diminish it by intensification of anxiety, insecurity, withdrawal, fantasy, or a combination of these and other reactions. Nevertheless, that deprivation of essentials provides fertile ground for innovation is indicated by the fact that in any state of crisis

. . . a familiar universe of associations and sanctions has been distorted or destroyed and must be reorganized. The wrenching away of any control mechanism . . . requires a reorientation. Unsettlement for any cause creates a fluid condition in which the old values are no longer operative. With the old sanctions and compulsives gone or of doubtful validity, the way is open for the creation and the acceptance of new interpretations.[25]

One study that illustrates and supplements this generalization is Laura Thompson's *Culture in Crisis,* an interpretation of the Hopi Indians of northern Arizona. It was conducted with the cooperation of the United States Department of the Interior and is distinguished by careful refinement of conceptual instruments. A cultural crisis is defined "as the manifestation of critical imbalance in one or more essential dimensions of a culture structure in environmental setting."[26] On this basis, Thompson analyzes the crisis confronting "Hopiland" into several components. It is traceable largely, of course, to the impact of white culture, beginning with the Spaniards in the sixteenth century, but aggravated by other conflicts. Thompson sees the core of the crisis to be "ideological"—that is, the Hopi symbolic system, logical and esthetic, is bound to be out of balance with the total environment in which it has been operating.[27] Hence she emphasizes the need to deal with the crisis holistically, for every element is interfused with every other. Although a small group of people, the Hopi constitute a microcosm of "meanings of planetary scope."[28]

Other anthropologists have been concerned with the nature of crisis less systematically and directly. The whole of Malinowski's *Freedom and Civilization,* to be considered later, is an impassioned interpretation of the crisis in freedom set off by the rise of totalitarianism.[29] Kluckhohn's *Mirror for Man,* while far from sharply focused upon the phenomenon of crisis, is not insensitive to the abnormality of our period of history. Thus: "Americans are at present seeing social change of a vastness difficult to comprehend . . . [The] depression and World War II appear to have destroyed the old equilibrium beyond repair."[30]

Finally, Morris Opler has attacked the reactionary character of organic or biological conceptions of history which, he contends, stem from a distrust of man's capacity to cope with cultural crises and to control his destiny. The organicists and racists "have lost their faith, if they ever had any, in mankind's ability to regulate social institutions thoughtfully and to harness culture intelligently"[31]—a loss of faith, he might have added, by no means wholly foreign to *sui generis* theorists of culture.

Reference to conceptions of history brings us back to the cultural philosophers some of whom, I have said, are more concerned with probing into the deeper significance of crisis both formally and concretely than are many other scholars. Take this statement from Sorokin: "The twentieth century, so far, has been the bloodiest period and one of the most turbulent periods . . . in the history of Western civilization and perhaps in the chronicles of mankind in general." Or take Toynbee as another example: even the summary of his position already given should be enough to reveal that he builds his theory around the core idea that the history of culture is one of recurrent crisis. His chief hypotheses, such as withdrawal-and-return, challenge-and-response, are instruments of this idea. Much of his work is reminiscent of the Hegelian philosophy of history and even of the Marxian, both of which are built on the premise that all reality, including culture, has been an intermittent process of conflict and resolution of conflict. As Josiah Royce said, Hegel's Absolute is "a man of war. The dust and the blood of ages of humanity's spiritual life are upon him . . ."[32]

Among American philosophers of culture, I know of none who has dealt with the substantive nature of crisis more forthrightly or brilliantly than has Lewis Mumford. He believes, and richly documents his belief, that ours is a time of disintegration but also of capacity for reintegration—for "renewal," to recall his own favorite term. "The age that we live in," he insists, "threatens worldwide catastrophe; but it likewise holds forth unexpected hope and unexampled promise."[33] But Mumford is not a confirmed meliorist; he does not believe that man will inevitably correct the evils now besetting him. Instead, he sees three courses open: one, to blunder along; two, to superimpose a program of enforced and artificial stabilization; three, to change the total pattern of modern culture. Although the world may choose any one of the three alternatives, the first two he himself rejects as futile and self-defeating; the third he recognizes to be difficult beyond words. Indeed,

Such a change does not come about purely by rational decision: it will come, probably, only as the outcome of a crisis so threatening, so calamitous in its possibilities, so empty of easier alternatives, that something like a spontaneous collective decision will be possible . . .[34]

Mumford believes that we are now at the threshold of the moment when this change may and should occur. Indeed, he is convinced that the crisis, both internal or personal and external or cultural, is already at the breaking-point:

The period through which we are living presents itself as one of unmitigated confusion and disintegration: a period of paralyzing economic depressions, of unrestrained butcheries and enslavements, and of world-ravaging wars: a period whose evil fulfillments have betrayed all its beneficent promises. But behind all these phenomena of physical destruction we can detect an earlier and perhaps more fundamental series of changes: a loss of communion between classes and peoples, a breakdown in stable behavior, a loss of form and purpose in many of the arts . . .[35]

Today, then,

The time has come for a new drama to be conceived and enacted . . . Now, as once before in the disintegrating classic and medieval worlds, the achievement of a new personality, of a new attitude toward man and nature and the cosmos, are matters of life and death . . . A crisis that has been faced and mastered gives the survivor a new confidence in his powers: thereby he reaches a higher point than he might have achieved through a more normal line of growth. There lies our hope.[36]

And there also lies Mumford's affinity with the "humanistic" attitudes toward cultural process in general, and crisis in particular, that are shared by anthropological authorities as diverse as Bidney, Malinowski, Kluckhohn, Opler, and Thompson.

CAUSATION AND PREDICTION

The final concepts I have selected as pertinent to the problem of human process are not as exhaustively treated by anthropologists as they ought to be. Typical discussions of causation and prediction are piecemeal at best, while even in most of the studies where one would expect systematic analysis—Barnett's *Innovation* is one—we are likely to find meager explicit consideration given to either concept. Keesing is undoubtedly correct when he asserts that the "problem of causation has engaged . . . the attention of philosophers, historians, and perhaps other groups of scholars much more than it has of anthropologists."[37]

Yet it is obvious that if we are to understand cultural process we cannot avoid the question of the causes that generate cultural change —a question that leads, of course, to the still more basic one in the philosophy of science of what is meant by "cause" and its twin concept, "effect." Of equal importance is "prediction": Can we, by careful analysis of the order and process of culture, predict a given course of cultural events? The close relation of this question to others —for example, whether we can deliberately control cultural change in desirable directions—is of paramount importance to education when conceived as one of the means of such control.

In keeping with the thoroughly experimental tone of recent anthropological investigations, the majority of experts look with suspicion upon any doctrine of causation and prediction that reduces cultural process to a mechanical sequence of cause-and-effect. While the influence of mechanistic physics continues in anthropology, as it does in all the behavioral sciences, the trend is away from this classical model of scientific research—a trend also resulting from the influence of the physical sciences. Curiously, however, the philosopher of science who comes perhaps closest to anticipating the assumptions of contemporary scientific theory regarding causation is one who lived some two centuries ago: the great David Hume. Causation for him, and for countless followers since, becomes a concept connoting solely the empirically observable relations between concomitant events. Since Hume the complexities involved in determining such relations have led to more and more emphasis upon their probability rather than certainty; in fact, an elaborate discipline based upon statistical and other methods for establishing probability has recently developed in both the social and physical sciences.

Thus, among many present-day anthropologists there seems to be agreement that no theory of cultural change traceable to a single cause—even to a limited set of specifically delineated causes—is sufficient to explain the intricate processes involved. The same generalization applies to other culture-theorists, especially if it may be assumed that their views are well represented in such collaborative works as *The Social Sciences in Historical Study*,[38] or in G. K. Renier's able *History—Its Purpose and Method*.[39]

It follows that if causation is treated so flexibly and cautiously, prediction would be also. A majority consensus apparently prevails that the scientific study of culture can produce tentative, hence only probable, predictions of the course of cultural change. "Inevitability" is a *verboten* term among most experts of our day.[40]

With such qualifications, however, causation and prediction continue to play a role in culture-theory. *Sui genersis* theorists such as White are most ready not only to trace the evolution of culture through a chain of objectively ordered causes and effects but to explain its dynamics by a single cause of that evolution. In his case this cause is "the technological system" for it is "both primary and basic in importance; all human life and culture rest and depend upon it." Social systems and philosophic systems are secondary; while they have retroactive influence they are at best conditions and not primary causes. But even White is unwilling to predict the future too assuredly: he speaks of "the next war" as though it were inevitable; but he also reveals a certain cautious hope that

. . . . the creative powers of the new technology [based upon radioactive energy] may be sufficiently great to rise up from the ruins and to enclose the whole world in a single political embrace. Then and only then will the curse of war be lifted and the way made free and open for a fuller and richer life. [41]

At the opposite extreme from White, yet alike in their efforts to trace cultural processes to a sufficient cause, are the psychoanalytic theorists. Róheim is perhaps the most vehement exponent of the view that cultures are determined by patterns of behavior established in infancy and derived from innate instincts. Here such familiar but influential theories as the Oedipus complex are utilized, Róheim having gone so far as to study firsthand and interpret aboriginal cultures of Australia from a Freudian viewpoint.[42] This approach, while anathema to White and to all theorists influenced by or close to the superorganic position, is nevertheless similar to theirs in the paradoxical ways that Marx and Freud are similar. As students of these giants of modern thought have observed, the former interprets man chiefly from the "outside in" and the latter from the "inside out," but both tempt us to accept a monistic as well as a materialistic theory of cultural causation—the one in objective economic forces, the other in subjective instinctual drives. Both approaches, therefore, are rejected by the majority of culture-theorists today in favor of the more pluralistic, flexible viewpoint discussed above.

Let us consider what this viewpoint involves. In their succinct discussion of causation, Kroeber and Kluckhohn call attention to the many non-cultural factors that affect cultural processes: those of the natural environment (inorganic as well as organic), of racial stocks, of gifted individuals who may "traceably influence" the cultures to which they belong, and of social phenomena such as population. Still more pertinent are cultural processes and structures themselves, for every given culture is the product of a long history. One important principle that follows is that of "circular causality"—the interaction of these processes and structures not only with themselves but with the natural environment, social factors, and with individual persons, gifted or not. Here is their answer to monistic theorists of the types just mentioned: Kroeber and Kluckhohn are at least as much opposed to "toilet-training" theories of causation as they are to economic or geographic theories, but they admit that personality affects culture at the same time that they stress the ways that culture affects personality.[43]

Elsewhere, Kroeber has recognized the principle of circular causality by utilizing the concept of "efficient cause," derived from Aristotle (by way of Bidney). By this he means the common-sense notion of an immediate relation between effect and cause, as in the case of a carpenter being the cause of building a house. In the same sense, individual personalities are the cause of culture: without them the culture would not occur any more than would a house rise without the work of a carpenter. But such *efficient* causes are not therefore *sufficient*. The culture has taught the carpenter how to build the house in the first place; actually it has done much more than that, for it has set the style of the house and shaped the arrangements for living characteristic of the culture. The form or pattern of culture that precedes and influences such style and arrangement is therefore called, again after Aristotle, "formal cause," and it is this which Kroeber considers the primary concern of anthropology.[44]

We can now better appreciate that "formal cause" is the primary postulate of his *Configurations of Culture Growth*—a study in which, it will be remembered, he makes no claims to having discovered "immanent causes" or laws that would enable him to predict future cultural configurations. He shows that cultures assume patterns of "florescence" and "deflorescence," but he is in no way certain as to why they do so. He only suggests that they become tired—an explanation that is hardly more sufficient than the fact of individuals being the "efficient cause" of cultures or carpenters of houses. While continuing to express uncertainty about aspects of the problem, he does clearly and forcibly epitomize his position:

What is therefore operative is a powerful system of circular causality. The human beings who influence culture are themselves molded; and they are molded through the intervention of other men who are culturalized and thus products of previous culture. So it is clear that, while human beings are always the *immediate* causes of cultural events, these human causes are themselves the result of antecedent cultural situations, having been fitted to the existing cultural forms which they encounter. There is thus a continuity of indirect causation from culture event to culture event through the medium of human intermediaries. These intermediaries are concerned, first of all, with relieving their own tensions and achieving their personal gratification; but in so doing they also transmit, and to some degree modify, the culture which they carry because they have been conditioned to it. In a sense, accordingly, a kind of cultural causality is also operative.

However, compared with the immediate efficient causality of men on culture, the causation of culture on culture is indirect, remote, and largely a functional relation of form to form.[45]

Within this frame of reference, he and Kluckhohn are, however, willing to go so far as to say that "reasonably accurate predictions of culture change" may be made "under specified conditions."[46] Here Kluckhohn's theory of implicit and explicit culture, noted in Chapter Five, is again relevant. For, if the patterns of an implicit culture can be discovered, then we have one important kind of causal relation with the more overtly observable patterns of the explicit culture—the latter being, in a meaningful sense, the effect of the former. The operational emphasis that we have earlier noted in these authorities also comes to the fore: "The patterns of the implicit culture are . . . purely inferential constructs. They are *thematic principles* which the investigator introduces to explain connections among a wide range of culture content and form that are not obvious in the world of direct observation."[47]

This operational emphasis calls for more consideration, and extends our analysis of causation further than Kroeber and Kluckhohn seem willing to go. In their legitimate concern to avoid monistic and mechanistic causation, they and most other present-day theorists of culture have in my judgment come near to throwing out the baby with the bath —that is, they have failed sufficiently to retain and to utilize the concept of causation as a creative instrument by which cultural and historical phenomena could be more fully explained and even predicted. The concept of implicit culture is one example of how it can be used in this fruitful way. But we might ask whether various other concepts, if they were reconsidered as "inferential constructs," could not assume a significance and fruitfulness that they cannot have so long as they are treated as, say, White or Róheim treats them. For example, economic causes of cultural change can be viewed in either of two ways: as hypostatized causal forces that soon take on the character of absolute laws; or as operating ideas that help, by careful utilization of the data of a given historical and cultural period, to clarify the meaning of that period in particular ways. Because anthropologists, like other culture-theorists including historians, have feared the consequences of the former, they have too often of late shied away also from the latter. Actually, it is doubtful whether the "technological" hypothesis, for example, has received anything like enough attention in explaining the present crisis besetting many cultures of the world. But if it has not, this is at least partly because of the oversimplified and dogmatic consequences that follow from its misuse.

Steward's *Theory of Culture Change* comes near to the position for which I am pleading. Consistently operational throughout, he insists that the "relativists" and "particularists" have gone much too far in their skepticism of causation as an instrument of cultural interpretation. Though he does not analyze the concept of law with sufficient care, he is convinced that it is entirely legitimate to hypothesize cultural regularities both of a sequential, historical type and of a functional type. He illustrates this conviction with technology itself, showing how "basketry, pottery, weaving, metallurgy, and construction" operate in a number of "formative eras" across the world. He considers diffusion too simple an explanation of cultural process, often failing to consider how cultures develop parallel types of basic technology and social institutions. As noted earlier, he is a "multilinear evolutionist": he rejects any "world scheme of cultural development or a set of universally valid laws," and he has no pet doctrine of ultimate causality (such as Spengler's or White's). But he does insist upon the propriety of "working hypotheses" that formulate recurrences of cultural types—that is, of cause-effect relationships empirically observable on different levels of culture in time and space.[48]

The need for this way of utilizing causation applies even to a work like Toynbee's. The vigor of his interpretations often tempts his reader to transform his favorite causal postulates into misplaced concretions. For this reason, historians of the empirical-pluralistic school are impatient with his work. Yet, if a concept like Toynbee's "withdrawal-and-return" is utilized operationally, it might generate challenging and meaningful judgments concerning historical processes. One's own assumption regarding causation will therefore strongly affect one's appraisal of Toynbee and other audacious interpreters of history. Operationally interpreted, they become significant in a way denied them so long as they reduce their legitimate hypotheses of historic explanation to illegitimate hypostatic absolutes.

In a cogent discussion of "causes in culture," Rushton Coulborn offers support, at least by implication, for this point of view. He calls attention to the value of the formal-cause approach, stressed by Kroeber, which focuses upon the causal relations of cultural forms or patterns. But he also argues that it is constricting to limit the scientific study of culture to this kind of causation—a point, we have seen, with which Kroeber agrees but does not implement in his primary studies. Other causal factors play a role too, and to take these into consideration on occasion (or, in my terms, to utilize these as operational constructs) is not only proper but unavoidable if the full scope of cultural process is to be embraced in theory and practice. So considered, the technological system, the Oedipus complex, and any number of other hypotheses deserve consideration not so much in opposition to as in supplementation of the culture-pattern, formal-cause approach that continues to be so productive.

Coulborn also brings us to the final question raised at the outset of this section: whether causation, as considered by culture-theorists, in any sense implies deliberate control of cultural processes. His own answer is affirmative. For, among the causes at work upon culture other than those purely *of* culture, one must include the "self-determination, however small, of the human participants . . ." Here the historian is of importance, for he is much more concerned with the novelty of events—especially those induced by human agents—than with the repetitiveness which anthropologists stress. (At this point he reminds us of White.) It is doubtful whether historians or anthropologists would be happy with this dichotomy, although Kroeber endorses it.[49] But when Coulborn urges that both disciplines be considered complementary rather than mutually exclusive, he deserves to be applauded not only because he invites an interdisciplinary approach to the problem, but because he points toward a resolution of the ancient conflict between "free will" and "determinism."

For he is saying that human agents play a creative role in cultural process—more of a role than the Kroeberian type of interpretation sometimes infers. At the same time he is insistent that the efficacy of either human will or natural environment in modifying cultural patterns is obviously not infinite. "The natural limitation of variation of culture patterns has probably contributed to the illusion that the culture develops its patterns without any regard at all to the individuality of the persons who make it."[50]

Bidney's too brief but brilliant treatment of causation leads him to a rather similar conclusion. Man and society are the "active, efficient

. . . originators and directors of the cultural process."[51] This does not mean that cultural patterns are not determined by preceding causes, both cultural and non-cultural: every effect requires "certain necessary and sufficient conditions for its existence" and in this sense every effect is determined by a cause. But this is quite different from assuming that we can deduce the effect *from* the cause; for causes may produce effects that are in no way necessarily established in advance of the effect's appearance. This is reminiscent of Hume. It leads to an "emergent theory of causality" that allows not only for the emergence of a distinctive level of nature called culture, but also for the operation of human agents who may help to shape the further course of cultural development. When we attempt to deduce cultural effects solely from cultural causes we are trapped into a kind of mechanistic determinism that prevents us from considering the role of human creativity either as a descriptive phenomenon or as a normative guide to further cultural change.

The scientific possibility of cultural prediction is thereby lessened, to be sure, for the chain of culture is constantly being reforged. Yet it is probable that, despite an inadequate treatment of causation, the general position taken by Herskovits would be shared by many culture-theorists: if "cultural laws" are regarded as "statements of process," then there is no reason why a certain degree of prediction as to particular cultures or phases of cultures is not legitimate.[52] Even though he might agree with Coulborn and Bidney that individual human agents can influence and thereby help to control cultural events, Herskovits would also certainly maintain that their influence is limited by the persistences and resistances of cultural patterns. The more such persistences and resistances can be recognized, the more prediction becomes possible; but so too, paradoxically, does the capacity of man to control culture through his knowledge of them, and thus to modify predicted outcomes. No less than in other areas of nature, scientific understanding of causal relations is integral to any operations that men attempt by which these relations may themselves be altered.

"EDUCATION AND THE CULTURAL PROCESS": RELATIONS OF THEORY TO PRACTICE

That the concepts considered in this chapter are of great significance for education should be obvious from the fact that they are manifestations *of* education. Not, of course, education in a narrow or formalized sense, but rather in the much more pervasive sense of the inclusive process by which people learn to mold their cultural behavior. One may even assert that culture-theorists, in the sparse degree to which they have thus far singled out education for intensive analysis as an institution of culture, have probably done so mostly at this focal point. Interestingly, one of the rare collaborative discussions of the field by culture-theorists and practitioners is entitled "Education and the Cultural Process."[54]

Yet it is, I hope, a fair judgment that some of the most fertile implications emerging from such concepts as discovery and acculturation are not so much those already appreciated directly for their educational relevance as those that may be inferred indirectly from the nature of cultural process itself. I emphasize this latter type here.

Builders of modern curricula on the elementary, secondary, and college levels, especially those organized in terms of the "problem approach," confront the endless task of selecting themes that are likely to motivate genuine, sustained interest and are sufficiently fundamental to justify the time and energy devoted to them. How shall we deal with problems so that they become meaningful to the young—so that they can be transfused into living experience, while at the same time be grounded solidly in the most reliable knowledge available about "nature and human nature"?

Let us begin with a simple example that gradually leads toward answering this large and serious question. As every parent knows, babies hardly a year old are fascinated by doorknobs, hooks, dials, switches, wheels, and hundreds of other gadgets common to our mechanized age. It is in accord with normal growth and interest to treat such culture-traits as opportunities for early learning—at first their simplest manifestations, and a bit later their relations within culture-complexes and their common uses. Still later, by the third or fourth grade, students may trace the main steps through which, for example, the automobile has evolved from the one-wheeled cart to its present form; they may review the changes it has brought to civilization "almost overnight"; and they will certainly want to inspect startling designs for "the car of tomorrow."

Thus is the ground prepared for systematic study (by, say, the fifth grade) of a great cultural phenomenon such as transportation.

Here the teacher may consciously utilize the concepts of *discovery* and *invention* to follow the evolution of boats and other conveyances through some of the early stages known to archaeology, to appreciate the inventiveness of people of nonliterate as well as literate cultures, and to dramatize the story of transportation with class-painted murals, cardboard or wooden models, and in other ways that teachers of art could suggest. The role of accident in discovery, the importance of natural resources, the beginnings of science and technology—all are problems that bear upon the theme.

Even the concept of *crisis* helps to increase the young student's understanding. The airplane as a mode of transportation is, of course, still more revolutionary in its impact upon cultural change than was the automobile. The use of the airplane by Australian ethnologists to increase their contacts with remote aborigines, its effects upon "national character," its terrifying contributions to globe-encircling warfare—these are instances of how, through transportation as a central problematic theme, the meaning of cultural crisis could itself be deepened.

Although this theme might be followed much further, let me turn to other concepts of process considered earlier. *Diffusion* enables students to view any number of transcultural phenomena in a new light—for example, by organizing "research" teams to study the myriad of objects that have been diffused through American culture from Europe and Asia. (Displays of these artifacts are one project that has already been successfully organized in a number of schools.) Ways to relate diffusion to cultural history are also numerous, both in courses dealing with specific periods and, on the upper levels, in large syntheses such as that of Toynbee who, incidentally, often utilizes the concept of diffusion.

Acculturation is equally fertile for learning. Here Unesco publications are graphic and contemporary, *Cultural Patterns and Technical Change*[55] being a good example. Not only are several cultures of different types described by this study in terms of the effects of Point Four and other programs, but particular fields undergoing rapid transformation are singled out for attention: agriculture, nutrition, maternal and child care, public health, industrialization, and fundamental education itself. In each of these fields, problems that arise from disequilibrium are considered, along with practical techniques for reducing resistance and encouraging acceptance. Moreover, the problem of force as a factor in acculturation is at least implicit. To what extent is it ever defensible to impose, say, American patterns upon another culture? Here is an issue that haunts the pages of this report as it does so many others that deal with problems of acculturation. That new skills are needed to deal with all these problems leads directly to the demand, in turn, for new types of training in "human engineering"—training that has scarcely begun to achieve recognition on the college and university levels either by the social sciences or by teacher education itself. In the latter field, centers of human-relations studies in professional schools are frontier opportunities.

Assimilation, we have found, is so proximate conceptually to acculturation that many of the issues lending themselves to educational attention are applicable to the former as well. One question raised in our earlier discussion was whether the process of assimilation can be deliberately accelerated or retarded by organized planning— a question that the above Unesco study, among others, answers with a guarded "yes." A reiterated warning of many of these studies is that efforts toward assimilation will boomerang unless carefully controlled; that is, such suspicion and antagonism can be generated that barriers will rise rather than lower between particular cultures in contact. This was one of the most startling effects of the Nazi invasion of Norway and France. Today, too, among countries within the communist orbit—notably, Poland and Hungary—resistance to assimilation is strong.

Apropos as such examples are, especially for studies in international relations, problems of assimilation on the level of the local community naturally seem more pressing to the average educator. How far, how rapidly, by what methods, shall "immigrant" children of, let us say, Puerto Rican background be absorbed into already established cultural patterns of a great city like New York? Shall they be taught only in the English language? Shall they be compelled to eat only foods prepared in school cafeterias according to American recipes? Shall they learn only American games and songs? Shall they be forced to comply as rigidly with American habits of punctuality as already assimilated children are?

Comparable questions arise with regard to rural-urban relations, to age groups, to class and status levels. Shall, for example, maximum assimilation according to the dominant middle-status standards of public-school faculties be assumed as a matter of course? If not, then how can alternative processes be planned and implemented rather than left merely to the often unconscious biases of an individual teacher? These questions, though surely disturbing, are not unanswerable. Not only do leaders in the field of intercultural education agree that blundering efforts to hasten assimilation in children will produce injurious results but, given a reconstructed teacher-training program of the sort to be proposed in Chapter Thirteen, there is no good reason why many such results cannot be corrected.

Turning next to *innovation*, it is striking, yet hardly unique in anthropological writings, that Barnett omits "education" from his extensive index. Nevertheless, his interpretation abounds with guidance for the educator searching for ways by which schools could become more effective partners of cultural change. His postulate that innovation is a natural, universal experience of culture is a direct challenge to those who contend that education is almost if not entirely a reinforcing rather than a reconstructing agency of culture. If, however, it is to be of the latter as well as of the former kind, certain rules are essential—for example, the rule (also stressed by Gillin) that acceptance of an innovative proposal must be tied to what people already genuinely want, and expressed in familiar terms. Abstractly, this is far from a novel recommendation; yet many a promising educational venture has foundered because its initiators failed to estimate the emotional and social attitudes of potential acceptors—children, teachers, and parents alike. Similarly, the rule that acceptance of innovations in curricula, in methods of evaluation, or other school practices must appeal to groups of people amenable to such changes is often overlooked by educational leaders. Instead of cultivating those sections of the community from which support of innovations is most likely to come—such as minority or other dissident groups who may justly feel that some of their needs are neglected by education—leaders too often cater primarily to middle- or upper-status groups better satisfied with customary policies.

Innovation provides opportunity also for organizing problematic approaches to subject matter. College students on the threshold of maturity are normally interested in changing habits and institutions. Many of them, given chances to participate in choosing and planning their studies, would benefit by careful exploration of how and why "mutations" or lesser innovations have occurred in the history of cultures, looking toward practical methods for sharing actively in innovations proposed or under way in their own culture. Here culture-theory and research could be fused with social philosophy, social psychology, political science, and related fields. The works of Kurt Lewin, John Dewey, and Thorstein Veblen (each cited in the *References*) exemplify interdisciplinary resources that could stimulate both intellectually and at the level of action.

Focus is an operational concept that helps to strengthen the educational value of innovation by calling attention to pliable areas in a given culture. Assuming that the focus of our own culture is technological, it does seem that in this sphere we are readier to examine methods and devices, to strive for improvement and innovation, than in such spheres as organized religion. Granting that the concept is debatable, it suggests to educators that if they are to have any kind of creative function, one of their first duties must be to determine as clearly as possible the precise character of the focus or foci of a given culture, and then to construct strategies of change geared to this character.

The concept of crisis, already exemplified in the project on transportation, is another neglected educational resource. There is no good reason, except timidity or irresponsibility, that prevents high schools and colleges from encouraging young people to analyze both the meaning of crisis theoretically and its manifestations overtly. Leaders ought accordingly to clarify their orientation here: they ought to face the issue of whether education is to be regarded as capable of sharing importantly in the control and resolution of crises, or as a pawn of overpowering material or spiritual forces beyond control and resolution. Barnett's point that crisis may serve either to restrict or to encourage innovations is also important; it could be illustrated *ad infinitum* from the experience merely of the past few decades—an opportunity, incidentally, for students themselves to explore the evidence afforded by such works as Thompson's on the Hopi Indian.

On the upper levels, stimulating cores of study in general education extending over a full year or more could center in one great problematic theme: "Is the world in the midst of a major crisis?"

Here the best available authorities, both pro and con, should be consulted—not only anthropological experts like Linton and Malinowski, but historians as well as philosophers of culture like Sorokin, Toynbee, Bidney, and Mumford.

In this perspective, the problem could be raised as to what attitudes such thinkers hold toward the educational process itself. Malinowski is more definite than most: we shall see that he regards education as the partner of cultural dynamics on all levels of sophistication—a position implied, though in different terms, by Bidney and Mumford as well. Toynbee makes the important if familiar point that education can as easily become a weapon to increase human degradation as it can become a power for human betterment. On the whole, nevertheless, both his and Sorokin's scattered comments on education reveal only narrowly conventional notions of its meaning and role.

By contrast, Park in his essay on "Education and the Cultural Crisis" points up the issues that need to be faced by problem-centered learning—issues generated in American communities by shiftings of population (as from South to North); by changes in one institution (such as the economic) at a more rapid rate than in another (such as the political); by severe disharmonies of value (as in sexual conduct); by racial and other minority frustrations and aggressions (as among Negroes and Jews). Can education do anything significant to alleviate these sources of conflict? Park believes that it can. Defining education as a "process by which a society renews and perpetuates its existence . . ." he goes so far as to assert that ultimately there is "no other means." In our time, education's responsibilities are heavy: they demand much stronger stress upon geography, geopolitics, languages, news and propaganda analysis, and world literature and other arts. Above all, they incite us to cure the "blindness" caused by ethnocentrism and provincialism.[56]

But whether the international or the local level is being considered, educators should not forget the admonition of experts that a crisis situation can be settled in more than one way. If schools remain largely so indifferent to the symptoms of crisis that now prevail, they will, in fact, continue to have their part in its resolution. As has often been pointed out, indifference to controversy is itself a choice among alternative choices. It means that education has chosen to allow other agencies—economic pressure groups are one—

to shape courses of action that it should itself be helping to shape. Resolution by default is neither the most responsible nor the most in accord with what culture-theorists are helping us to learn about education as a tool of culture.

The preferred attitude toward *causation and prediction,* the last in our series of concepts of process, should be apparent from the preceding statement. In accordance with an "emergent theory of causality," I would urge educational theory to reject an unqualified determinism, certainly of the classical model: its premise is a hypostatic, mechanistic cultural reality that, in Part II, we have found defective. This is not to say, obviously, that cause-effect relations are not fundamental to culture change and therefore to education. It is to say with Bidney that, while all cultural and educational effects derive from sufficient causes, the infinite variables of human experience are often such as to prevent deduction of specific cultural effects from knowledge of the cause alone. Whether we conceive of education as an opportunity to encourage and strengthen these variables or merely as the transmission belt of a cultural process bound to a fixed chain of causes and effects makes a fundamental difference *to* education.

Two qualifications to this attitude would increase the educational importance of the concept of causation. One is the fertility of the "formal cause" postulate that Kroeber has clarified so well. The search for sequences that reveal the forms of culture according to various patterns of relationship, with minimum regard for individual personalities that still remain their "efficient causes," explodes the spurious belief so widespread especially in the American implicit culture that education singlehandedly can accomplish almost anything. A more reasonable viewpoint is suggested by Kroeber's and Kluckhohn's concept of "circular causality," though I should myself wish to see more stress placed upon the causal role of organized social action through education than would be congenial to those who find patterning to be the master principle of cultural process.

The other qualification was anticipated by the discussion in Chapter Six of philosophies of cultural history as helpful leads to integrated programs. I proposed there that Toynbee and others, considered cautiously and undogmatically, could provide exciting insights and perspectives that history courses commonly lack. This proposal relates to a second one made earlier in this chapter for more straightforward causal hypotheses in the study of cultural history. Here I suggest that both proposals be combined into fresh interpretations of *educational* history. To take but one example: a "technological interpretation of education" might provide a great deal of new insight into the causal factors at work upon the evolution of schools as cultural institutions. The use of such cultural hypotheses is partially exemplified in Freeman Butts' *A Cultural History of Western Education.*[57] But its causal hypotheses are frequently vague, and there is much less sustained or systematic effort to apply them to great educational movements than there is concern to emulate the irresolute pluralism currently fashionable among historians.

Either of these qualifications to an "emergent theory of causality" is compatible with the need for educators to practice with the concept of prediction. Leaders will strengthen their contributions to the processes of culture as they learn more expertly to anticipate and prepare for future changes. (The effects of increased populations and rising age-levels in the schools are two examples that are already receiving attention). Similarly, the operational utilization of causal hypotheses such as the technological could help education to predict, if not *the* way the schools will move, then certainly the more likely ways. (The effect of automation on jobs and leisure time is an example.)

In sum, just as culture-theory is beginning to understand and to operate with scientific principles of causation and prediction, so education must do likewise if it ever expects to utilize the processes of culture with comparable skill.

CHAPTER NINE

PERSONALITY IN CULTURAL PROCESS

THE CULTURE-AND-PERSONALITY FRONTIER

No study of contemporary culture-theory could justify a claim to inclusiveness that did not give attention to the relations of personality to culture. Considerably less than thirty years ago, this assertion would hardly have been true. In not much more than a decade, the culture-and-personality field, as it may be called, has become one of the most conspicuous, exciting developments in the human sciences—a development that has affected not only anthropology but sociology, psychiatry, and psychology. The interdisciplinary character of the movement is one of its salutary features.

The relevant literature, both theoretical and experimental, that has emerged in such a brief span is already so overwhelming that it would be impossible even to survey it, much less to appraise it with competence. I confine my interpretation, therefore, primarily to one aspect —namely, to how personality, as interpreted by culture-theorists, bears upon the problem of human process. This aspect is sufficiently central to disclose something of the wider compass of concepts, data, and issues.

The polaristic character of culture-theory is once more revealed by the fact that problems raised by the culture-and-personality movement have been clamoring for attention. In our examination of the problem of cultural reality we saw, for example, that experts are in conflict over whether, and, if so, how, individuals are significant to the meaning of culture. If pushed, even *sui generis* protagonists would agree that without human personalities there would be no culture, although this is not to admit that the sum of human personalities is all that culture means. For them (and indeed for those of less extreme view) the sum is not only greater than its parts; it is qualitatively different.

The problem emerged even more plainly in the preceding chapter when we examined the concept of causation. There we found that the author of the superorganic theory of culture, Kroeber, now recognizes willingly that individual persons are the "efficient causes" of culture and in this exact sense are both its creators and manipulators. But he is unwilling to agree that anthropology must accordingly be reduced to anything like psychology. On the contrary, he is as insistent as ever that it is not the relation of personality to culture, but the relation of the forms of culture to one another, that remains the anthropologist's distinctive and important concern. And even Kluckhohn, one of the pioneers in the culture-and-personality field, joins with him in asserting that it is a fair question whether the study of culture "does not tend to be more effective if it is abstracted from individual or personality factors . . ."[1] More emphatically,

. . . the well tried and mainly impersonal methods of pure culture studies still seem more efficiently productive for the understanding of culture process than the newer efforts to penetrate deeper by dealing simultaneously with the two variables of personality and culture—each so highly variable in itself.[2]

Kroeber and Kluckhohn do not deny that cooperation between psychology and anthropology may produce fruitful results in the future, and their concept of "circular causality" supports this admission. They are inclined to the judgment, however, that efforts thus far are sometimes premature, forced, and indefinite. Thus we approach the problem with appreciation not only of its complexity but of the still exploratory status of culture-and-personality studies as one subdivision of cultural process.

THEORIES OF LEARNING AND PERSONALITY

A central aspect of this subdivision is the nature of learning. All culture-theorists agree that personalities would not emerge at all if human beings were unable to learn. For personality is not an innate or inherited phenomenon of human nature; it is in great degree the product of complex influences derived from its cultural environment. True, the individual possesses inherited characteristics which are now well recognized by psychologists and biologists—one being the *capacity* to learn. But these characteristics by no means constitute personality. Kluckhohn and Henry A. Murray (the latter a psychiatrist and psychologist, not an anthropologist) remind us that every personality is " 'like all other men,' 'like some other men,' 'like no other man' "[3]—that is, it possesses constitutional determinants such as appetite for food and sex that are universal in the human species; it holds group memberships and plays roles that are similar to those of various other members; and it finds itself in situations that are unique and that affect it uniquely. But these determinants are also interrelated in a variety of ways—the pattern of interrelations that emerges constituting the particular personality.

The function of learning in the shaping of this particular personality is the problem in which we are now interested. As Kroeber and Kluckhohn have shown, some culture-theorists even consider learning to be the chief differentia of culture. Benedict, for example, is quoted to the effect that "culture is the sociological term for learned behavior, behavior which . . . is not given at birth, which is not determined by his germ cells as is the behavior of wasps or the social ants, but must be learned anew from grown people by each new generation."[4]

An apt term for cultural learning, as anthropologists view it, is *enculturation,* defined by Herskovits as "in essence a process of conscious or unconscious conditioning, exercised within the limits sanctioned by a . . . body of custom."[5] Such learning continues through life, although in the earliest years it is mainly concerned with fundamentals like eating and with the aim of cultural stability, while in later years it extends to more complex, abstract aspects of living and is more conducive to cultural change. Herskovits makes too sharp a distinction between the two functions of enculturation: we shall see that there is no *a priori* reason why it need be as exclusively devoted to conformity in its earlier stages as he implies. His insistence, however, that cultural learning—indeed, *all* learning—is a process of conditioning is of crucial importance to the role of personality in cultural process. Nor is it surprising that Boas, as Herskovits reminds us, called ethnography a "behavioristic discipline."[6] Behaviorism, based as it is on a theory of conditioning, has influenced culture-theory to an enormous extent—more, if Hallowell is right, than any other psychological school.[7]

This influence is illustrated by the approach of the Yale University group, which has probably given more painstaking attention to learning theory than any other American group of experts in the culture-and-personality field. One of their central interests, however, has been their attempt to fuse psychoanalysis with behaviorism, while modifying the more orthodox formulations of both theories. By comparison, the influence of organismic, gestalt, and field theory, and of more recent theories that are developing from the research of psychologists like Adelbert Ames and Hadley Cantril,[8] appears to be as yet secondary. This judgment, in the degree that it is accurate, is of importance for education: it means that the theory of learning emphasized by anthropologists has encouraged a type of education committed more to cultural adjustment than to cultural reconstruction, and thus to a type of education of which this volume is critical. But the predominant orientation, however influential, is by no means exclusive, and the entire effort of culture-theorists to deal with learning is still so exploratory that diverse educational implications may be drawn from various approaches to the problem.

A clear formulation of the Yale approach is provided by Gillin.[9] He makes the cogent point that since culture is entirely learned, it is high time that anthropologists beg the question no longer but ask what they mean. For Gillin, what they mean must be couched in terms of habit-formation which, in turn, derives from stimulus-response, pleasure-pain postulates characteristic of behaviorist theory as expressed, not in its orthodox form, but chiefly by C. L. Hull and his associates. It is unnecessary to review this theory. The crucial importance of trial-and-error as the basis of all learning in men as well as other animals, the role of primary and secondary drives, the function of reward and punishment—all of these will be familiar to students of American psychology.

The bearing of learning, so conceived, upon personality requires consideration also of psychoanalytic theory—a consideration developed with telling effect in the work of Dollard.[10] That the process of habit-formation is by no means primarily a conscious one is recognized, of course, by behaviorists themselves. But the work of Sigmund Freud and his school enriched this recognition: his concept of the unconscious, and his analysis of the interworkings of id, ego, and superego, demonstrated that every personality acquires constellations of habits that are the products of its whole history, especially its childhood history. The training one receives from parents and other

surrogates of the culture, much of it in his first years, shapes his outlook upon the whole of life; yet it does so with scarcely any awareness
on his part that his habits are being formed, his emotional and
intellectual character being set, his adult reactions being molded.

The significance of the marriage between behaviorist and psychoanalytic theory is epitomized by Gillin: "[The] same basic principles
of stimulus, drive, reward, and punishment apparently apply not only
to conscious but also to unconscious and subconscious activity."[11] It
is exemplified and tested in a growing body of research, one of the
most interesting examples of which is the cross-cultural study *Child
Training and Personality,* by the anthropologist John W. M. Whiting,
and his associate, Irvin L. Child.[12] The point is the implications of
this marriage for culture-theory itself. These are, to paraphrase Gillin:
first, that culture provides both the conscious and unconscious conditions for learning—conditions available from infancy onward;
second, that culture encourages certain conscious and unconscious
responses and discourages others, depending in turn upon habits
previously established; third, that culture reinforces these responses
by systems of reward and punishment; and fourth, that culture tends
to perpetuate itself by means of the learning that thus occurs, although
cultural changes may also occur as stimuli and responses are themselves modified or altered.

The cultural equivalent of habits is *custom;* in Whiting's and
Child's terms, custom is "a characteristic habit of a typical member
of a cultural category of persons."[13] They would agree with Gillin
that customs, too, are in a sense unconscious at least as often as they
are consciously held by a cultural group—an extension of Freudian
theory that reminds us of Sapir's early essay, "The Unconscious Patterning of Behavior in Society,"[14] of Kluckhohn's theory of implicit
culture, and thus of the concept of culture-configuration discussed in
Chapter Five.

The meaning and role of personality, as it develops in the milieu
of culture chiefly because of learning, are probably the dominant
interest of anthropologists who have worked on the culture-and-
personality frontier. Gillin's definition of personality is: "an internal organization of emotions, attitudes, idea patterns, and tenden-
cies to overt action."[15] This internal organization manifests itself in
a continuity of experiences that may be called the individual's "stage

of life": it is an amalgam, harmonious and/or inharmonious, of the three dimensions of genetic, cultural, and unique determinants analyzed by Kluckhohn and Murray in their own detailed conception of personality mentioned earlier. They summarize this conception as "the continuity of functional forms and forces manifested through sequences of organized regnant processes and overt behaviors from birth to death."[16] Other anthropologists, such as Sapir, who is often considered to be the leading instigator of the culture-and-personality movement, offer still different definitions. Perhaps the simplest of all such definitions, however, is John J. Honigmann's: personality means "the actions, thoughts, and feelings characteristic of an individual." But because these characteristics are so strongly affected by the individual's culture, we may say that at least in part "personality means culture reflected in individual behavior."[17]

Let us follow Honigmann's study of cultural learning a little further, since his book *Culture and Personality* is a competent if eclectic survey of the field. He emphasizes that the anthropologist is interested in learning as it occurs because of an individual's group-memberships or, in other words, because he is largely a culture-shaped being. The concept of pattern, already studied, here assumes a fresh importance if we recognize that it is really *patterning* that largely shapes the individual into a personality. The influence of behaviorist-psychoanalytic theory is strong in his review: terms like reward and punishment, primary and secondary drives, the conscious and unconscious, are emphasized. Honigmann also calls attention to the fact that learning is both direct and indirect: the former is the familiar process of deliberate instruction, the latter the much more influential process of learning that occurs by the sheer inevitability and often unconscious exposure to the welter of habits, attitudes, and practices that envelop every individual. One of the commonest sources of personality conflict is, of course, the discontinuities and contradictions between what one learns directly and what one learns indirectly—a phenomenon recognized by every psychiatrist but especially serious in cultures undergoing rapid change. Another important emphasis is the role of symbols; for learning is largely a symbolic process, and personality consists to a great extent of the individual's symbolic portrayal of himself and his world. Honigmann concludes his review with an unfortunate topic-head, "Patterning versus Learning," for what he goes on to show is that the two are not at all antithetical. He writes, for example, of "physiological personality patterns" such as digestive processes and posture that are shaped by cultures in different ways. These are "standardized non-deliberately, unconsciously, or so casually that the ordinary notion of learning does not apply."[18] But the "ordinary notion," whatever that may mean, is deficient if it suggests that learning is to be separated from the *total* process of personality formation. Both behaviorist and psychoanalytic theories have pointed toward a more inclusive and adequate conception. Other culture-theorists, whom we shall now consider, point even more clearly toward that conception.

The need for the latter was anticipated in a pioneering inter-disciplinary conference on culture-and-personality held in 1947.[19] Significantly, three of the non-anthropological contributors are famous for their reformulations and supplementations of both behaviorist and psychoanalytic theory: Gardner Murphy, Erich Fromm, and Harry Stack Sullivan. Murphy's work on personality[20] is, of course, implicit in his statements here. His approach is primarily based on "field" theory which, as was shown by way of Benedict earlier, reflects revolutionary developments that have taken place in physical science and are being adapted by the social sciences. He questions the assumptions that have governed behaviorism, for example, by showing that these (the stimulus-response concept is one) are modelled upon a mechanistic philosophy of science now becoming outmoded. He insists that culture-and-personality must be considered as a field of forces within one encompassing matrix of experience, in which each is relational to the other—a "bi-polar relation of organism and environment."[21] Therefore he is as much concerned with the role of personality in shaping culture as he is with the power of culture to shape personality. Implicit in his argument is a severe challenge both to the *sui generis* doctrine of cultural reality and to the conception of learning as adjustment that both behaviorist and psychoanalytic theory have encouraged.

Fromm and Sullivan are the outstanding American spokesmen for the neo-Freudian school of interpersonal psychiatry.[22] Like Murphy they question, much more than would orthodox or even various "modified" Freudians, the notion that child-training is *the* cause of personality structure, or the notion that the cure for serious personality maladjustments is in a type of psychoanalysis that leads the individual toward acquiescence in a given cultural pattern. "Freud's concept of man . . ." Fromm points out, "saw the individual as an isolated entity, endowed with certain drives rooted in his inner chemistry. The theory of interpersonal relationships . . . explains human personality in terms of the relatedness of the individual to people, to the world outside, and to himself."[23] In his insistence that the key to personality is the social structure, Fromm does not deny the importance of child-training, but he contends that each form of the latter is itself derived from social structure, and therefore from the matrix of economic, political, and other relations that in Murphy's terms constitute a "field."

Also like Murphy, Fromm would be in agreement with anthropologists who emphasize the enormous influence of custom upon learning. But the total effect of his theory is to encourage a creative conception of personality that is less apparent in the bulk of anthropological approaches to the problem.

These three non-anthropologists are mentioned in order to re-emphasize that the predominant orientation of culture-and-personality studies by anthropologists has been perhaps too circumscribed by the influence of behaviorist and psychoanalytic theories. It is not apparent that the positions represented by such innovators as Murphy, Fromm, and Sullivan have as yet made the impact upon such studies that they deserve to make. Honigmann's overview, for example, though it mentions the first two of these writers, fails to show that their overall positions have been at all systematically incorporated either into culture-theory in general or into learning-theory in particular; references to them chiefly bear upon some detail. Perhaps the nearest approximations to a more adequate appreciation of how their kinds of approach would affect the problem of culture-and-personality as seen by culture-theorists are to be found in the work of Hallowell, Kluckhohn and Murray, and Bidney. The theory of learning that may be held by these authorities will not be considered as such, but its implications for the problem will be numerous. We are concerned now to obtain further understanding of the role of personality in cultural process by moving toward the broader formulations represented by these authorities.

THE CONCEPT OF PERSONALITY: RECENT EMPHASES

To begin with Hallowell, a statement such as the following at once sounds a different note from that of the majority of anthropologists who have concerned themselves with culture-and-personality: "Individuals are the dynamic centers of this process of interaction" called acculturation. "By capitalizing on his capacity for invention and learning, . . . man created a new world, a human world, one that depended upon the character and efficiency of the cultural instrumentalities that man himself invented and learned to use."[24] In the essay from which this is quoted, Hallowell, too, reveals a strong behaviorist and psychoanalytic approach to learning, although in the reprinting of it ten years after its original appearance he deletes a number of passages, perhaps because of doubt as to their continued adequacy.

In more recent statements he has moved further. He still recognizes the invaluable contributions of the two theories he previously stressed, but he now seems more aware of the significance of organismic philosophers and psychologists—Whitehead, Dewey, Cassirer, Lewin, Fromm, Murphy, Sullivan, and others—who profoundly challenge traditional formulations. His reference to Dewey, particularly, highlights by contrast the disregard of this great philosopher of culture by many other culture-theorists. He is, moreover, critical of the neglect of gestalt and other deviations from behaviorism.[25]

Hallowell pays attention, as does White, to the crucial role of symbols as the supreme instrument of cultural process. He stresses, as does Fromm, the sociocultural matrix of personality thereby questioning an over-simplified Freudian interpretation, and he affirms that "human personality structure is a product of experience in a socialization process and . . . the resulting structure varies with the nature and conditions of such experience . . ."[26] He even approaches, without directly referring to, the "transactionist" psychology of Ames, Cantril, and others, when he reminds us that the world we perceive is deeply affected by our habits of social perception—habits that, in turn, derive largely from customary ways of looking at the world.[27] While stressing, as any anthropologist should, the personality structure that results from learning the ways of culture, Hallowell nevertheless strikes again a distinctive note: man, he reiterates, is the "creator and re-creator of the kind of life that is his most distinctive attribute . . ."[28] But he reminds us that cultures are by no means identical in the way they encourage this attribute: some enhance adjustment to new conditions more readily than others, so that acculturation as a major way by which personalities cope with the processes of change varies tremendously from culture to culture.

A clear epitomization of Hallowell's over-all position is the following:

Viewed functionally and historically, it appears to be the indeterminate aspects of man's nature that makes him unique, the inherent potentialities of which, under the necessary motivational conditions, may lead to new and varied forms of social, cultural, and psychological adjustment . . . Human behavior *is* relative to traditional culture patterns and historic circumstances but, at the same time, it is relative to unrealized potentialities that inhere in man's human nature and which permit the emergence of novelty in his mode of life.[29]

Kluckhohn and Murray, at least as strongly as Hallowell, are critical of the mechanistic overtones of behaviorist theory, although like him they recognize its great contributions. A few of their statements seem to be misleadingly idealistic—for example, when they speak of "*personality,* or mind."[30] Also, their treatment of psychoanalytic theory takes insufficient account of neo-Freudian developments of the kind mentioned above. Yet on the whole their position is much more influenced by the "field" theory of personality, as exemplified by Murphy, than is typical of most specialists in culture-and-personality. Among the numerous invaluable concepts to which they pay careful attention, the following are germane to this chapter:

1. Personality is a process. In a sense, its history gives its meaning.

2. Personality is directional. It is goal-seeking, although specific goals in the form of need-satisfactions may be unconscious as well as conscious.

3. Imagination plays even a more important role in motivating the quest for goals than does perception. The role of symbols is, of course, paramount in imagination.

4. One of the important needs of personality is to play roles in congenial groups having goals harmonious with its own.

5. There are two major classes of goals or need-satisfactions: more or less immediate ones that are more or less regularly satisfied; long-

range ones that express more ultimate and comprehensive purposes.

6. Learning directed to goal-seeking and goal-achieving is more important than stimulus-response learning.

7. The reduction of need-tension by attaining equilibrium between a need and its satisfaction is the corollary of goal-seeking. This function involves "scheduling" so as to assure choice of the most enduring satisfactions—that is, the more desirable ones.

8. The id of psychoanalytic theory is the source of "all the basic energies, emotions, and needs . . . some of which are wholly acceptable and some wholly unacceptable"[31] to a given culture at a given time.

9. The superego may be constricting, but it may also invite a "conception of an ideal future world, or at least a better world, to be constructed by stages . . ." while the ego ideal "is an inviting conception of an ideal future self, or at least a more able or better self, also to be attained by stages."[32]

10. Culture predominantly selects the range of tension-reducing functions that are permitted the average personality, which learns to conform to them. The process by which this learning occurs may be termed "socialization."

11. But culture also consists of patterns that provide a variety of opportunities for goal-seeking or tension-reducing functions, some inconsistent with others.

12. Resentment, anxiety, frustration and aggression, and similar negative experiences are the consequences of conflict between these patterns, or between a need and its satisfaction within any single pattern.

13. Personalities may regard the compulsions of a culture that deny tension-reduction to be so unwarranted as to challenge them "to attempt to modify the culture patterns which are most objectionable to them . . . In doing this, the individual will usually be identifying with others who, like himself, have suffered from the hurtful culture patterns."[33]

14. It follows that the "ego-controlled" personality, as against both the "id-dominated" and "superego-dominated" personality, is one achieving a dynamic equilibruim between the source of its energies and the patterns of its culture. It is a culture carrier, but also a culture creator. The "goal of the socialization process is the dis-

position and the ability to reciprocate and cooperate with members of the society who are conserving its most valuable patterns as well as with those who are endeavoring to improve them."[34] This is related to the "ego ideal" of (9) above.

I have chosen Bidney as the last spokesman for a more inclusive approach to the concept of personality because, as seen in other pages, he is skillful in synthesizing partial views. His critique of the super-organic concept for its failure, until radically modified, to account for psychological factors in culture prepares the ground for his view of personality in cultural process: "The individual," he insists, "is not merely the passive carrier of social culture, he is also an active agent in originating and modifying his culture." Nowhere does Bidney examine the concept of learning with precision, but his orientation is clear:

. . . human culture may be understood to comprise, in part, the art of human self-cultivation or self-conditioning, with a view to the development of human capabilities in relation to a given environment . . . Whatever is learned is cultural, including the ability to learn itself . . . Hence, a dynamic psychology is concerned with the growth and development of human potentialities in the process of education and cultural conditioning . . . In brief, my theory . . . is in complete accord with the biological determinism of modern genetics, but allows scope for the active intervention of man in utilizing his biological equipment in accordance with his cultural requirements and preferences.[35]

Bidney argues cogently that various definitions of personality offered by anthropologists are inconsistent, often failing to reconcile psychological with anthropological premises. (Something of this is evident in a formal definition such as Kluckhohn's and Murray's, cited above.) He insists that personality must be regarded as

. . . a determinate psychocultural action and reaction pattern, whether overt or covert, which is typical or characteristic of an individual (or organization of individuals) in the performance of his sociocultural role at a given stage of development . . . A person is a polaristic entity in the sense that he comprises two distinct elements, namely, the element of human nature and that of culture.[36]

Such a polaristic interpretation prepares the way for a creative theory of education in which personalities are, throughout, both passive and active agents of cultural process.

MODAL PERSONALITY, NATIONAL CHARACTER, AND CULTURAL CHANGE

Having reviewed, first, the most emphasized approaches to learning and, second, the meaning of personality as largely a product of learning—it is now important to ask specifically: What contributions to our understanding of personality have been provided by culture-theorists working in the culture-and-personality area that will help to sharpen the problem of process itself?

It may be argued that their most distinctive contributions cluster around one concept, that of the "basic personality type" or "modal personality" that is revealed by the study of human beings living in any culture. It is understandable that anthropologists would be interested in developing this concept, for it reflects their concern with cultural order and hence with such prolific concepts as pattern, social status, and configuration. As Bidney points out, ". . . psychologists have tended to stress the uniqueness of the person, while the cultural anthropologists have drawn attention to the common elements, or traits, to the 'basic personality structure,' or 'modal personality,' which the individual shares with other members of his cultural community."[37]

Here once more the interrelations of our study are apparent. Benedict's and other important works, noted in our examination of cultural order, are in a fundamental sense concerned also with the nature of modal personalities. The postulate common to these works is that modal personalities differ as the cultural learning to which they are subjected differs. Behaviorist assumptions operate more or less in all of them, as do psychoanalytic assumptions in many. Moreover, the gestalt approach to modal personality is inherent in both Benedict's and Mead's pioneering studies, among others. As Hallowell points out, Benedict brings into relief "the question of how we are to conceptualize and study the 'wholeness' of cultures, in contrast with an analytic approach . . ."[38] This "wholeness" is manifested also in her interpretation of personality types which are a corollary of her culture types. We conclude that rarely is any one psychological theory utilized exclusively by influential students of culture-and-personality (Róheim, the orthodox Freudian, is an exception), although not all approaches are equally explicit or equally emphasized.

Next to Sapir, Linton is perhaps most noted for his theoretical contributions to personality typology; his book *The Cultural Background of Personality*[39] is a classic statement. Some of the earliest research in the field was done by Abram Kardiner (a psychotherapist of strong Freudian leanings with an interest in anthropology) collaborating with Linton. In his introduction to Kardiner's *The Psychological Frontiers of Society* (aided by three anthropologists), Linton summarizes the postulates of the "concept of basic personality types" with exceptional clarity:

1. That the individual's early experiences exert a lasting effect upon his personality . . .
2. That similar experiences will tend to produce similar personality configurations in the individuals who are subjected to them.
3. That the techniques which the members of any society employ in the care and rearing of children are culturally patterned and will tend to be similar, although never identical, for various families within the society.
4. That the culturally patterned techniques for the care and rearing of children differ from one society to another.[40]

Linton is certain that these postulates are backed by an abundance of evidence and that, since the members of any culture will have early common experiences differing from one culture to another, the personality norms of various cultures will also differ. His formal definition of basic personality type is "that personality configuration which is shared by the bulk of the society's members as a result of the early experiences which they have in common."[41] It is not, of course, identical with the *total* personality of the individual, nor is it productive of identical behavior among similar personality types. These generalizations are supported by Kardiner's interpretation of several cultures investigated firsthand by collaborating anthropologists. In the case of one, the Alorese, which had been studied by Cora DuBois, the validity of the findings are strongly corroborated by Rorschach tests administered to members of Alorese society and independently analyzed by an expert in projective techniques.

Let us select a few of the pertinent emphases that appear in recent literature on modal personality. Doubtless the hypothesis that has received most attention is that patterns of child-training are crucial to the development of modal personalities. Because these patterns are by no means similar among cultures, however, neither are the modal personalities that result from them. What all modal personalities do have in common is the circular causal relation that operates between them and child-training patterns: the adult personality types that emerge from these patterns tend to perpetuate themselves by repeating similar patterns of child training in succeeding generations. Beyond this, there is not, except among Freudians, much agreement as to the reasons for one pattern as against another pattern. For example, almost no attention has been paid to Marxian or pseudo-Marxian theories of economic causation, at least in America. Rather, as we have seen in the preceding chapter, the whole problem of causation is far from clarified in culture-theory, and the same ambiguity exists in causal explanations of modal personalities. Beyond a tacit consensus that causal factors are plural rather than singular, and that a circular causal relation operates between child-training and modal personality, we are left pretty much in the dark.

Another interest centers in group membership as a condition of modal personality. Here theories similar to George Herbert Mead's[42] have had some influence—that personalities are role-players, that their several roles as they become stylized also become expressive of modal personality, and that these roles always reflect the expectations of the groups to which people belong. While little research has been guided directly by Mead's own conception of the "self-other" process, research of this kind might seriously modify the child-training hypothesis by viewing modal personality in terms of a more or less harmonious synthesis of roles (social-class, family, vocational, etc.), some of which do not develop until adolescence or even later. In complex cultures, particularly, the multiple roles often demanded of group members may result in an even more complex modal personality than might be typical of the comparatively homogeneous cultures that have remained the traditional concern of anthropological research. Group-membership research would probably show that childhood-training patterns, while of great importance certainly, are necessary rather than sufficient conditions of modal personality. Moreover, just as personalities may develop their particular configurations in different cultures over spans of time that vary in length from only a few years to several decades, so too may modal personalities develop over varying spans of time that could extend deep into adult life.

The complexity of research into modal personality as shaped by membership in groups is highlighted by an even newer field designated by the term "national-character studies." According to Margaret Mead, a forerunner in the field, the distinguishing features are of two kinds: in national-character studies the group under examination is that of a sovereign state rather than a culture or subculture, and the method of study is "at a distance"—that is, less by direct observation than by the use of interviews, analysis of films, books, and any other indices of national attitudes, habits, and institutions. Her review of the field shows that learning theory and all major principles utilized for the study of personality in culture are pertinent here, but that methods applicable to relatively small, simple, stable cultures are often inapplicable to nations. She contends that the study of any national culture should precede the study of national character as it develops within a given culture. The aim of the latter study is

... to trace the way in which the identified cultural behavior is represented in the intra-psychic structure of the individual members of the culture, combining cultural theory and psychological theory . . . into a new psycho-cultural theory to explain how human beings embody the culture, learn it, and live it.[43]

She is aware, as is Geoffrey Gorer,[44] another forerunner, that serious difficulties stand in the way of scientific study of national character, but she defends it as potentially fruitful. Its findings may be validated by various methods, particularly that of "fitting" the delineated national character to the national pattern in both its cultural and psychological perspectives. The most elaborate studies thus far attempted have been of Japan, Germany, Britain, and the Soviet Union.

One of the serious problems arising from many modal-personality and national-character studies is the prevalence of conflicts that manifest themselves in neurotic patterns of behavior. For example, even the modal personality of a relatively "simple" culture may be fraught with insecurity largely induced, according to Kardiner's psychoanalytic interpretation, by repressive sexual habits and values. By comparison, Western cultures are still more conducive of personality types that suffer from disharmony—Kardiner's analysis of "Plainville, U.S.A." being a case in point.

Mead has paid attention to this kind of problem in her *Male and*

Female and other studies.[45] Perhaps more than any other contemporary anthropologist of note, she has been able from firsthand research to expose the wide divergences in personality structures among living cultures and to show how our own culture generates psychological disturbances. She attributes these largely to an abnormal rate of cultural change, one result of which is a chronic discrepancy between modal personalities of parents and cultural patterns to which growing children are exposed. "Age-grade standards" become a substitute for parental standards. But the latter nevertheless continue to affect young people, with resultant anxiety induced by guilt feelings among adolescents. The concept of crisis, already discussed, is enriched by Mead's examination of the inner turmoil often suffered not only by the American personality but by other types that are being subjected to abnormally rapid rates of acculturation.

Her observation that age-grade standards are tending to replace parental standards anticipates the famous thesis of David Riesman that the American personality type is increasingly "other-directed"— that is, governed by the wish to win approval of peer groups with which it is associated, but at the cost of considerable conflict with the earlier configuration of "inner-direction." Although Riesman is not an anthropologist but a sociologist, we mention him because he reinforces the thesis of Mead and others that "psycho-cultural" conflict is chronic in our culture, and because he has been frequently cited by anthropologists since his *The Lonely Crowd*[46] was published in 1950.

George Spindler, for example, has tested Riesman's thesis of other-directedness with college students and has found that their "emergent values" include "sociability," "consideration for others," and "conformity to the groups." An anthropologist keenly interested in education, Spindler argues that this transition helps to explain some of the present confusions in American education that are due to friction between traditional and emergent values. He does not contend that school personnel universally accept the latter and reject the former. Rather, they are on a continuum—school boards and the general public being closer to the traditional end, younger teachers and students being closer to the emergent end.[47]

Still other hypotheses and issues are associated with the concept of modal personality. Honigmann's review of the field demonstrates that the emergence of modal personality is conditioned by many factors that vary in different cultures—fear of punishment, attitudes toward wealth, injury to self-esteem, sex and sex roles, old age, hostility and aggression, class and status roles, and others.[48]

Perhaps, however, enough has been said to justify this assertion: the study of modal personality enables us to deal more negatively than positively with the problem of cultural process. That is, we are helped more often to appreciate how resistant modal personalities are to modification once they are formed, and we are given more information as to some of the conditions that bring them about, than we are helped to understand how to engage in the process of modifying either them or the cultural patterns that produce them. True, a few anthropologists (we have cited Mead as perhaps the most prominent) have paid perceptive attention to this latter question. Moreover, we recall here the work of Barnett on innovation, discussed in Chapter Eight, in which he shows how personality types vary from "acceptors" to "rejectors"—the former tending to be the advocates of innovation, the latter, opponents. His analysis of these types is not, however, directly enough integrated with recent culture-and-personality studies to help us very much.

The same generalization must be made of the work of Linton and of those associated with him in studying basic personality types. As he himself points out:

Unfortunately, we have had few opportunities so far to investigate the interrelations of basic personality and culture in changed situations, but there can be little doubt that the basic personality type plays an important part in determining a society's reaction to innovation. Innovations which are congenial to the personality type probably are accepted and incorporated into the society's culture much more readily than those which are uncongenial.[49]

This statement also epitomizes one of Barnett's central contentions, but it does not tell us how to proceed. Linton admits the "urgent need for study of the reactions of particular societies to particular innovations and of the way in which basic personality type influences the acceptance or rejection of new elements."[50] There is little evidence, however, that this need has been satisfied since 1945 when he challenged anthropologists with it. On the contrary, a survey of the field gives one the impression that anthropologists are more concerned with the relative permanence of types of personality in culture than they are with the serious obstacles to needed change which this permanence may itself induce. Their main contribution thus continues to be the indispensable one of establishing that any effective answer to the question of conscious, controlled cultural process must first come to grips with the meaning of modal personality and its habits of resistance *to* that kind of process.

PROBLEMS OF CULTURE-AND-PERSONALITY IN THE EDUCATIVE PROCESS

1. Turning again to the significance of our study for educational theory and practice, let us first reiterate the conclusion at which we have just arrived. The study of modal personality is of importance, not so much in helping educators to discover ways to accelerate cultural process as in providing them with a reassessment of the stubborn difficulties that must confront them in any such undertaking. The modal personalities of students, for example, though they differ markedly in different cultures, are alike in the respect that they are usually firmly structured, according to the majority of experts, at an early age. Moreover, we are told that it takes two or three generations to change modal personality in any fundamental sense, although under special circumstances one generation is possible.[51]

This is not a new finding for this study. All through the discussion on cultural order the same generalization was often at least implicit, so much so that the polaristic relationship of modal personality and cultural patterning should be underscored. Each, in a sense, provides a different perspective upon the same inclusive phenomenon of man-living-in-culture.

Nevertheless, the concept of modal personality enhances the educator's concern with process in more positive ways. First of all, it deepens his grasp of the human situation he is dealing with—a truistic observation, to be sure, but one made without apology. One of the appalling deficiencies in the typical training of teachers and administrators lies here: not only has there been a dearth of understanding of those modal personalities most like their own, but almost no opportunity is provided to help them interpret modal personalities shaped by cultures or subcultures unlike their own. This point was exemplified in a different context when we examined cultural order in its vertical dimension and noted something of the conflicts and confusions generated by differences between the lower- and upper-middle status of typical teachers and that of students who come chiefly from lower-lower or upper-lower groups. Even more serious, perhaps, are the frictions that result when either teachers or students migrate to cultures or subcultures with customs and habits unfamiliar to them. At a time when teacher-exchange programs are on the increase, when tremendous movements of people often occur in a brief period, ignorance of and among modal personalities suddenly thrown into close contact is bound to create greater friction, suspicion, or hostility, than would occur if even our present limited knowledge were included as an essential part of professional training. National-character studies are equally relevant here: rapid cultural changes now occurring place upon education as one of the major avenues of international relations an unprecedented obligation to familiarize the personnel of an agency like Unesco with the growing body of resources in this frontier field.

In the second place, the study of modal personality directly bears upon the problem of cultural process through education, by helping us to understand variations in modal personalities upon which it may be desirable to effect some kind of change. (The problem of cultural goals is, of course, anticipated here, for "desirable" assumes a criterion of value.) As Hallowell among others has stressed, some types of personality are more resilient than others, just as some cultures are. The concept of focus, noted in the previous chapter, may also apply to modal personalities: that is, within the latter there are spheres of greater amenability to modification than are other spheres—a commonplace of psychiatric theory. To locate these spheres and to work there for initial change of habits and customs would seem to be as good a rule to follow when we are approaching process through modal personality as when we are approaching it on an objectively cultural plane. It is likely, for example, that habits of personal sanitation are more easily reshaped than deep-seated moral habits, just as they are in cultures themselves. But through re-educating people in the ways they keep themselves clean, opportunities are also opened to modify their ways of engaging in, say, sexual practices that may have unhealthy psychological or physiological effects.

In the third place, the prevalence of modal personalities that are inharmonious, often to the point of psychotic behavior, compels the educator to consider therapeutic measures. Mental hygiene, a field that is receiving more and more attention in teacher-training programs, should be broadened to include modal-personality research of the type to which Mead has contributed. The cultural conditions of personality conflict are still sparsely treated in most mental-hygiene courses. Even more inadequate, if that is possible, are the clinical services for dealing with unhealthy student personalities: not only are such services unavailable in the great majority of schools, but those that are available are deficient in staff personnel familiar with the cultural foundations of mental therapy.

The Riesman hypothesis may be selected to point up this deficiency. If he is right, the trend toward other-direction is one of the most significant phenomena in American culture today. Yet, to what extent are those charged with the emotional and intellectual well-being of adolescents concerned with the disturbances that this trend generates? Mead sees in it a good deal of danger: it invites blind followership— crowd adulation of the demagogic leader or "parent surrogate" who will assuage their feelings of anxiety and guilt. But she also sees an opportunity:

If educational leaders became sufficiently aware of the possibilities of using this mass willingness to follow a congenial solution, a willingness which is so characteristic of young people today, and if they were able to enlist young people in the task of creating new patterns of living congruent with the aims of a democratic society, this readiness for any new path might be used in building a more democratic state rather than a less democratic one.[52]

In terms of mental health, the over-arching problem is then to find a way of channeling other-directed personalities toward constructive, realizable ideals commensurate with the demands of an age in swift transition. Unfortunately, however, it is not only mental-health experts who often lack such an orientation. Riesman himself lacks it. Despite his plea for "utopian" thinking and planning, his own educational predilections are toward adjustment and conformity. Speaking of "Teachers amid Changing Expectations," he insists that "their function is limited—primarily, to teach a subject . . . They must see that . . . schools can never reform society, but only put brakes on it . . ."[53] Such opinions as this may please culture-theorists who prefer to end their study of modal personality with description rather than with attack upon the problem of how to modify it when or if it is adjudged undesirable. They may also please the kind of educator who is only too ready to find rationales for his own conservatism. But they will not please anyone who regards education in a more creative light.

For example, Van Cleve Morris, an educational theorist, draws different inferences from Riesman's thesis. Granting that other-directed personalities are with us increasingly, Morris contends that the task before education is to broaden the scope and worth of other-direction rather than either to retreat into some inner cloister of dubious "autonomy"—Riesman's favorite solution—or to return to the old-fashioned, subject-centered school. Morris writes:

What makes other-direction so distasteful is its narrowness, its limited perspective, its short-range expediency and shallowness . . . But we must also remember that other-direction has its long-range dimensions as well. We can receive signals from sources other than our immediate peer group. We can receive them from other social classes, from individuals in other occupations, in other religions, in other races . . . And these distant signals . . . may come from across the street in our own community or from the other side of the world . . . Every culture has its own message to transmit, its own value scheme to offer as hypothesis for value-seeking man. If anthropology has told us anything, it has told us this . . . We can hardly build a better social order until we have clearly in mind what it is we want to make of our American society, and it would seem that a full-scale, other-directed attempt to come into a working understanding of the values and ideals . . . of other peoples would be a most effective starter . . .[54]

Morris is saying, if I understand him, essentially what Mead has said in other terms. The conflicts, the superficial conformities, the constrictions that accompany other-direction—assuming it to be a revealing symbol of personality in contemporary American culture—also demand frontiers for education that are as unprecedented as they are intriguing.

2. If education is not to fail, however, the culture-and-personality field must itself offer more by way of conceptual assistance than our search has thus far yielded. Turning back to other problems and concepts raised in this chapter, we saw, for example, that learning

theory is far from unified—on the contrary, that it is often eclectic if not old-fashioned.[55] Mechanistic-behaviorist psychologies, particularly, seem to lag behind the most advanced theory and practice in educational psychology. The gestalt and transactional approaches, the orientation connoted by such symbols as "organismic," "functional," and "field," these may already have had more impact upon education than they have had upon culture-and-personality theory and practice in their dominant formulations. If I am correct in this opinion, then there is special need for synthesis here. More perhaps than in any other aspects of our study thus far, educational theorists not only can learn from culture-theory, aided by general psychologists, sociologists, and philosophers, but they can also help to broaden and vitalize that theory.

The kind of synthesis I mean is anticipated by the work of psychologists like Murphy, Fromm, Sullivan, Murray, and, among anthropological theorists, by Hallowell, Bidney, and Kluckhohn. The core of their approach is, we have found, to regard learning as a more creative experience than is likely to be inferred by the Yale type of behaviorist-psychoanalytic theory. For the latter, learning too much emphasizes and at least inadvertently encourages a process of acquiescent responses to stimuli selected and reinforced by parental and other surrogates of culture. Educationally, despite qualifications, the stress is upon transmission, with the teaching process, formal or informal, thus becoming largely a way of conditioning children to given cultural patterns.

For "field" psychologists like Murphy the implication is otherwise. The indispensable role of transmission is not ignored, of course, and the Yale type of theory is appreciated for its contributions. Nevertheless, Murphy's postulate of culture-and-personality as a dynamic field of forces within which each conditions the other invites a conception of learning that, to a much greater degree, conceives of personality as a "stimulating" as well as "responding" human entity. In terms anticipated by Dewey half a century ago, learning becomes a "reflex arc": the widely flexible responses of which personalities are capable condition further cultural stimuli just as often and as richly as cultural stimuli condition responses of the personality. Learning, in short, is truly interactive—a "self-other" process throughout. The first task of education, psychologically, is to draw

180   CULTURAL FOUNDATIONS OF EDUCATION

upon this principle by constructing school programs that afford opportunity to work upon, to shape and reshape, culture at the same time that learners learn to live in and with its given forms.

Comparable lessons for education can be inferred from Hallowell's interpretation. Indeed, his appreciation of the relevance of distinguished non-anthropologists for culture-and-personality theory highlights all the more pointedly their neglect by some of his contemporaries. Cassirer is an excellent example. Aside from Bidney,[56] who has paid close attention to him as a "philosophical anthropologist," no culture-theorist so far as I know has tried to evaluate in Cassirer's own terms or in painstaking fashion the central thesis of his philosophy—namely, that the differentiating characteristic of the human species is its symbolic function. Hallowell himself does not thus examine Cassirer's thesis. Yet, in focusing as he does upon the importance of this symbolic function as central to personality in culture, there is little doubt that Hallowell could agree not only with much of Cassirer's general point of view but with its educational suggestiveness. This suggestiveness, which I have examined in detail elsewhere,[57] provides education with the kind of integrative principle that it must have if it is not to remain a hodgepodge of odds-and-ends of knowledge and skills. It is a principle by which personality may be both studied and expressed in many interwoven dimensions, as myth-maker, artist, religionist, scientist; a principle by which human evolution studied through the history of cultures is provided continuity by the universality of the symbolic function; above all, a principle by which man comes to be seen by the student as the creative, imaginative, symbol-making and symbol-using animal.

In commenting on Hallowell's viewpoint, Robert Redfield reveals much the same general attitude. Culture, he says,

is . . . an expression of human creativeness . . . I find it easier to see man creating, expressing himself, representing his inner state, and I come to see that man not only receives stimuli or submits himself to the constraints of custom or adapts or adjusts to others in a network of social relations, but he is also a dreamer, a mythmaker, a fantasy-producer. Symbols are seen not merely as the clues to social control and the mechanism of communication, but also as products of the symbolizing nature of man—something accomplished by man, not merely acting upon him . . .[58]

Redfield's attitude is developed more fully in his discussion of "Creation" in *The Educational Experience*[59]—a series of lectures in which, unfortunately, there is little additional evidence of a theory of education that has directly profited either by recent culture-theory in general, or by his own abundant anthropological contributions in particular.

Consider next the educational implications in Kluckhohn's and Murray's view of personality in its cultural relations. Any theory of education adequate for our day would have to take into consideration every one of the chief concepts that they delineate: for example, the dynamic, temporal character of personality; its goal-seeking proclivities (discussed in the next Part); the tensions arising between the personality's grasping for satisfaction of its wants and the constrictions placed upon it by every culture; the conception of "ego-controlled" personality as an operational ideal to be contrasted with both the "id-dominated" and "superego-dominated" personality. The educational norm inherent in their interpretation is, like Murphy's and Hallowell's, creative and reconstructive. The child is a creature with boundless potentialities, and the duty of the school is to release and channel these as richly as it can—a duty to which various educational psychologists and philosophers alert to recent theory and research have already been demanding our allegiance.[60]

The position of Bidney invites a similar outlook, as indeed does that of Fromm and Sullivan. Rather than reiterate the value of their ideas for our understanding of cultural process—important as these are—I wish to turn to certain educational problems that are inadequately clarified either by them or by others who have contributed to the field of culture-and-personality.

3. One problem centers in the relation of individual and group action. None of the writers cited—indeed, none in the entire field considered in this chapter—gives anything like the attention it deserves to the question of how personalities as culture-creators as well as culture-carriers enhance the former of these roles by the power and effectiveness derived from active cooperation with others of like interest. To be sure, group membership is given consideration, and such theories of role-playing and self-other relations as Kurt Lewin's, J. L. Moreno's and G. H. Mead's[61] have not been by-passed.

For the most part, however, culture-theorists seem satisfied to note rather casually (as do Kluckhohn and Murray, for example) that the individual needs to identify himself with others if he expects to modify "hurtful culture patterns." The consequence is that such theories as group dynamics and psychodrama, which have recently influenced educational experimentation, have received little bolstering from most culture-theorists, least of all from the anthropologists.[62] Kenneth Benne, one of the leaders in the field of educational group dynamics and an educational theorist, states that he knows of no "significant collaboration" of this kind. This opinion is shared by the social psychologist, S. Stansfeld Sargent.[63] True, Margaret Mead has acknowledged her indebtedness to Lewin (as well as to Moreno, the "father" of psychodrama) and she indicates that the Society for Applied Anthropology, in which she has been active, has been concerned with group problems.[64] Yet it remains unclear as to precisely how Lewin's or Moreno's basic concepts of intra- and intergroup process have fed either into her own theoretical formulations or into those of other experts in culture-and-personality research. Such an authoritative work as *Small Groups*, to which a large number of social scientists have contributed, contains only one brief section by contemporary anthropologists; they are E. D. Chapple and Carleton H. Coon.[65] The review of the literature of "primary groups" by Edward H. Shils likewise mentions but one present-day anthropologist, W. Lloyd Warner.[66] Equally sparse is any explicit anthropological theory in the frontier explorations of George C. Homans in his *The Human Group*,[67] although Mead tells me that Homans has worked closely with applied anthropologists. Nor do we find adequate analysis of the problem in the comprehensive symposium *Anthropology Today*. Only a few pages by Chapple can be said to deal more or less directly with it. And yet Edward A. Kennard and Gordon Macgregor (writing of "Applied Anthropology in Government: United States") declare: "The great opportunity for the anthropologist lies in the problem of the extent to which purposive change can be introduced, how rapidly, and with what consequences to different segments of the society."[68]

Here then is another striking example of the synthesis urged (under #2) above. The school is a human-relations resource of unparalleled fertility. Its classrooms are potential intra- and intergroup laboratories that mirror (although they may distort) the culture surrounding it. Sociometry, the methodology of analyzing and interpreting these patterns in terms of the interactions of personality and group vectors, has already made contributions by utilizing the human data for research that classrooms provide. Role-playing, as a practical and dramatic method of learning, has also been utilized by hundreds of the more modern schools throughout America as well as England, and all the way from kindergarten to the college level. What is needed next, then, is investigation of how concepts like modal personality, to which culture-theorists have contributed most, can be integrated with these methods of learning—integrated, not only for the purpose of understanding children better, but for the purpose of changing attitudes and behavior when or if such changes are considered to be preferable to established attitudes and behaviors.

The other-directed personality may again be chosen to exemplify the need. As Morris has pointed out, the great problem confronting education here is not how to suppress or emasculate this personality type; it is to broaden and enrich its own character, to develop appreciation of and identification with peer groups other than one's own immediately narrow one of age, status, and class.

But how precisely is this to be done? It is to be done, first, by understanding as much as possible about the nature of a given modal personality and how it is manifested in specific group patterns; second, by providing learning experiences that test its comparative resistance or resilience to change. The famous Lewin-inspired experiment of Ronald Lippitt in changing classroom responses toward autocratic and democratic leadership exemplifies the kind of controlled group process that is fruitful here.[69] So, too, is the experimentation of Herbert Thelen and others.[70] Role-playing, designed to sensitize students both to their close associates and to other groups (such as ethnic, economic, national, religious) "at a distance" from their own is one fruitful process. Organized efforts to work with and strengthen a movement of long-range purpose, such as world government, is another. The hypothesis that the other-directed modal personality can be redirected through the small-group relations typical of classrooms is in itself pregnant with experimental possibilities that no one, so far as I have learned, has begun to test. It is a hypothesis which challenges the Freudian theory of early child-training as the key to modal personality by suggesting that other conditions, some of them not becoming influential until fairly mature years, are also at work—conditions of almost equal causal potency.

4. Another problem in culture-theory of great relevance to education arises from the concept of enculturation as learning. Herskovits, we remember, defines this term as the process of conscious or unconscious conditioning within the limits of customary sanction. But he distinguishes sharply between the kind of enculturation that occurs in childhood and in later years when there may be deliberate and systematic concern with change of custom. The point is well taken in the sense that of course children must be socialized by learning to accept and behave according to the rules and routines of the culture they are born into. So, too, must adults. It is dangerous, however, to infer that there need be a kind of cleavage between the earlier and the later stages of enculturation. Rather, if we accept the creative approach to cultural process that Herskovits himself usually does, it is much more consistent to think of a *continuum* of learning in which the degree of inculcation is greatest in the first years but in which, from the beginning, the basic orientation is toward an active rather than passive way of coming to terms with one's culture.

This active way is, again, in accord with gestalt and organismic theory more than it is with either behaviorist or orthodox psychoanalytic theory. It assumes that children of nursery-school age can begin to think, to decide, and to act both for themselves and by sharing with other children. It assumes, too, that habit formation is of more than one kind—that while cultural experience is impossible without habits, and while habits are essential to the efficient performance of innumerable functions, the individual can also acquire the habit of reflective, critical behavior. This is a major postulate of one of the classic works in American social psychology, Dewey's *Human Nature and Conduct*,[71] and it is applied specifically to education both by him and by such brilliant disciples as Boyd Bode.[72]

This postulate takes fundamental issue with any dichotomous implications in the concept of enculturation. And it assumes that the attitude with which teachers approach the task of habit formation even—or rather, especially—in the elementary school makes a great deal of difference to the mature attitudes and habits that develop toward cultural stability and cultural change. To believe that creative intelligence is cultivable, that such cultivation cannot begin too early, and that modal personality can incorporate habits of experimental change, has consequences for learning, teaching, and the curriculum that are revolutionary. But they remain unassimilated into the research and outlook of numerous leaders both in education and in the theory of culture-and-personality itself.

But educational philosophy as propounded by Dewey and his followers is to be criticized, too. The concept of modal personality, for instance, with all that it implies as both a fact of and an incitement to cultural process would, if incorporated into their thinking, sharpen their analyses and help them to realize that cultural change through education is by no means as facile as they sometimes suppose. It is probably true, moreover, that they have incorporated into their philosophy not nearly as many of the findings of psychoanalytic theory and practice as have most of the culture-theorists here cited. At the same time, both progressive educators and culture-theorists have much to gain by bringing recent studies in the field of group behavior into close relation with their own formulations. As I have sought to show,[73] progressive educators, at least, have neither weighed realistically the cultural obstacles blocking democratic group action in behalf of cultural change, nor considered sufficiently how such action could effect cultural alterations in ways that individual effort finds impossible.

5. Our concluding problem brings us again to the need of an experimental framework for educational integration—a need considered in Part II. Here, however, I wish to consider integration, not primarily in terms of the schools as a whole, but by anticipating Chapter Thirteen which deals with the professional training of teachers.

The "foundations of education," developed in recent years in several institutions, are an attempt to provide such a framework by reviewing and interpreting the major findings of the psychological and social sciences. The guiding assumption of these foundations courses—that teachers, if they are to serve the school as a cultural institution, must acquire broad knowledge of the sciences of man— is one that most culture-theorists would applaud.

Nevertheless, weaknesses remain. Foundations courses often divide the psychological and social sciences into separate divisions of subject matter rather than recognize, in accordance with the regard of their own organizers for "field" theory, that a more consistent approach would synchronize the two into one unified interpretation.

This does not mean that the psychological and social sciences do not also require separate and focused treatments. But if the central aim of the foundations of education is to provide teachers, not so much with specialized knowledge as with understanding of the inter-related character of human experience, then a more productive way of achieving this aim is to accept a premise of the culture-and-personality field. To construct the foundations of education so that *both* aspects are continually, not merely intermittently, treated as polaristic is a logical conclusion from this premise.

The theory and research of culture-and-personality are unable, of course, to provide all the rudiments of the foundations of education. What they do provide is a unified, field approach to the problems that are, or at least ought to be, focal to teacher-training—namely, the problems of the human being as he lives with other human beings. Such an approach is possible only through the cooperation of all the sciences of man, of which psychology and anthropology are two of the most fecund, most controversial, and most indispensable. If education is ever to become the powerful spearhead of cultural process that most leaders in the foundations of education want it to become, then the hangovers of compartmentalized and dualized subject matters that remain in these foundations are out of date.

The needed experimental approach is provided by another non-anthropologist, Lawrence K. Frank, whose contributions to culture-and-personality theory are far from sufficiently appreciated. In *Nature and Human Nature*, particularly, Frank has opened the door to the reconstructed way of studying man in culture. Operational and functional throughout, Frank begins with man's geographical environment, moves on to his internal environment (the human organism), from there to the cultural environment and the social environment of group living, and concludes by returning to the personality as it emerges from and reacts back upon all of these environments. His dynamic synthesis compels us to recognize, as few books have, how artificial and mechanistic are all approaches to man in terms of any single science or any other single discipline. As Whitehead has done in a much more speculative fashion, Frank has suggested a design for life itself—an organic design by which teachers could learn to approach their great responsibilities more assured both of themselves and of the human world which is the school's most important business.

The heart of our answer to the first problem of this chapter is offered by Frank more succinctly than by any other writer from whom I have learned:

For centuries we have believed that culture was a superhuman system or organization, something given to man from on high . . . Today we can assert with full conviction that culture is a human creation, man's attempt to order and pattern his personal life and to provide for orderly group or social living. Moreover, we are recognizing the dynamics of culture, of how it operates in human beings, who learn to think, to act, to feel according to what they are taught in childhood and youth when they are culturized by parents and others . . . This indicates that culture is not a superhuman system, final and unchanging, beyond man's reach and control; also, it shows that we can and do change culture by modifying what we think and do and feel and what we teach and how we rear our children . . . Thus we must free ourselves of the older conception of man *and* culture as separate entities and try to grasp this two-way, reciprocal or circular, dynamic relation: that man himself carries in his organism-personality his ideas and feelings which we call culture. By translating these into functional patterns and social conduct, into buildings, tools, weapons, art and a way of group living, man and his fellows both create and are responsive to culture.[74]

Elsewhere, speaking of "personality and culture" in still more explicitly educational terms, Frank concludes:

. . . it is imperative that those who are genuinely concerned with the longer-term program of education . . . utilize all the understandings and insights offered by psychiatry, and psychological disciplines and by cultural anthropology to help children and youth. These new ideas and insights provide the reorientation of thinking required for modifying our traditional culture and the dominant character structure of individual personalities . . . More than ever before the schools must provide more than academic instruction and training to help the bewildered children today who need aid in meeting life courageously and sanely.[75]

PART IV

THE PROBLEM OF HUMAN GOALS

CHAPTER TEN

CULTURAL GOALS—PREVIEW OF THE PROBLEM

THE GOVERNOR of Puerto Rico, Luis Muñoz Marín, was speaking of what he considered to be the next great stage in the program of reconstruction of which he is leader. Let me paraphrase him: "For several years, we have been engaging in Operation Bootstrap. We have been trying to find ways by which we can lift the economic standards of our people as high as possible above the impoverished levels on which we have suffered for centuries. This has required all sorts of new methods and policies—in mass housing, for example, and in special incentives to manufacturers—that a country like ours simply must undertake so that change can occur rapidly.

"But we know that, no matter how successful we may be, all this is not enough. We must begin now, even while Operation Bootstrap is at full momentum, to plan for what I may call Operation Serenity— for a way of life full of satisfaction, a way of life in which decent standards of housing, food, shelter, clothing, health, continue to be provided, yet not merely these. The people want and deserve esthetic creativity and enjoyment that are harmonious with our own traditions and ideals. In an age of increasing automation, we should have opportunities for recreation that are equally creative and enjoyable. We need a kind of education that will help us to discover our own resources for personal happiness and for cooperative living as intrinsic ends."

Governor Muñoz was contending, of course, that no culture is a phenomenon of means or of process only. It is equally one of goals— of purposes and ideals that in long range justify the means. Although more articulate and sensitive than many political leaders of our time, he was expressing a conviction that would be shared by other able leaders. At the same time he was pointing toward one of the most baffling, most disturbing issues that any culture confronts.

That the issue of goals is central to education is, as the Governor himself recognizes, also evident. For education, like the culture it serves, is both "how" and "what," means and ends, process and goals. True, education is not always dynamically balanced between these two poles. American schools, particularly, have been so obsessed with process that teacher-training institutions are now under heavy fire for their overemphasis on pedagogical techniques. Nor is the most influential educational theory in America without blame for this imbalance: progressive education as expounded by Dewey and his followers is, without doubt, more vulnerable in its central concern for scientific methodology than at any other point, and this despite either the great merits of its case or the distortions of its principles in the hands of belittlers.

But the problem of goals in American culture-and-education is far from limited to the habit of de-emphasizing them. Chapter Two suggested several others: the lack of agreement as to what the goals of our age are, much less what they should be; the doctrine of the relativity of cultures which tends to justify the parity of all cultural values, however different; the challenge of totalitarian systems with their fierce commitments to their respective goals; the question of whether and how far international, intercultural goals are possible and, if so, which are to be preferred; the conflict between verbal acceptance of values like freedom and our notorious failure to practice them.

These examples are in themselves sufficient to justify the task we now confront. For none of the perplexities that education faces in the area of goals are merely educational. Like problems of human order and of human process, they are first of all problems of the culture. They must be considered in this environment if they are to be considered effectively at all.

Also like the two major problems that this study has thus far considered, the problem of human goals is inextricable from either of these others. At the outset, it was emphasized that values would permeate every phase of this discussion. It was emphasized, too, that the question of norms was one toward which educational systems such as the American were neither positive nor consistent even though, paradoxically, education is a normative enterprise throughout.

Thus the polaristic character of order, process, and goals, which has frequently been stressed, is highlighted for a final time. The order of culture can no more be divorced in actuality from its over-arching goals than the multiple processes of culture can be divorced from order. In the following discussion the guiding threads of the preceding chapters are pulled together in terms of the ways that values have already been emerging.

The problem of human order is perhaps the most objective problem of culture-theory. Even here, however, the issue of whether or not the human individual is privileged to choose between different ways of coping with cultural reality involves the issue of value judgments whenever he is faced with two or more alternatives each of which may seem desirable to him. It will be remembered that some culture-theorists, while recognizing the ubiquity of cultural values, hold that individuals are constricted both in opportunity and capacity to choose between such values, for the simple reason that the culture has largely if not entirely chosen for him first. That other theorists disagree with this determinist doctrine became apparent when we dealt with concepts like causation. The variables of human experience in shaping desirable goals and in effecting changes in the means to attain them are more heavily defended by Coulborn and Bidney, for example, than they are by White. The consequences for educational values are accordingly different also: Shall we accept the implication of *sui generis* theory that education as a servant of culture can and should do little more than transmit and reinforce the personal and social values that it has inherited from cultural reality? Or shall we support the implication of operational theory that education has a singular responsibility toward molding and directing these values?

When we turned to the spatial model of cultural order, the problem of values began to loom in additional ways. The functional position, which we associate especially with Malinowski, approaches cultural behavior from the springboard of human needs and wants; and human needs and wants, as we shall see more fully, are crucial to the meaning of values. Benedict, influenced by functionalism, highlights another axiological category: the esthetic patterns implicit in cultures. Sapir, Kluckhohn, and others carry the pattern concept further into the realm of values when they write of culture-configurations; these are, of course, saturated with implicit beliefs about what is good, right, and beautiful. As for the vertical dimension, exemplified by Warner's hypothesis of status levels, he has already been quoted to the effect that "class is present in a community when people are placed by the values of the group itself at general levels of inferiority and superiority . . ." Equally valuational is the concept of class in the Marxian theory; indeed, classes in one sense are considered to be the root of all cultural evil. All of these problems of spatial order, furthermore, raise normative responsibilities for education—among them, that of building integrated programs based upon problems of human relations ranging from family to community to world, that of creating educational designs that express indigenous "ways of life," and that of coping with the biases of teachers who equate middle-status values with the goal of "success."

The temporal model of cultural order embraced value issues no less comprehensively. All of the classical theorists supported a progressive view of cultural evolution. We have cited Tylor, for example, for believing that "the history of the lower races, as of the higher, . . . has on the whole been forward"—a statement which of course makes a value judgment while neglecting to tell us here what is meant by "forward." And though most recent culture-theorists suspect any such melioristic doctrine, the idea is far from obsolete. A few, such as Childe, continue to reflect the classical influence. At the same time, we shall see that even such careful authorities as Boas and Kroeber do not deny that progress (itself intrinsically a value term meaning change for the better) may be utilized as a criterion by which to judge the development of cultures, so long as we define the kinds of progress we mean.

The role of values in temporal order likewise entered our discussion of the selected philosophies of cultural history. Each of the four "substantive" theories deals with values throughout. Kroeber's avoids value judgments more than the others, though much of his subject matter involves values (for example, of the fine arts). Sorokin is probably least successful. But Spengler's dislike of industrial civilization and Toynbee's plea for a Christian renascence are confessions of their own lack of objectivity. Among the "methodological" philosophies of history, Muller's point regarding the importance of the future is especially apropos of the problem of human goals. And all of the theorists of cultural history to whom we have referred create opportunities for education—above all, the opportunity to vitalize historical study in general education by means of great conceptions of man's destiny. These conceptions, while deflating any superficial faith in progress, view the struggle of humanity as essentially a normative struggle motivated by only partially expressed beliefs about the deepest goals of life.

Human process, embracing our second main cluster of problems, is equally germane to the issues we now face. All of the selected concepts—discovery and invention, diffusion, acculturation and the others—are affected by values if for no other reason than that, as Malinowski would contend, the desire to satisfy needs and wants is integral to every effort of a people to change. Yet resistance to change is significant, too: it means, at the least, that a given group cherishes the values to which it is accustomed and resents the efforts by another value-motivated group (Christian missionaries, say) to modify or undermine them.

Still further issues are raised by the concepts of process. Cultural pluralism versus cosmopolitanism or universalism is one: pluralism insists that a wide variety of values is both a fact and a good; cosmopolitanism agrees to the fact of variety, but questions both its meaning and desirability for the "one world" that is now emerging. Another issue is raised by focus and innovation: since cultural change usually if not always occurs either toward or away from values that are accepted by some groups and rejected by some others, the urgent issue that these concepts raise is again not the fact of change but rather how successfully change can be effected toward what new foci, what innovations. Or consider the concept of crisis: Does not a crisis in culture often manifest itself even more gravely as a conflict between opposing patterns of belief and action about human ends than about human means? In this kind of situation, is cultural choice between alternative ends still possible? And if still possible, what can be done by education to facilitate the choice—to reduce the margin of error, to increase the likelihood of the *better* choice, and to generate the human power essential to attainment once the choice is made?

The brief exploration in this work of the field of culture-and-personality as it relates to process is no less pertinent. The whole function of enculturative learning is essentially valuational in that it is, above all, the values of a culture that must be imparted to initiates. Drives, reward and punishment (with their concomitants of pleasure and pain), custom, and other aspects of learning are similarly toned with value elements, as are the concepts of "national character" and "modal personality." The theory of creative personality stressed by Hallowell, Murphy, and other experts in this field recognizes the potentialities of man to achieve the high value of self-fulfillment; while for Kluckhohn and Murray the goal-seeking, directional character of personality is central to their whole analysis. Comparably relevant, of course, is Mead's critique of our anxiety-inducing culture, as is Riesman's theory of other-direction as an impelling norm of middle-class America.

Problems of human process, no less than those of order, are chronic also to education in its normative role. Programs of intercultural understanding are always motivated by at least implicit criteria of desirable goals—of respect for peoples of varying ethnic and racial backgrounds, for example. Grave educational issues arise from clumsy, impulsive attempts at acculturation and assimilation of children with diverse cultural values—a truth reconfirmed in Southern states since the Supreme Court ruling on racial integration. Even more difficult issues are raised for education by the concept of modal personality. To mention but one: How far should a certain type of personality also become the norm, the "ego ideal" of an educational policy and program; and how far not? And, if not, how do we go about changing a given modal personality toward what more desirable norm?

Here we face head-on the third and last of our great problems—that of human goals. For, assuming agreement that cultures and the personality types that epitomize cultures are inherently goal-seeking, teachers and their students still have the right to ask authorities: *"What goals do you mean?"* As a normative endeavor, education cannot be content merely to describe the phenomenon of goal-seeking. Its obligation extends further: not only to help personalities come to terms with the dominant goals of their respective cultures but to help them analyze, express, implement, and often reconstitute these goals as fully as they are able and as comprehensively as they see fit.

To be "able" and to "see fit" are also, of course, normative terms. They imply that healthy personalities as members of healthy cultures have the capacity, latently at least, to deliberate about whatever goals may be open to them, to choose at a specific time the most desirable goal, to reach proximate agreement upon that goal, and to move concertedly toward its consummation.

In this normative framework, education differs from culture-theory at least as it is represented by a majority of contemporary anthropologists. Since Boas especially, anthropologists have usually classified themselves as social scientists—hence as neutral searchers for the truths of culture unwarped by value judgments. Perhaps as much as any reason, this explains why the first systematic formulations of the concept of value in anthropology were not, we are told, undertaken until the early nineteen-forties and why no consensus is available as to the best formulation.[1] Today, while interest in the problem increases, a descriptive—that is to say, an ostensibly impartial and objective—study of cultural values continues to predominate. Only rarely have authorities been candid enough to admit that some set of important values underlies their own contributions; still more rarely have they taken pains to analyze or vigorously defend its nature. The plea of Bidney that the scientific study of culture become deliberately normative remains unheeded by most anthropologists.

I stress this distinction between a descriptive and normative study of cultural values because it means that if education as a normative enterprise is to learn here from anthropologists it is likely to learn most from their descriptive contributions. That this can still be substantial is seen not only from our summary above but from the evidence to be presented in the next two chapters. The prevailing view is succinctly expressed by Kroeber:

It follows that if we refuse to deal with values, we are refusing to deal with what has most meaning in particular cultures as well as in human culture seen as a whole . . . What we have left on elimination of values is an arid roster of culture traits . . . Other things being equal, a descriptive or historical approach would accordingly seem more readily fruitful, in scientific inquiry into values . . .

Values . . . can obviously be described; their differential qualities as well as common characteristics can be compared; their developmental phases, sequential relations, and connections can be investigated . . . [In] apprehending cultures the most essential thing to apprehend is their values, because without these he [the student of culture] will not know either toward what the cultures are slanted or around what they organized.[2]

From the array of research and discussion on this important subject, which aspects should be selected for more careful scrutiny? The answer is hardly easier than it was in Parts II and III; as Keesing has shown in his extensive survey of *Anthropological Contributions to Value Theory*,[3] the range of topics and issues is already wide. Therefore, once more, I demarcate by the yardstick of educational relevance even though certain contributions must be ignored.

One demarcation follows from the term "human goals." Although some culture-theorists use "value" and "goal" interchangeably, I shall not press for their identity. One may contend that, while all values connote what should be or ought to be—and in this sense they are always norms, standards, ideals, ends, goals of human endeavor toward which people strive—the converse proposition that all goals connote values is not equally correct. You may set yourself the task of walking from one point to a second, accurately calling the latter a goal; yet you may find no value whatever in finishing the chore. Also, it is possible that many goals are partly valuable and partly not. In the example just given, your destination as such may be devoid of value, yet the feeling of radiant health that you obtain as a result of your exercise may still have value whether or not you perceive it to be valuable. One need not, in short, contend either that all goals are values or that values are equivalent to goals because the latter may possess ingredients of value. One should simply be concerned with those qualities of value that one is able to discern in the cultural pursuit and attainment of goals.

The final demarcation is the choice of crucial problems as foci of this discernment. I have chosen two. One, to which the next chapter is devoted, is the problem of the relativity versus the universality of human values. The other is the problem of freedom—the theme of Chapter Twelve. Reasons for their selection should become clear as they are weighed more carefully, and as a cultural *and* normative design for education emerges. A guide to the remainder of this Part is Malinowski's dictum that "The whole system of education is determined by value."[4]

CHAPTER ELEVEN

HUMAN GOALS AS RELATIVE AND UNIVERSAL

THE CASE FOR CULTURAL RELATIVISM

WHY IS THE problem of relativism and universalism selected for interpretation, rather than one or more of a dozen other problems? The answer is fourfold. In the first place, it has probably received more sustained attention from anthropologists in recent years than any other problem of values. In the second place, experts in other fields concerned with values—philosophy is one—have been especially influenced by anthropologists at this point. In the third place, it cuts a channel through various dimensions of the problem of human goals. And, finally, it has importance for education both as theory and as practice.

The focal issue may be simply stated. Are all values relative to particular cultures, and hence to the particular times and places in which these cultures exist? Or are values universal—that is, are the basic purposes, ideals, norms, goals of people cross-cultural or trans-cultural in the sense that, regardless of place, race, ethnic character, social institutions, habits or customs, they are common to many if not to all cultures? Or is there a third alternative?

Influenced profoundly by Boas, it was Benedict doubtless more than any other anthropologist who brought cultural relativism into prominence and who, through the popularity of *Patterns of Culture*, has persuaded innumerable students that the answer to our first question is affirmative, the second negative. One corollary of her position invites a kind of ethical neutrality. In her own words, there are "coexisting and equally valid patterns of life which mankind has created for itself from the raw materials of existence."[1] The logical consequence of her position is, as Kluckhohn has said, that "one is compelled to accept any cultural pattern as vindicated precisely by its cultural status . . ."[2]

Although Kluckhohn doubts that most culture-theorists now accept this consequence, it is difficult to understand why they are unwilling to do so as long as they tacitly admit its premises. Abraham Edel in his illuminating study of the problem insists that "unavoidable indeterminacy" is inherent in relativism as an ethical doctrine.[3] That is to say, if the only values we can have or know are limited to the particular experiences of particular individuals and groups, then they are indeterminate because always challengeable or negatable by contradictory or conflicting values.

We must, I think, appreciate the great contribution that cultural relativism has made to a sophisticated approach to values. If students of culture were ever to get anywhere as scientists, the first necessity was to purge themselves as much as possible of their own ethnocentric biases. In this sense anthropological research like all social science had to learn from the natural sciences. Objectivity—the absence of emotional, religious, political, or other distorting factors—is a prerequisite of any legitimate scientific effort.

To assume the norm of objectivity is, however, to imply that objectivity itself is a value, or more precisely that scientific truth made possible by objective research and discovery is desirable. Another value perhaps less often admitted but obvious as a practical effect of relativistic ethics is a respect for and tolerance of people different from ourselves. The legitimacy of both of these values is stressed in the "code of ethics" adopted by the Society for Applied Anthropology, which also includes the values of "integrity" and "responsibility":

To advance those forms of human relationships which contribute to the integrity of the individual human being; to maintain scientific and professional integrity and responsibility without fear or favor to the limit of the foreseeable effects of their actions; to respect both human personality and cultural values . . .[4]

The values explicit in this statement might be justified on the ground that, as Herskovits points out, applied anthropology is quite different from pure anthropology in that it is concerned with "engineering"—with practical effects that involve human welfare.[5] Yet even "pure anthropology" is not, we have just seen, entirely devoid of values: the least it affirms is that scientific research is a worthwhile end in itself.

To admit, however, that this kind of value crosses cultural boundaries wherever science operates is by no means to admit that most other values do so. Herskovits is militant in his defense of cultural relativism as the only legitimate position. He insists that it is "tough-minded" (i.e., empirical) rather than "tender-minded" (i.e., rationalistic).[6] It avoids the dangers of ethnocentrism—"the point of view that one's own way of life is to be preferred to all others."[7] By contrast,

. . . cultural relativism is a philosophy which, in recognizing the values set up by every society to guide its own life, lays stress on the dignity inherent in every body of custom, and on the need for tolerance of conventions though they may differ from one's own . . . [The] relativistic point of view brings into relief the validity of every set of norms for the people whose lives are guided by them, and the values these represent.[8]

He does not deny that "certain values in human life are everywhere accorded recognition, even though the institutions of no two cultures are identical in form."[9] But Herskovits opens himself here to a charge of ambiguity if not inconsistency since, as Bidney points out, "no objective standard of comparison" is provided.[10] His arguments for cultural relativism are more persuasive. He shows how questionable are all efforts to rank "primitive" and "civilized" cultures in terms of norms, and hence why the neutral terms "nonliterate" and "literate" are preferable because devoid of ethnocentric value judgments. Polygamy, for example, may be just as "good" for the Dahomey culture of West Africa as monogamy may be "good" for ours. So too with the definition of "normalcy": the trances or possessions that occur in certain religious rites may be considered abnormal by us but not by their practitioners; on the contrary, they fall "entirely in the realm of understandable, predictable, *normal* behavior."[11]

Of many other culture-theorists who have worried over relativism, Kroeber and Kluckhohn may be chosen because of both strong sympathies and serious doubts. Kroeber, for example, is quoted by Herskovits in its support:

Anthropologists now agree that each culture must be examined in terms of its own structure and values, instead of being rated by the standards of some other civilization exalted as absolute—which in practice of course is always our own civilization . . . This anthropological principle leads, it is true, to a relativistic or pluralistic philosophy—a belief in many values rather than a single value system . . . But why not, if the facts so demand?[12]

One of the important points that Kroeber and Kluckhohn make in their collaborative work, hitherto cited, is scarcely treated by Herskovits: the fact of plural value patterns not only between but within cultures—a point with which Steward, Warner, and others would surely concur. Florence Kluckhohn is cited to the effect that "Variation for the same individual when he is playing different roles and variation between whole groups of persons within a single society are not adequately accounted for . . ." by students of cultural values.[13]

Still more emphatic is their agreement that

. . . sincere comparison of cultures leads quickly to recognition of their "relativity." What this means is that cultures are differently weighted in their values . . . and that true understanding of cultures therefore involves recognition of their particular value systems. Comparisons of cultures must not be simplistic in terms of an arbitrary or preconceived universal value system, but must be multiple, with each culture first understood in terms of its own particular value system and therefore its own idiosyncratic structure . . . Cultural relativism has been completely established and there must be no attempt to explain it away or to deprecate its importance because it is inconvenient, hard to take, hard to live with.[14]

Their position is fortified by parallels with modern biology and physics, both of which they regard as relativistic: biology, in the classifications of living forms; physics, in such phenomena as the space-time continuum. The fluidity of nature revealed by the concept of physical relativity is an important postulate also of the science of culture.

We shall soon find, however, that Kroeber and Kluckhohn together qualify their relativism in true polaristic style. Meanwhile, it is important to consider Kluckhohn's own further thinking, for he has recently concentrated upon the problem of values with both thoroughness and persistence. He says:

No anthropologist . . . doubts that the theory of cultural relativity is in some sense forced by the facts and meaningful. There is an exuberant variation in ethical codes, and surely a satisfactory interpretation of morality must be able to account for the moral judgments found in all cultures.[15]

Having thus paid tribute to relativism, Kluckhohn goes on to attack its limitations. The only defensible position, he believes, is one that counterbalances cultural pluralism by a scientifically defensible universalism. Let us examine, then, the meaning of the latter concept as he and others have come to grips with it.

THE CASE FOR CULTURAL UNIVERSALISM

Kluckhohn puts both the question and the direction of his answer concisely: "But can any values be conceived, if not as basically absolute, as at least universal? Or are all values inherently relative . . . ? . . . To me it is clear that the answer to these questions must be given not in an 'either-or' but in a 'both-and' form."[16] Here then is a "third alternative" to relativism as such, and universalism as such.

Of course, says Kluckhohn, some values express personal or group taste and preference. Yet it does not follow that because some are relative therefore all must be. Rather, "neither extreme relativism nor extreme absolutism is tenable as a guiding hypothesis for further empirical enquiry."[17]

Universal values are more difficult to ascertain than relative values because they require cross-cultural investigation safeguarded against the danger of generalizing from limited perspective, especially ethnocentric distortions. Nevertheless, Kluckhohn contends that certain common values are already demonstrable. In part, they derive from biological similarities of all human beings. Negatively, for example, no culture approves of human suffering as a good *in itself*. Similarly, none condones rape or incest; none tolerates indiscriminate lying or stealing; none permits such extreme abnormality that an individual's behavior is completely unpredictable to the group. Positively, all cultures value reciprocity, restitution, mutual obligations between children and parents, and "many other moral concepts . . ."[18]

In his collaborative survey with Kroeber (some of which he also incorporates in his lecture, "Universal Values and Anthropological Relativism"[19]), Kluckhohn maintains, following Wissler's[20] early statement on the problem, that

. . . the broad outlines of the ground plan of all cultures is and has to be about the same because men always and everywhere are faced with certain unavoidable problems which arise out of the situation "given" by nature. Since most of the patterns of all cultures crystallize around the same foci, there are significant respects in which each culture is not wholly isolated, self-contained, disparate but rather related to and comparable with all other cultures.[21]

The ways in which universal values are spelled out in practice vary, of course, from culture to culture. This is especially so for such abstract values as "truth" and "beauty." Nevertheless, if the phrase "a common humanity" is meaningful, then common values are indigenous *to* humanity.[22] Just as each personality is both different from and common with all others, so too is each culture. "Not only is *human* social life inevitably a moral life in theory and to a large extent in practice, but ethical principles are the fundament of most of the rest of the culture."[23]

Kluckhohn's theoretical defense of universalism is bolstered by research of his own. In his "Universal Categories of Culture," he surveys the literature in English for evidence of cultural universals and comes to the general conclusions already summarized. He reminds us that anthropologists have long assumed universals, but that their own research has been "directed overwhelmingly to the distinctiveness of each culture and to the differences in human custom as opposed to the similarities."[24] He pays tribute to Freud and other psychoanalysts for having depicted correctly various universal characteristics of motivational life. Nor should this be surprising to anyone but "an anthropologist overindoctrinated with the theory of cultural relativism": after all, "many of the inescapable givens of human life are also universal."[25] The fact of two sexes, of infantile helplessness, of competition for the affection of parents, illustrates what Kluckhohn means by "givens." But others, such as those of social organization, may also be discovered; indeed, research already points toward their likelihood. Kluckhohn is not dealing here with values alone; he is concerned only to gather together the extant research on universal characteristics. Since, however, he assumes that cultural life is saturated with values, it follows that if there are demonstrable universal characteristics in culture, then there are demonstrable universal values. The examples he offers in this important paper abound with ethical and esthetic ingredients.

Among the anthropologists whom Kluckhohn is able to cite in support of his position, Linton paid special attention, toward the close of his life, to the value problem and took a pro-universalist stand perhaps even stronger than Kluckhohn's. In his essay, "Universal Ethical Principles: An Anthropological View," Linton puts the issue sharply: "Behind the seemingly endless diversity of culture patterns there is a fundamental conformity. To discover what the common factors are and to plan culture change in conformity with them is the most important task of the social scientist."[26]

Linton does not deny that a great deal of comparative research is demanded by this task. Yet he is prepared to state that the differences among cultures, which hitherto have been the principal interest of anthropologists, are already known to be less than the similarities. Among the similarities with value implications are: marriage as a life-long ideal; responsibility of parents to children and vice versa; personal property and eminent domain; charity; economic obligations involving goods and services; opposition to murder and sex violence; and psychic as well as physical security. Thus he concludes, "The resemblances in ethical concepts so far outweigh the differences that a sound basis for mutual understanding between groups of different cultures is already in existence."[27]

Linton reiterates his conviction in a second essay, "The Problem of Universal Values." While unduly critical of philosophic analyses of the problem, he is justified as an anthropologist in pleading for more scientific study of the universal values of culture. Such study, he contends, shows that the commonest and in some ways most pronounced of all values is associated with supernatural religious belief, although the precise meanings of supernaturalism and of such closely related ideas as faith in an after-life are widely disparate. Since this point is not equally considered by Kluckhohn or other axiologically-oriented culture-theorists, Linton's conclusion is important:

The only universal features which can be derived from such a wide variety of beliefs are those of man's universal sense of inadequacy in the face of many situations and his belief that there are beings whose powers exceed his own and who will give him the aid which he so vitally needs, if he can learn the correct methods of approaching them. To this may be added the well-nigh universal belief that the individual's personality is not extinguished in death.[28]

Another emphasis in the essay that I have not found elsewhere is Linton's recognition of the universal value attached to leadership, although again the ways leadership is manifested differ sharply. Still other values are knowledge, curiosity, and "extreme teachability." These, like all values, are arranged in hierarchies which, though universal, vary in the order of importance attached to certain values; some cultures place chastity, for example, on a much higher level than do others. The same variation is found in the value of individual initiative—a value so high in the American tradition that it is difficult for many of us to realize how low it may be elsewhere.

Kroeber criticizes this essay both negatively and positively. Negatively, he characteristically opposes the deliberate injection of Linton's own value judgments: ". . . a problem like that of universal values is intellectually fundamental enough to warrant attention in its own right, rather than because we are alarmed about our future."[29] Positively, Kroeber is ready to agree largely with the validity of Linton's list of universal values (some of which are also found in the other essay, mentioned above), but he is again negative both in considering the list vague and in regretting the stress on cultural similarities at the expense of cultural differences. Here Kroeber reflects his sympathy for cultural relativism and pluralism—a sympathy which often seems more strongly polaristic to universalism in his own thinking than it does in Kluckhohn's.

Kroeber cites George P. Murdock as an anthropologist whose approach to the problem, so far as careful research is concerned, surpasses that of Linton. While Murdock has not theorized systematically about cultural values, he has contributed to our understanding of them by his years of study of cross-cultural phenomena, many of which reveal ethical or other valuational factors. His *Social Structure* is, I am reasonably sure, the most meticulously documented examination of "the nuclear family" that has been made by an anthropologist. Its universal character, based upon data obtained from two hundred and fifty societies, is epitomized in this summary statement:

> In the nuclear family or its constituent relationships we thus see assembled four functions fundamental to human social life—the sexual, the economic, the reproductive, and the educational. Without provision for the first and third, society would become extinct; for the second, life itself would cease; for the fourth, culture would come to an end. The immense social utility of the nuclear family and the basic reason for its universality thus begin to emerge in strong relief.[30]

Variations in the structure of the nuclear family are, of course, wide. Yet the striking fact is not so much the variations as the similarities: incest taboos, marriage with accompanying sexual privileges, division of labor by sex and age, economic cooperation, child care and social rearing, rules of descent and residence—these are present in every society investigated.

But Murdock and his co-workers at Yale University have gone much farther in cross-cultural research than the nuclear family. In his essay, "The Common Denominators of Culture," Murdock offers an explanation for cultural universals that reflects the theory of learning criticized in Chapter Nine. Aside from the issue of the validity of this theory, his partial list of elements common to all known cultures still deserves quotation, for ethical and esthetic values permeate most if not all of these elements:

. . . age-grading, athletic sports, bodily adornment, calendar, cleanliness training, community organization, cooking, cooperative labor, cosmology, courtship, dancing, decorative art, divination, division of labor, dream interpretation, education, eschatology, ethics, ethnobotany, etiquette, faith healing, family, feasting, fire making, folklore, food taboos, funeral rites, games, gestures, gift giving, government, greetings, hair styles, hospitality, housing, hygiene, incest taboos, inheritance rules, joking, kin-groups, kinship nomenclature, language, law, luck superstitions, magic, marriage, mealtimes, medicine, modesty concerning natural functions, mourning, music, mythology, numerals, obstetrics, penal sanctions, personal names, population policy, postnatal care, pregnancy usages, property rights, propitiation of supernatural beings, puberty customs, religious ritual, residence rules, sexual restrictions, soul concepts, status differentiation, surgery, tool making, trade, visiting, weaning, and weather control.[31]

In more limited fashion than Murdock, but with comparable thoroughness, Richard B. Brandt has contributed to the problem of universalism and relativism in his study of *Hopi Ethics*. The study is ground-breaking in its systematic application of philosophic categories to anthropological data. His conclusion, so far as our present problem is concerned, is that Hopi Indian values both differ from and are similar to white American values. He finds, for example, that they differ in their greater tolerance of sexual relations and of cruelty to animals. But they are similar in such values as avoidance of injury to others and to oneself, obligation to care for children and the aged, respect for private property, equitable rewards for useful service, and responsibility for intentional acts.[32]

Brandt's conclusion that relative and universal values, so far at least as two cultures are concerned, are both demonstrable brings us back to the "both-and" point of view held by Kroeber and Kluckhohn in their joint study. It is reiterated again by Kroeber's review of the discussions of value that took place at an international conference of anthropologists:

Acceptance of relativity of morals and values invests our conceptualization of each culture with a certain degree of autonomy. It is a cardinal point of anthropological doctrine . . . On the other hand . . . the fact that all men have an essentially common anatomy and physiology . . . makes a pervasive generic similarity of cultural values expectable . . . The problem is neither: Is there some absolute uniformity? nor: Is relativistic differentiation unlimited? The proper form of the problem is: How much similarity and how much dissimilarity are there? What the quarrel has really been about is that we tended to see it as an all-or-none distinction: either relativism was true, or it was false. Whereas it is really a question of how far similarity and dissimilarity extend . . . Values, then, are both particular and relativistic and universal and permanent.[33]

RECENT PHILOSOPHIC APPROACHES

Thus far, our study of relative and universal values has been limited almost entirely to anthropologists. That the question is of interest to experts in adjoining fields is, however, indisputable. Many cultural philosophers, for example, have given it attention; indeed, Kluckhohn reminds us that it arose some twenty-four hundred years ago in Plato's dialogues. Basically, the problem is the ancient one of whether, how far, and in what ways ethical standards transcend time and place. The most influential answers in the history of philosophy have probably been more often on the universal than on the relative side—one of the most famous exponents in ancient times being that of Plato himself, in modern times that of Kant. Yet, the counter doctrine also has been popular especially in recent years, associated as it is with such influential thinkers as Dewey, Mead, and other pragmatists. In all probability the cultural relativism popularized by some anthropologists and the ethical relativism of some philosophers have tended to support each other.

Though we should be wandering much too far afield to review the major philosophic issues related to the problem, we may benefit by the comparably relevant but highly disparate ideas of five present-day philosophers: David Bidney, Ralph Barton Perry, F. S. C. Northrop, Charles Morris, and Abraham Edel. All of these thinkers are selected for their familiarity with and utilization of the several disciplines, including anthropology, which converge upon the problem.

Bidney takes a forthright stand with cultural universalism. Like Kroeber and Kluckhohn, however, he does not think that we have to choose entirely between universal and relative values. He does point out that just as in science there is cumulative knowledge of nature so in our understanding of man there may be cumulative knowledge of what is universally desirable:

The practical effective alternatives are not cultural absolutism versus cultural relativism . . . but rather rational norms with a potentiality for universal acceptance . . . The only effective alternative to a mythical relative absolute is a better, more rational and more objective ideal of conduct and belief . . . [If] anthropology is to attain the stage of making significant generalizations concerning the . . . values of civilization, then comparative studies . . . must be made in order to demonstrate universal principles of cultural dynamics and concrete rational norms capable of universal realization.[34]

Perry's *Realms of Value* is distinguished both for its axiological analyses and for their application to many practical aspects of human life. He too is convinced that any dichotomy between universalism and relativism is unjustified, whether we are thinking of economics, politics, art, or of culture as a whole. Perry uses the apt term "culture-centric predicament" to emphasize that all interpretations of culture are relative to culture, for no one can escape the fact that he is conditioned by it and hence views his own and every other culture in the perspective of his relations to it. To infer from the culturecentric predicament, however, that value judgments are necessarily arbitrary and subjective is to fall victim to a "vicious relativism" that is no more justified in the case of cultural values than in any other kind of judgments about nature and life. The task of establishing universal judgments is, to be sure, "a perpetual endeavor, never perhaps wholly successful, to eliminate the distortions and limitations of experience by bringing them to light and putting them where they belong. It rectifies the distortions and supplements the limitations."[35]

Perry argues further that a culture may even establish as part of its own character the norm of emancipating itself from its own biases. This may be attempted from within the culture itself, but also with the aid of standards external to it. Always, however, the aim is to make sure that all standards, internal or external, are as explicit as possible so that they may be criticized and corrected in the course of their operations.

Turning to Northrop, we find him defending a viewpoint which has influenced a number of anthropologists, including Kluckhohn. In *Anthropology Today*, Northrop approaches the problem through theories of law, notably those of positivism, pragmatism, Kantian idealism, functionalism, and "naturalistic jurisprudence." All but the last, he argues, force us to make relativistic value judgments—even the idealist theory does so—because they fail to provide any universal criterion of value beyond themselves that is workable in practice.

His own position, naturalistic jurisprudence, tries to provide this criterion in "the inner order of nature as revealed by natural science."[36] This is essentially the position he also takes in a symposium on relativism (with Kluckhohn and Cantril) before the American Philosophical Association.[37] In both papers, as well as in other writings, his central argument is that "the values of a culture are the fruits of living according to the basic philosophical assumptions used by a people in conceptualizing the raw data of their experience."[38]

But Northrop's position is open to difficulties. I have tried to show in Chapter Four that he commits the "philosophic fallacy" of interpreting cultures in terms of their philosophic systems and then regarding these as if they were virtually causal of the cultures themselves. To resolve the problem of values in terms of scientific conceptualization is equally oversimplifying. No doubt it is true that every culture does have its conceptual underpinnings, whether explicit or implicit; the importance of discovering and enunciating these has been stressed repeatedly in the present volume. But to argue that we can logically deduce "second order facts" (referring to "culture and living law") from "first order facts" (referring to "nature and natural law") raises more questions than it answers. Particularly serious is the question of the *counterinfluence* of the second order upon the first. Just as the meaning and role of, say, the economic institutions of culture are not established by insisting upon the "relativity of culture to philosophy" as against "the relativity of each philosophy and its particular ethic to culture," so the relations of values to culture are not established by that insistence. Moreover, the issue of relativism and universalism is left unresolved, for, while Northrop writes of the possibility of a philosophy of science that would account "for the first order facts of all theories," he also admits that "Where the initial theories of first order facts differ, there are different artifacts and hence different living laws and cultures."[39] In short, there are different systems of value.

Morris attacks the problem in a different way. He has devoted several years to research, utilizing refined statistical techniques, in the effort to demonstrate how values may be subjected to scientific inquiry. The study from which I shall draw, *Varieties of Human Value*,[40] is the outgrowth of two earlier studies of a more purely philosophic nature;[41] it examines with painstaking care the value-orientations primarily of college students in three cultures: those of the United States, India, and China (with lesser reference to Japan, Canada, Norway, Pakistan, England, New Zealand, and Italy). The study demonstrates that carefully controlled research can be successfully accomplished even in so complex an area as intercultural ethics.

To what extent does Morris strengthen or weaken the case for cultural relativism? The answer is far from black and white. His data consist primarily of sample responses to thirteen "ways to live," each described in a succinct paragraph, that express such influential goals of human life as self-control, enjoyment, withdrawal, and sympathy for others. The results are subjected to various kinds of comparison, with numerous limitations and uncertainties. One of the most enlightening results is that each of the three major cultures ranks the different "ways to live" in different orders.[42] The United States sample ranks "Way 7" highest in terms of means scores: "integrate action, enjoyment, and contemplation." The Indian sample ranks "Way 1" highest: "preserve the best that man has attained." And the China sample ranks "Way 13" highest: "obey the cosmic purposes." The Japan and Norway samples are still different, both ranking "Way 3" ("show sympathetic concern for others") highest. The ways of life ranked lowest are also striking: the United States and Japan samples rank "Way 13" lowest (at the opposite end of the scale from China); India and China rank "Way 9" ("wait in quiet receptivity") lowest; and Norway ranks "Way 11" ("meditate on the inner life") lowest.

The case for universal goals certainly does not thus far seem to be strengthened by these findings. It even seems difficult to generalize about either East or West, much less about culture on a world scale. Not only do Japan and Norway agree on the highest ranking, but Japan and the United States agree on the lowest. Yet when the data are further analyzed, certain similarities, at least within the Eastern and Western cultures, respectively, begin to appear. For example, India and China agree in ranking "Way 7" (highest for the United States) about in the middle; they also agree in ranking "Way 9" lowest. Moreover, when the scores for all thirteen "ways to live" are compared and grouped, Morris finds (though with qualifications) that Eastern groups "are more tolerant of cultural diversity than the Western groups" while "Western groups are more tolerant of diversity within the individual (pschological diversity) . . ."[43] On the whole, Western students are more self-centered than Eastern students, the latter being more society-centered. Still more significant in terms of our problem, when the "ways to live" are grouped in larger categories, all of the cultures with minor exception rank "social restraint and self-control" and "enjoyment and progress in action" higher than "withdrawal and self-sufficiency" or "receptivity and sympathetic concern."

Morris also examines the social, psychological, and biological "determinants of value" to ascertain whether and how far these condition the "ways to live" of the several cultures. His answer is that all three are fundamental, although the social or cultural is most so. The high correlation among the various samples taken in each culture demonstrates that "the main determinant of the ratings is a social one, that modes of life deemed desirable by individuals are the modes of life approved in the culture to which they belong."[44] Yet it is impossible to say that any one causal factor, such as the economic, is primary; rather, the findings support the pluralistic view of causation that we have found predominant among culture-theorists. Within each culture, moreover, certain differences are noticeable: in India, Brahmans and non-Brahmans are by no means wholly agreed on their goals; in the United States, Negroes and whites are not. Also, one of the most striking of all inferences from the social determinants is that, contrary to traditional opinion, the Chinese and Indian cultures (at least as represented by young adults) appear to be less complacent, more vigorously concerned with social reconstruction, than does the United States.

Psychological and biological determinants of value are less influential but equally revealing. To take one instance, the eclecticism of "Way 7," which predominates in the United States sample, suggests the kind of psychological insecurity and anxiety that Mead earlier called our attention to as itself culturally induced. To take another instance, Morris is persuaded that such biological determinants as age and physical type affect preferences for alternative goals, but he is also persuaded that "if bodies are determinants of values, values will in turn be determinants of how bodies act . . ."[45] —a good transactionist principle. At the same time, the differences between individuals and groups within cultures, while significant, tend to be less marked than the differences between cultures—a reconfirmation of the primary influence of culture as a determinant of human goals. "Thus the social system as well as the personality [and biology] system must be kept in the forefront of attention in the study of values."[46]

The strongest impression that one receives from the Morris study is that hasty conclusions about either universal or relative values are untenable. The thirteen "ways to live" appeal to some persons in all cultures—so much so that it is always a question of "less or more" rather than "all or none." The cultural processes now accelerating so rapidly also undoubtedly affect current preferences—a fact particularly marked in the reactions of Chinese, Indian, and Japanese respondents, but by no means absent from those of the United States. Whether, in view of the crisis character of our age and the rate of acculturation and assimilation, more similarity of goals will emerge in the future is a prediction that cannot be made with any certainty on the basis of this work.[47]

The admirable caution with which Morris presents his findings is also conspicuous in the study by Edel. The question to which he addresses himself is this: Can the human sciences throw light upon the conflict between universalism and relativism? In order to answer, he ploughs the fields of biology, psychology, history, anthropology, and sociology. In all of these he finds qualified evidence in behalf of universal values. I shall dwell chiefly on the last two fields as most pertinent.

Edel reminds us to begin with that some phenomena are inherently cross-cultural—scientific knowledge being the most familiar—and that the "dignity" of all cultures, which the relativist Herskovits also allows, at once presupposes a value judgment that is no longer relative. So, too, do such value judgments in Benedict's relativistic apologia as condemnation of war and absence of violence in sex relations. Edel's more original exposé of relativism, however, centers in his answers to four searching questions: (1) Can we discover "invariant values"? (2) Can students of culture learn here from the biological and psychological sciences? (3) Are there "invariant tasks" in every culture? (4) Are there "specific sociological determinants and functions" of a cross-cultural character?

In answering the first question, Edel argues that the non-appearance of a value up to a certain time does not necessarily disprove its potential universality. To take an example of my own, many people do not follow a properly balanced diet, but this in no way establishes that they would continue to prefer an unbalanced one if they understood its effect upon health or if better food were available. More subtle values, such as esthetic creativity or respect for knowledge and justice, are more difficult to demonstrate as invariant, especially since they are manifested in such variable ways, but cultural research that endeavored to do so might well reach affirmative results. "Invariant evils," such as killing or disorganization, are perhaps more conspicuous than invariant goods, although here, too, research is still insufficient to allow quick generalizations.

The second question, as to whether biology and psychology can lead toward cultural universals, is answered more positively. Health—physical and mental—may be one such universal. Equally so is the negative value of disease and low life-expectancy. Even "happiness" with all its ambiguities and variables is by no means devoid of empirical demonstration in terms of the satisfaction of human needs. If it is too much to expect scientists to formulate a "happiness-inventory," it is not impossible to hypothesize that there are "invariant necessary conditions in institutional patterns productive of happiness, that is, appropriate social relations whose violation entails a human failure to secure real happiness."[48]

Edel's third question—Are there invariant tasks?—is also answered positively. Control over nature, reproduction, social control, pooling of knowledge, and communication are among the tasks that no culture can avoid and still survive. We have noted others in an earlier citation from Murdock's work. These tasks are frequently related to cultural goals and thus acquire value both as means and as ends. They are not in themselves sufficient to establish universals, for frequently they also generate conflicting goals (of economic organization, say). But they are indispensable because they underscore the cultural similarities that anthropologists like Linton have insisted upon as inseparable from values.

In dealing with the question of "sociological determinants and functions," Edel seems less clear. He is trying, I believe, to ask whether, and, if so, how far, values are dependent upon economic, political, or other institutions and practices. His answer is that there are such dependencies, but that it is often very difficult to trace them in any historical cause-effect sequence. It is easier to understand values as functions of, say, economic life—a viewpoint with which Malinowski and other functionalists could happily agree. The significance to me of Edel's answer to his fourth question is that, while "ethical indeterminancy" is not eliminated by specifying the dependence of values upon economic and other social institutions, it is reduced both by the fact that these institutions are themselves universal and by the fact that they are universally appraised by cultures in terms of their effectiveness to accomplish the respective tasks for which they are established.

Edel epitomizes his conclusions:

We have seen thus far that there are several clear avenues along which invariant [i.e., universal] elements may be sought by the social sciences to act as a basis for transcultural evaluation. There may very well be invariant values of a highly general character. The use of established biological and psychological knowledge about human needs and processes has overturned the kind of ethical relativity that was based on a conception of complete human plasticity. Cultural forms are therefore capable of being estimated for their satisfaction of human needs, their interference with human processes, their contributions to human happiness. Further bases of evaluation are provided in part by seeing how well cultures perform the tasks that every society engages in. These become more specific as knowledge of social determinants and functions grows. What has already been learned shows that it is possible to evaluate a moral pattern in part by the way it fits into or helps advance basic productive and organizational aims of men in society.[49]

How shall we react to the five philosophers taken together? Clearly, they agree with such leaders in anthropology as Kroeber that "relativism *versus* universalism" as an issue must be replaced by the less simple but more meaningful issue, "relativism *and* universalism." While Morris and Edel are the most meticulous in their use of evidence, Bidney, Perry, and Northrop also ground their conclusions in exceptional knowledge of cultural fields. Of the five, Morris is compelled to emphasize relative values probably the strongest, Bidney to emphasize the universal strongest. The least convincing in my opinion is Northrop, and the most convincing, both because of his comprehensiveness and the limitations he places upon his own conclusions, is Edel. The educational significance of their studies, as well as those earlier considered, is the next concern.

CULTURAL RELATIVISM AND UNIVERSALISM: THE RESPONSIBILITY OF EDUCATION

Education, as a normative institution, has a responsibility to deal with the issues raised by the problem of relativism and universalism. This responsibility comes to focus in the disturbances of our time. The question of whether human beings can join together in a common front of means dedicated to a common ground of ends, or whether they must continue to hate and even destroy one another, is as everyone knows no longer academic but sternly immediate. True, education does not as yet even ask the question persistently, much less answer it. The obligation to do so nonetheless grows in gravity not only from year to year but, quite literally, from day to day.

If the best answer we can find is that the values and hence the goals of men living in cultures are and must inevitably be wholly relative to particular time and place, then education influenced by such an answer has reason to support one important kind of teaching and learning about this issue. It has reason to teach and learn that the values of cultures are not only different from one another but that we should tolerate these differences, neither condoning nor condemning but rather respecting them for whatever they are.

In short, cultural relativism lends credence to the view that all nations and all races are equal in the sense that each possesses its own pattern of values none of which can be adjudged to be better or worse than any other pattern. The result is a kind of benign intercultural laissez-faire: let each culture be itself and then, as Adam Smith said of capitalist enterprise in the eighteenth century, the best of all possible worlds will most surely result. Educationally, cultural relativism thus encourages a policy of impartiality toward the values of different cultures, one corollary of which is a sociopolitical neutrality and an isolationism that would be welcome to many school leaders.

To hold, on the contrary, that educators professing such impartiality are often partial to their own ethnocentric values, to hold that no educational system actually is or could ever be normatively neutral because it cannot avoid taking sides with and acting to win certain goals at the same time that it opposes others—to hold this kind of policy is to regard education from a point of view profoundly at odds with the intent and consequences of the relativistic point of view. It is, however, the policy that I believe now to be imperative.

This is not to say that cultural relativism is without educational merit. We have found two interrelated lessons that may be learned from it. One is the lesson of objectivity. Granting the subtleties of the latter term, education can perform a service in teaching and respecting the canons of scientific research in the study of cultures. That it does not thus far do so effectively, that innumerable students are indoctrinated rather in beliefs that tend to reinforce their prejudices, is a commonplace not only of American schooling but of that of other countries. Thus the teaching of history, art, politics, religion, and many other fields needs to be more strictly governed by the indubitable principle that, in one sense, people of different periods, places, customs, and creeds are *not* to be judged deficient or inferior by virtue of their differences. The strongest case for relativism educationally speaking is that, since even this much sophistication is atypical, to plead for a universalism that is still more difficult to prove or even to comprehend is premature indeed.

The other lesson lies in the values of tolerance and respect for cultural diversity as educational goals. Though we have found that these goals, because they are transcultural, already belie the relativistic doctrine, they do nonetheless deserve attention from the first years of learning. Appreciation of people who practice ways of living unlike those immediately familiar is a guidepost of all educational programs that consider "intercultural and international understanding" to be something more than a phrase.

As specialists in such programs would probably agree, one of the practices that has weakened them most is that of teaching tolerance and diversity in terms of what may be called the "folklore approach."[50] Altogether too frequently children are introduced to cultures or subcultures other than their own by means of "quaint" customs—wooden shoes, exotic costumes, pretty dances—with virtually no concern for more fundamental institutions, practices, and beliefs: their economies, for example, or their religious and moral patterns. Aside from the fact that often the examples chosen are obsolete and atypical (picturesque dress, so commonly portrayed in social-studies textbooks, is oftener than not worn only for the benefit of tourists or on national holidays), the folklore approach accomplishes little if anything to enhance the very values it claims to enhance. The principal effect is likely to be whimsical curiosity on the part of learners rather than genuine respect for the plurality of cultures.

Objectivity and tolerance nevertheless continue to be two admirable norms for all levels of education. Relativism is, indeed, paradoxical in its support of these norms: its proper application as an operational concept is integral with rather than contradictory to the concept of universalism. For, to know cultures as objectively as possible, to appreciate the multiplicity of values thereby discerned, is prerequisite to any universality that emerges from such knowledge and appreciation.

What kind of universality, then, may education properly consider? There is nothing difficult about understanding the long list of common values compiled by Kluckhohn, Linton, Kroeber, Murdock, and other anthropologists. Also, the biopsychical equipment of man, the "inescapable givens" of his motivational and physiological life, provide resources through which to integrate psychological and biological with cultural knowledge of these values. In the social studies, cross-cultural opposition to such "disvalues" as human suffering or indiscriminate dishonesty could help to purge the teaching of "moral and spiritual values" of typical innocuousness. So, too, could cross-cultural support of positive values such as reciprocity, mutual obligations between young and old, marriage as an ideal relationship, emotional and bodily security, and respect for property (not necessarily private). At proper age levels, study of sexual and marital practices and ideals in various cultures could assist growing learners to appraise intelligently the types of custom (analyzed by Mead, Kardiner, Whiting, and others) that produce anxiety and turmoil, as well as those that produce well-adjusted, harmonious relations between "male and female." Likewise, acquaintance with child-rearing practices in various cultures—so heavily stressed by anthropologists in the culture-and-personality field—could help young adults on the threshold of parenthood to avoid those practices that produce mental illness and to encourage those that produce mental health.

Linton's concern for the universality of religious belief leads us to the thorny issue of whether, in the perspective of culture-theory, public schools in a democracy such as ours should deal forthrightly with religion at all, or whether the separation of church and state requires them to by-pass the subject. The answer, in my view, is that we cannot honestly choose the second of these alternatives: as long as we assume that one of the purposes of responsible education is to familiarize children with *all*, not merely *some*, aspects of the human life with which they must cope as cultural beings, then the real problem is not whether religion should be taught but rather in what manner.

Of course, public schools cannot indoctrinate any creed or faith and remain loyal to the principles of democratic and scientific learning. What they can do, given teachers trained to handle this flamboyant problem (very few are available at present, to be sure), is to encourage students to investigate and evaluate the meaning of religious life in all its cultural expressions. Study of religious orders, processes, and goals—"primitive" and "civilized" alike—could loosen the minds of learners from dogmatic, often superstitious outlooks. It could increase tolerance and respect for "the varieties of religious experience." But it could also assist learners to reappraise their own hitherto preferred beliefs, leading toward more universally, more logically, and hence more defensibly established beliefs than they held before.[51]

Other guides emerge when we turn to the philosophers of culture.

Bidney's plea for the study of more "rational norms with a potentiality for universal acceptance" raises, in one sense, our foremost education problem: Can and should the means-centered, process-geared curricula characteristic of American and many other schools in recent years achieve more dynamic balance with ends-guided, goal-centered policies and practices? Bidney's implied answer is "yes." To implement that answer, however, education must incorporate much more of the findings of the human sciences—findings that point toward and undergird the potential as well as actual universal values of cultural life.

To fail in this obligation is to invite the kind of "vicious relativism" which Perry repudiates but which, I am afraid, education has itself frequently endorsed. This is not to contend that education must therefore become committed to static or otherwise absolute goals. As Perry says, the attainment of comprehensive values is never completed, never fully successful. Yet, whether education settles for short-term, "practical" activities and contents or whether it accepts the obligation to search for and discover long-term, universal goals may have the gravest import for the future of mankind.

With Bidney and Perry, the philosopher Northrop would doubtless concur in the indictment that too many countries especially of the West neglect this latter alternative. While his own approach is largely through the philosophy of law, his critique of pragmatism (which, of course, underlies the theory of progressive education) is germane to our present interest. The pragmatic concern with scientific problem-solving—in Dewey's terms, with the centrality of intelligent inquiry—exposes it to Northrop's charge of providing no universal criteria by which values may be judged.[52] His own solution, if hardly more satisfactory, does perform the service of calling attention both to the need of such criteria and to the likelihood of finding these in a naturalistic approach to cultural experience without recourse to supernatural metaphysical absolutism. Thus far he is in accord with Dewey himself, as well as with all culture-theorists studied in this chapter: if universal values are to be established at all, they must be established through scientific investigations of the nature of man as cultural being. One of education's first responsibilities is to channel these investigations into the mainstream of learning.

An excellent instance of this kind of education is afforded by

Morris's research. Courses in ethics could be charged with vitality if his thirteen "ways to live" became the central theme and if, at appropriate times, comparisons were made between the preferences of a particular class and those of other college students both in America and, say, India or China. Relativism and universalism as concepts could thereby descend the "abstraction ladder" to the ground of empirical meaning. Differences between young citizens in their life goals could be sharpened, but so too could their similarities. The problem of the determinants of value—cultural, biological, and psychological—could likewise become more meaningful if not left dangling in abstraction as it is in conventional courses in philosophy.

Edel's study suggests indirectly how students, even in the grades, might begin to develop greater self-awareness both of their own goals and of those cherished by other cultures. A core project on the high-school or undergraduate level dealing with such a theme as "What do we hope to obtain from life?" should be governed not by preconceived answers but by cooperative discussion of the students' own values—couched, of course, in language familiar to them. I have discovered from several attempts to introduce value study into the core curriculum that initial reactions to such a large question are trite and ambiguous. ("Success" and "happiness" are typical answers.) Accordingly, the teacher should press for specificity and simplicity, beginning with such biological goals as adequate food, shelter, clothing, and sex, moving from these to psychological goals such as recognition and security, and eventually to such elusive but meaningful goals as creativity. The teacher meanwhile should guard carefully against imposition, both by frankly revealing his preferences for and by inviting vigorous dissent from his own pattern of values. Indeed, dissent and criticism should always be encouraged in the process of attaining any consensuses that might still emerge as the group explores this intriguing question.[53]

Learning by the dynamics of discussion and reinforced by solid content also encourages students to look beyond their personal experience. Here the sort of data and conclusions provided by Edel could again become resources. To what extent "invariant values" are defensible; to what extent biological, psychological, and cultural knowledge provides reinforcement for the values of a particular student; to what extent "invariant tasks" and "sociological determinants and functions" serve to ground values in cross-cultural events and institutions—these are the kinds of questions that education, aided by the human sciences, can now begin to answer. And as they are answered, the learner's own values radiate outward from his limited circle of experience. By discovering his likenesses with as well as differences from not only his own associates but people elsewhere in the world, universalism becomes more than a generality. It becomes related to definite values that he discovers are as important to many other people as they are to himself. "The human roots of world order"[54] are thereby fertilized, and the likelihood that he will gravitate toward a cosmopolitan outlook upon the issues of our crisis-age is manifestly strengthened.

In view of the need to translate cultural values into workable learning experiences of the kind just indicated, we can only regard as unfortunate the sparse attention explicitly paid to education by the anthropologists cited in this chapter.[55] Linton, to be sure, mentions the universal values of knowledge and teachability—values of obvious importance to our interest—but he does not develop their meaning or significance. Similarly, despite his pronouncement that cultural change devoted to the common values of mankind is the "most important task of the social scientist," he offers little help either to social scientists themselves or to educators who might wish to cooperate with them in implementing that task. Murdock, after listing education as one of four fundamental functions of the "nuclear family," says very little about it thereafter in any explicit way, and even the nearest comparable concept (socialization) is treated meagerly. Only Kluckhohn among our anthropological authorities departs from the role of objective scientist long enough to address the educator directly in a serious way. He says:

. . . all talk of an eventual peaceful and orderly world is but pious cant or sentimental fantasy unless there are, in fact, some simple but powerful things in which all men can believe, some codes or canons that have or can obtain universal acceptance . . . Yet we need a new set of success values that is better geared to economic and political realities. No social order is secure in which a high proportion of adults feel cheated of goals which they had been taught as youths were rightfully attainable by every-one who worked hard and intelligently.[56]

Kluckhohn quotes Eldridge Sibley and G. T. Robinson in behalf of the educational imperative for which he pleads. Says Sibley: ". . .

the colleges must undertake to lead the American mob out of the mire by helping it see what it is semiconsciously striving for, by focusing its attention on ultimate goals and values rather than on the details of the passing moment." Says Robinson: "It is not piecemeal answers that inspire men, . . . it is a total conception of the good life . . . In this situation, there is urgent need for philosophic reconstruction and renewal."[57] But Kluckhohn's own words are still more disturbing to educational complacency:

One of the broadest and the surest generalizations that anthropology can make about human beings is that no society is healthy or creative or strong unless that society has a set of common values which give meaning and purpose to group life, . . . which fit with the situation of the time as well as being linked to the historic past, which do not outrage men's reason and which at the same time appeal to their emotions.[58]

We have seen that Kluckhohn, both through his own research and in collaboration, is convinced that a good deal of evidence is already available for such a "set of common values." In this conviction, he might well agree with the French anthropologist, Pierre Teilhard de Chardin, that mankind is "not only continuing to diverge and differentiate as any other animal group but, in addition, to become more and more irresistibly united into a single, natural whole." Teilhard may or may not be presupposing some metaphysical direction in stating this conviction; he need not do so, certainly, in order to defend the hypothesis that "the specific characteristic of the modern world is no longer divergency but acceleration of a process forcing man to become economically, technically, and morally one." On this hypothesis, Teilhard contends that anthropology is now in a position to "supply modern man with an objective basis for a new ethics, which we need so desperately: a basis . . . established above any subjective preference on the unquestionable fact of natural human convergency."[59]

Here is an exciting mandate for education with which to close this chapter: to deal in the future as earnestly with far-reaching cultural ends as it has dealt in the recent past with near-reaching cultural means. It is a mandate not only to study as objectively and thoroughly as possible the evidence for and against "natural human convergency," but to join with other institutions in crystallizing, supporting, and achieving whatever universal values may emerge from such study. To become thus wholeheartedly involved would mean both a culture-conscious and a goal-dedicated education.

CHAPTER TWELVE

HUMAN FREEDOM AS CULTURAL GOAL

PROBLEMS OF MEANING

AT THE CONCLUSION of the preceding chapter, we reached a crucial stage. We were confronted with the demand to develop a "new ethics" based upon scientific knowledge of man and upon any perceptible trend toward cultural unity. This stage has beckoned us from the outset of this study. Chapter Three, for example, anticipated it by asking whether modern man can achieve unity—there called human order—yet at the same time preserve and enhance freedom as a goal of life. With the help of culture-theory, let us channel our search for the new ethics by considering more carefully the significance of this magnetic goal.

Preceding comments on the problem may justly be criticized on the ground that they have begged a key question: What do we mean by freedom? Few symbols are as fraught with ambiguities and platitudes; none are more loosely bandied about by educators all of whom, of course, are abject in their devotion to it. Equally few symbols, however, have received more profound attention by philosophers concerned with human values. Throughout the history of ideas they have sought for the definitive answer, but they have never agreed that it has been found. One difficulty is that their formulations have usually rested upon metaphysical or otherwise speculative and unverifiable presuppositions that are denied by philosophers holding alternative (and often equally deniable) presuppositions. Another difficulty is that their formulations may unconsciously but no less basically reflect varying cultural patterns—patterns that express freedom differently because the ways men actually live individually and collectively likewise differ.

Any relevant philosophy of education-and-culture for our age, guided by the goal of freedom, should therefore try to correct such deficiencies in traditional interpretations. It should build firmly upon whatever knowledge of man the behavioral sciences are able to provide. And it should take into account the patterns of culture that now prevail across the earth and adjust its interpretation of freedom to them in such a way as to reinforce as well as to assist in directing their course. The evidence of culture-theory and research gathered in these pages is sufficient to afford hope that the framework for such an interpretation can now be constructed.

Two additional questions must, however, first be faced. One question is: Why human *freedom*? Why not some other encompassing goal—love, for example?[1] I am forced to admit an element of arbitrariness in this selection, but my defense is that given the kind of planet we live upon today no other value is of equal urgency. The reader is reminded again, though he surely needs no reminding, that the strife between totalitarianism and democratic patterns of culture is no passing historic incident; it is a fierce reality that in some way affects every human being actually or potentially wherever he resides. I remind him, too, that authoritarianism, theocratic as well as political, is everywhere vigorous, even militant, in its policies and programs. The question therefore of whether man can retain, much less increase, the modicum of freedom he has thus far won is now the most disturbing issue that he can raise or try to resolve. Whether man can attain much more of the right and opportunity to live according to his own deepest rational and emotional resources, or whether these resources must be suppressed and mutilated if not destroyed by impersonal and overwhelming forces beyond his control and indifferent to his worth, is what I mean essentially by the problem of human freedom.

The second preliminary question is if anything still more fundamental: What do we mean by the term, value, of which freedom is one paramount symbol? The discussion thus far may be criticized for having, to some degree, begged this question also. To speak of relative and universal values without having defined the term common to both is, at the least, inadequate. But the delay has been intentional: by considering, with the help of Linton, Morris, and other authorities, the kinds of values that are held by people both intraculturally and transculturally, we have located at least some empirical evidence with which to construct an inductive conception—that is, one that harmonizes with and encompasses observable human experience. The search here for such a conception of value will be limited to culture-theorists with whom we are acquainted.[2]

DEFINITIONS OF CULTURAL VALUE

A singular commentary both on the influence of Kluckhohn and on the comparative dearth of attention that has been paid to value theory by other anthropologists is the fact that his definition of value, far more than any other, has recently been cited by his peers. "A value," says Kluckhohn, "is a conception, explicit or implicit, distinctive of an individual or characteristic of a group, of the desirable which influences the selection from available modes, means, and ends of action."[3]

Although the implications of this definition are many, six may be singled out. (1) Values are constructs involving both cognitive (that is, logical or otherwise rational) processes and cathectic (that is, impulsively attractive or repellent) processes. (2) They are always potentially but by no means always actually verbalized. (3) While primarily cultural products, they are uniquely expressible by each individual and by each group. (4) Because particular desires may be either disvalued or valued, it is essential to make sure that values are equated rather with the *desirable,* defined according to "the requirements of both personality and sociocultural system for order, the need for respecting the interests of others and of the group as a whole in social living."[4] (5) Choice among alternative values is made both in terms of available means and available ends. And (6) values exist—they are facts of nature, man, and culture at the same time that they are norms of the as-yet-unrealized.

Kluckhohn also introduces the concept of "value-orientation," defined as "a generalized and organized conception, influencing behavior, of nature, of man's place in it, of man's relations to man, and of the desirable and nondesirable as they may relate to man-environment and interhuman relations."[5] Both value and value-orientation are characterized by certain "dimensions." They may be, for example, positive and negative; esthetic and moral; instrumental and intrinsic; specific and general; categorical and hypothetical; dominant and deviant; implicit and explicit; idiosyncratic, personal, group, and universal.

Moreover, as Edel and Morris have shown, values must be approached through many channels—not only through philosophy, art, and religion, but through biology, psychology, sociology, anthropology, and all the sciences of man, each contributing indispensable aspects to the total conception. Finally, among the many distinctions that Kluckhohn treats, at least two are of direct interest to us: that between needs and values, and that between goals and values. Following Dorothy Lee, Kluckhohn recognizes that, while the two are closely related, values "*both* rise from and create needs"[6] since values also involve cognition, social approval, and other factors more inclusive than needs as such. Following a study at Cornell University, Kluckhohn also agrees that values are aspects of goals rather than identical with them—a position close to the delimitation noted in Chapter Ten above.

Keesing's compilation of anthropological treatments of value reveals additional definitions and aspects that help to enrich without contradicting Kluckhohn's. Gillin's definition, for example, deserves quoting because of its simplicity: "A value is the worth of a thing as compared with something else. It is obviously the result of training or experience and arises out of satisfactions associated with the thing valued." Another fruitful definition, from the Cornell study, is: ". . . value includes a continuum ranging from 'desires' (or 'interests' or 'preferences') . . . all the way over to . . . intense convictions, ideals . . ." Firth's discussion underscores an important aspect of value: the "quality of being something wanted and felt to be proper to be wanted." Finally, Kroeber makes the useful distinction between value judgments and values: the former "are decisions for action; they take sides as acts of will. Values are things one feels in order to apprehend and describe as objectively as possible." Keesing finds "the most constant threads" in these and other statements to be "(1) culturally defined relations of individuals toward phenomena of experience, (2) involving normative factors of actual or potential judgments and choice, (3) based on affective elements of approval or disapproval, of desirability or otherwise."[7]

Among the philosophers of culture from whom we have learned, Perry, Morris, and Edel are unusually helpful. Perry's theory of value, one of the most famous in American philosophy, evolves from the simple idea that a value is any object of any interest. This idea is examined in terms of its psychological roots and its manifestations in society, science, art, history, education, religion, and human life generally. The whole approach is empirical and sophisticated. I find no aspect of Perry's thought that would seriously contradict the kind of delineations that we have been studying; what it does do is to expose the untenability of Linton's opinion, mentioned earlier, that formally philosophic analyses of value are likely to be of little use to the behavioral scientist.[8]

Morris, recognizing value to be a "multiple and complex" concept, distinguishes between three aspects: operative values, conceived values, and object values. The first refers simply to the "actual direction of preferential behavior toward one kind of object rather than another." The second refers to "preferential behavior directed by 'an anticipation or foresight of the outcome' of such behavior." The third refers to "what is preferable (or 'desirable') regardless of whether it is in fact preferred [i.e., an operative value] or conceived as preferable [i. e., a conceived value]." As I understand Morris, the following experience includes all three kinds of value: if I like candy and reach for a piece of it, I am expressing an operative value; if I am conscious of the energy in it and deliberately eat it to help me as I write, I express a conceived value; if this is in fact the case, whether I am aware of it or not, then the candy is an object value. The common denominator is "preferential behavior," and axiology is regarded as the science of such behavior.[9]

Edel nowhere in his study offers a formal definition of value, but he does aid us with several original and pertinent concepts. One is that of "phase-rule"—a generally accepted "rule of reckoning" by which a value is attained or a disvalue avoided. He points up his meaning with the example of the act of killing: "Thou shalt not kill" is not an absolute value, for there are instances in which (the consequence of, say, a greater saving of lives through a single death) killing may be justified. A phase-rule, then, is an "operational universal" which we "break-only-with-regret." As an operation or process, killing may be considered to be universally wrong; in actual experience, consequences sometimes prove that such is not the case. Edel shows that the numerous phase-rules of conduct are reinforced by scientific knowledge of human experience.[10]

Another concept is that of the "valuational base." Here Edel refers to the amalgam of evidence from the human sciences, such as phase-rules, that provide "moorings to which a morality may be fastened, and sailing-charts for its general course." The base contains "value conclusions or guiding principles embodying the fullest available knowledge about men's aspirations and conditions." Because it fuses both "universal and local elements . . ." it supports the "both-and" position considered in Chapter Eleven. Like phase-rules, the valuational base provides no infallible criterion; many variables and contingencies remain. Yet Edel is persuasive in his conclusion that through "the use of science in ethics," man is capable not only of having values but of making value judgments that resolve the ancient dilemma between (a) pure indeterminacy and arbitrariness, and (b) pure absolutism and dogmatism.[11]

We are now better prepared to return to our central problem. The unavoidable abstractions above will become more meaningful and integrated as we operate with them upon human freedom as cultural goal.

FREEDOM AND THE "NORMATIVE SCIENCE OF CULTURE"

The history of culture-theory, in its concern for values, may be viewed in three gross overlapping periods. The first period was typified by the late nineteenth-century anthropologists—most notably, Tylor, Morgan, and Spencer—all of whom presupposed without carefully analyzing or validating their value judgments, especially the value of unilinear progress.

The second period, led by Boas, reacted violently against the speculative, often wishful thinking of these and other classicists. More precisely, however, this period is better subdivided, again grossly, into earlier and later halves. The earlier half (its heyday was perhaps the nineteen-twenties), following the prevailing practice of other social sciences, tried to exclude consideration of values entirely—or at the most to say that values, though proper to the humanities, are outside the scope of scientific relevance. The later half, starting with about the mid-nineteen-thirties, began to treat values as primary data of culture-theory and research but no more than this. Value judgments that would commit the anthropologist to certain preferences as against others remained strictly taboo. Cultural relativism, despite inconsistencies, was a product largely of this period.

The third period, which is only now at the threshold of careful attention (it would still be resisted by most culture-theorists) is a synthesis on a new level of the first and second. It continues to respect and practice the canons of objective research, and it rejects the naiveté of classical anthropology toward such values as inevitable progress; but it also deliberately incorporates definite, conscious value judgments into its total conception. Therefore commitments to desirable goals are part of its own theory of culture.

Although Bidney and Edel—significantly, both philosophers—see this kind of synthesis emerging perhaps more explicitly than any other authorities studied thus far, it is a commentary on the vision of Malinowski that he anticipated it at a time when most anthropologists were only beginning to take values seriously. He anticipated it, moreover, by dealing with the problem of freedom itself. His *Freedom and Civilization,* published posthumously in 1944, remains today the most inclusive study of this problem by an anthropologist. It deserves extended attention.

Malinowski's direct motivation was the Second World War and the threat to freedom which he rightly feared in the encroachments of totalitarianism. His conception of value, if not as refined as some others we have noted, points in the same naturalistic and goal-centered direction. A value is:

. . . that attitude which organizes drives, emotions and the impulse to possess other people and objects. It is the culturally determined ability to see the end and the appreciation of the range of ends . . . Through value, man is thus able to choose among the existing systems for the carrying out of a well-determined purpose, to learn how to use the means and to reach results.[12]

The relation of freedom to this conception is immediate. Indeed, freedom for Malinowski is not so much an instance as it is the core of all human values. For "freedom lies in choice of purpose, its translation into effective action and the full enjoyment of the results."[13] The key terms here are choice, action, and results. In different language, but inherent in this idea, we may say that man is free when he is able to consider and select that goal which among alternative goals is most desirable to him, to implement his choice by appropriate practice, and finally to have the satisfactions inherent in its achievement.

Malinowski, consistent with his anthropological orientation, is thinking of man not as an isolated individual but primarily as cultural. Of course he recognizes, as do all culture-theorists, the biological and psychological roots of value. Particularly crucial is the role of needs and wants: it is the quest for their fulfillment that is the driving force of all human experience. But needs are not simply organic; they are largely derived—that is, determined by cultural patterns. "As soon as man begins to exploit the environment through the round-about method of using artifacts, organizing concerted activities, and living in socially constituted groups, new needs arise . . . They are new dynamic factors in the cultural process . . ."[14] It follows that in broadest scope "freedom is the successful unimpeded course of the cultural process, bringing full satisfaction of all needs."[15]

The concept which best connotes for Malinowski the group's organized development of needs is the "institution." Families, municipalities, tribes, age groups, voluntary associations, occupational groups, and status groups are the main types of institutions. The satisfaction of needs occurs in and through each institution according to its "charter"—that is, the collective purpose or goal that governs its activities and provides satisfaction of the needs derived from it. The institution is thus the core of culture normatively conceived in terms of freedom.

Malinowski does not deny that institutions may also negate or inhibit freedom. They do so, however, only when they lack the kind of charter just described. The distinction between free and unfree institutions is important to our problem:

When the purpose is chosen by the group as a whole; when the action is taken by autonomous responsibility; and when the results are shared among all the members of the group, we find freedom within that institution. When the purpose is accepted by command or instilled by indoctrination; when the action is controlled by coercive authority; and when the results of the activity are doled out for the advantage of those in authority, we find a denial of freedom.[16]

The relation of cultural freedom to cultural order (a relation about which we were worried in Chapter Three) now becomes crystallized. Instead of regarding the two concepts as antithetical, Malinowski treats them as completely reciprocal. Here his functional philosophy of dynamic interaction is especially close to Dewey who, in *Freedom and Culture*,[17] argues cogently for the same bipolarity. Law, discipline, and authority (of parents, playmates, community, and finally the state) are not only entirely compatible with freedom so long as they are cooperatively formulated and maintained in terms of common purposes; they are mandatory. Freedom of speech is essential to them also: through it choices are more often based upon criticized knowledge, so that the chances of error are reduced.

Malinowski next tries to demonstrate (again, as does Dewey) that democracy alone guarantees the kind of cultural goals he has been expressing. Indeed, the three constituent elements of freedom, noted above, are all inherent in democracy as the encompassing institution of culture. For democracy

... gives, first, freedom and scope for the formation of purposes ... Democracy secondly gives freedom of opportunities, of instrumentalities and of action, for the translation of collective purposes into organized collective behavior ... Thirdly, democracy gives the freedom of enjoyment, through an equitable distribution of tasks, of rewards, and of rights to power, wealth and privilege ... Thus democracy can be defined as a cultural system devised so as to allow the fullest opportunities to the individual and to the group to determine its purposes, to organize and implement them, and to carry out the activities upon which they are intent.[18]

By the same token that democracy is the means and end of cultural freedom, totalitarianism is its antithesis. Malinowski is thinking primarily of fascist totalitarianism, but it is probable that in various respects he would compare the latter with the Russian dictatorship. Authoritarian rule-making, the concept of a master class, the ruthless exercise of force for the maintenance of power, education as indoctrination of "the one true doctrine," these have been typical thus far of both systems.

By contrast, Malinowski pleads for a world-wide conception of democracy. "The state today," he contends, "has to abrogate some of its sovereignty ..."[19] An international police force and court, and world-wide economic planning, have become imperative. "Instead of the doctrine of a master race and master nation, we postulate complete independence to be given to all races or nations and all cultural minorities ... [as a] culturally united, integrated group ..."[20] Convergency, to which Teilhard earlier called our attention as a demonstrable cultural goal, is clearly inferred at the conclusion of Malinowski's work.

But, though persuasive, it is open to the charge of some inconsistency. Bidney has pointed out that Malinowski at times mingles normative with descriptive assumptions. He "employs the concept of freedom within civilization as an ideal objective for mankind to pursue and at the same time speaks as if freedom were actually realized in the course of cultural process."[21]

Bidney puts his finger on the most perplexing issue confronted by culture-theorists who, like Malinowski, aim to synthesize the first and second stages (considered at the outset of this section) into a third stage where an openly normative interpretation of culture is fused with a descriptive scientific one. Malinowski only partly succeeds in doing so; in other words, he does not always distinguish between his anthropological study of values as facts of culture and his value judgments about those facts. Yet this is understandable in view both of the extreme difficulties of his task and of his impassioned concern with the crisis through which the world was passing in the 1940's—a crisis which, though its manifestations have altered, continues unabated today.

Whether or not Bidney is more successful in achieving a synthesis, he is at least explicit. His own viewpoint, we have seen, is frankly normative at the same time that it pays careful attention to the findings of cultural research. He speaks of "the concept of a normative science of culture . . . concerned with the formulation of cultural ideals as possible means and ends of sociocultural life." Such a science would deliberately deal "not only with what is the case actually and historically but also with what may be and ought to be, with possible alternative ideals suggested by the facts of cultural experience and natural science . . ."[22] Like Malinowski, Bidney is gravely troubled by our crisis-age and by the need to transcend the sometimes irresponsible neutralism of "purely" objective research:

Unless science can provide potentially universal cultural values capable of winning ardent adherents, other methods will be found to fill this need, such as the mythological appeal to race, class, or nationality . . . Only a cultural unity based upon a core of rational values and brought into being by voluntary deliberate consent can endure indefinitely.[23]

Does such a normative science of culture give further support to the goal of freedom? Bidney is convinced that a theory of culture can be developed that "will provide a rational, as well as empirical, foundation for the ideal of a common humanity."[24] The main strength of such a theory derives from science which, being self-correcting and self-disciplining, is free to reach whatever conclusions the evidence demands.

The free process inherent in scientific inquiry is exemplified by Bidney himself when, following Rousseau, he distinguishes between three types of freedom. The first is "natural liberty"—the psycho-biological tendency of the individual to do whatever he desires. The second, presupposing but also limiting the first, is cultural: it provides patterns of conduct within which its members act according to established rules and customs. The third is moral freedom, "defined as action in accord with the rational good of the individual or his society."[25] Bidney does not believe that any one of the three is synonymous with the others: thus cultural freedom as such is relative to the particular culture, while moral freedom is a universal ideal. Yet, as we have seen earlier, his position as a whole is not as dualistic as this statement might imply. His concept of normative culture tries to harmonize natural, cultural, and moral freedom, and his argument that the authority and power of a group are not necessarily antithetical to the self-expression of personality suggests the view of Malinowski and Dewey that freedom and order are complementary values.

Bidney's disjointed presentation, however, does sometimes lead his readers astray, and his efforts to create a working partnership between the descriptive and normative components of culture-theory are not entirely successful.[26] In the same direction Edel seems more successful, if only because he more painstakingly holds to the evidence of the human sciences and less often allows himself relapses into speculative and unconfirmed assertions.

Although Edel does not dissect the value of freedom in any systematic way, there is no doubt that he would agree upon its paramount importance. He speaks of the "need for a common-human morality" —of the "ideals of human dignity and human freedom." He is hopeful that, as we face the possibility of humanity's destruction, "the great issues of the modern world can be faced with the confidence that there are solutions available to reason and experience."[27] If, with Malinowski, we regard freedom not as an esoteric concept or as a hypostatized absolute, but as a constellation of experiences involving cooperatively achieved purpose, action, and satisfaction of maximum wants, then Edel's search for a "valuational base" is indeed germane to our problem.

The fruits of this search were reviewed in part in the previous chapter, but fields such as biology and history were scarcely touched upon. Assuming with many ethical theorists that on the whole expression of drives or impulse is a good,[28] Edel shows how, in biological perspective for example, health is almost universally regarded as a good, and illness as an evil. Psychologically, mental health is as positive a value as frustration is negative.[29] Indeed, as with many other values the human sciences have reached more negative evidence than they have positive; in this case, they know more about the causes of frustration than they do about the causes of mental health. For related reasons they are better equipped to diagnose unhappiness than they are happiness. Nevertheless, the range of agreement thus far is wide, as it is with the knowledge of healthy personalities that was surveyed in Chapter Nine. Speaking of "phase-rules," Edel concludes that "the possibility of establishing generalizations . . . [is] a rich one, though on the whole the harvest . . . [has] yet to be gathered."[30]

The valuational base of a great ideal like freedom can also be strengthened by specifying universal needs and wants of the type mentioned in our study of universal values. Edel speaks of such demonstrable psychological needs as affection, sympathy, cooperativeness, and growth. He speaks, too, of the "perennial aspirations and major goals" of mankind that are revealed by anthropology and history—including such broad goals as "the love of beauty and the desire for friends." He examines the "central necessary conditions" of value—such as place, order, work, and education—which are equally instrumental and intrinsic to the fulfillment of these broad goals. And he is strongly inclined to believe that on the political level "only some actual democracy can in the long run provide the widespread initiative required to keep going the large-scale collective efforts and enterprises that are themselves an integral part of modern life."[31]

Among all the experts included in our study of values, Edel comes most directly to grips with the issue that has disturbed us as we grope for a defensible synthesis of the "is" and the "ought"—the descriptive and the normative dimensions of value theory in general and of freedom in particular. In his own technical language: To what extent can we *validate* the valuational base? He does not answer this question with complete satisfaction (he would readily agree) but he does show how, *given the knowledge we possess of the nature of man and his striving for fulfillment, some values are much more universally consistent with this knowledge than are other values.* More human beings converge upon the goal of peace, certainly, than they do upon that of war. More human beings cherish the goal of human brotherhood than they do that of mutual hatred. More human beings consider desirable an economic order that will produce abundance than they do one of scarcity and poverty. By the same token, more human beings value freedom as the goal of providing concrete opportunities for their development than they do slavery or degradation. All of these values, moreover, are increasingly global in scope.

Edel concludes by reminding us that, though science thus provides a foundation for a new ethics based upon human convergence, science does not itself create values, only men do. Likewise:

Science does not give us goals, but men use their knowledge to broaden and refine and increasingly to achieve their human aims. And they use their growing knowledge of themselves to work out what their aims are and to distinguish increasingly the spurious from the genuine. A full scientific understanding thus molds their way of looking at the world. They see themselves at every point as active creators out of the past and into the future.[32]

In other words, they see themselves as free.

THE CONCEPTS OF PROGRESS AND IDEOLOGY

Of numerous ramifications from the problem of freedom that might be chosen for further consideration, two are unusually pertinent: one, the concept of progress; the other, the concept of ideology.

The concept of progress has broken through the implicit level on several previous pages, but it has not been examined sufficiently. In our present context the question is whether any support by culture-theory can be mustered for the common belief that humanity is moving toward greater freedom for itself than it has possessed thus far. Certainly the classical thinkers in anthropology implied an affirmative answer. So, too, does the immensely powerful doctrine of historical materialism. But even such painstaking authorities as Childe sometimes lead us to think we are justified in a qualified belief that cultural progress is on the whole occurring.

It is unlikely, however, that any strong consensus outside of com-munist-dominated cultures could now be obtained among culture-theorists in behalf of this belief. On the contrary, its tenability would be more widely denied than affirmed. Recall, for example, that the "substantive" philosophers of cultural history, earlier considered, agree that the course of development by civilizations—far from being unilinear—is characterized rather by curves of progression and regres-sion, of upswings and downswings. True, a Sorokin sometimes forgets his major postulates long enough to predict that an "ideational" cul-ture will follow our "sensate" one, and that this will be (for him at least) progress toward greater freedom. On the whole, nevertheless, their doctrines are anti-melioristic, as are those of such "methodo-logical" philosophers of history as Cohen.

The best that the majority of culture-theorists would concede is that progress occurs only in specific ways, in terms of specific criteria. Boas, the arch-empiricist of anthropology, states this point of view: "Progress can be defined only in regard to the special ideal we have in mind. There is no absolute progress . . . In an objective study of culture the concept of progress should be used with great caution."[33]

Kroeber, true to this admonition, points out that progress as a value is not even commonly accepted by non-Western civilizations. He con-cedes that if we identify progress with quantitative accumulation (of population, say), then there is progress. But who is prepared to equate sheer bigness with betterness? Kroeber also concedes, however, that progress has occurred in three defensible ways: in the decrease, by and large, of magic and superstition and the increase of rational methods of solving problems; in the diminishing "obtrusion of physiological or anatomical considerations into social situations"[34] (e.g., human sacrifice, puberty crisis rites, deformation of feet and heads by pressure); and in the growth of science and technology.

Despite his usual reluctance to do so, Kroeber here is not only studying the value of progress but is making value judgments of his own about its cultural meaning. More than this, if we accept such dilineations as Malinowski's and Bidney's then there is little doubt but that all three of these progressive cultural achievements enhance free-dom itself, because they strengthen man's capacity to control nature and so to control himself as a part of nature.

But Kroeber would agree with a philosopher like Cassirer that to eg.ghi

generalize about progress on the basis of, say, the expansion of science and technology would be foolish indeed. Totalitarianism has demonstrated that the products of technology—radio is one—can be used in behalf of magical and other irrational attitudes and practices quite as easily as they can be used in behalf of scientific ways of thinking and acting. The "myth of the state"[35] symbolizes a regression to pre-rational behavior; yet the speed with which it has been able to share in the destruction of democratic, cooperative political structures and processes is a sinister reality of contemporary history.

The most comprehensive although rather neglected study of the problem of progress by any culture-theorist—*Culture and Progress,* by Wilson D. Wallis—reinforces this judgment. (Significantly, the book was published more than ten years before most other anthropologists were dealing carefully with values of any kind.) It is science, says Wallis, "which enables man to attain a finer paradise or to create a fiercer hell . . . Indeed, practically every power which is capable of increasing the good is capable also of increasing the evil . . ."[36]

Wallis is not pessimistic, however. His work, which unites philosophy and anthropology, and which traces the history of the idea of progress from its earliest inception, repeatedly emphasizes the legitimate "possibility" of human betterment. But, like Boas and Kroeber, he demands precision in formulating the meanings by which any kind of progress can be discovered in culture. Particularly apropos of our concern with goals, he is aware that progress

. . . implies at least a desirable goal and this means more than a desired one. It means a goal which embodies a desirable end and one which, in the long run, brings satisfaction. A desirable goal presupposes a choice of goals, a choice made with discrimination . . . [The] highest progress involves the choice of the most desirable goal and the best means of attaining it.[37]

Wallis's own choice of such a goal is similar to that of others studied in this chapter. Though he pays only brief attention to freedom as such, it is nonetheless inherent in his preference for values that enable human beings to express themselves as fully and richly as their potentialities permit. For the same reason, he would oppose any *sui generis* notions of cultural progress: "Collectively, individuals can fashion their world as they will. Men have as satisfying a life as they deserve; when they deserve better it will be theirs for the asking and the taking."[38]

To sum up our discussion of progress, let Perry speak again. Because there are "many value-coordinates," the most we can affirm is that as history moves ahead in time "it may move up in some respects and down in others." There is no doubt that progress has occurred in the past two centuries toward humane working conditions, control of disease, increase of literacy, and in various other respects. Yet, however admirable these improvements are, we cannot therefore establish any universal principle of progress toward freedom. Rather, they are the product of "a happy conjunction of circumstances" confined to "a limited area of the earth's surface, a fraction of its inhabitants, and a selected aspect of their lives. It would be quite possible to draw another and less favorable picture." Depressions, world wars with their ugly attending evils, and the rise of the modern monolithic state may more than offset any of the gains. Is there then any over-all course? "The answer is yes and no. The final balance must await evidence which is not available."[39] So, too, with human freedom.

The second concept, ideology, is borrowed from Mannheim a sociologically-oriented culture-theorist to whom, regrettably, too little attention has thus far been paid in this study.[40] By ideology Mannheim means in general the word-picture of beliefs, ideas, attitudes, purposes, and customs that more or less completely and accurately expresses the practices of a given culture. An ideology hence serves, also, as a symbolic rationale of what a group of people at a give time regard as their most indigenous values. In American culture, progress itself is widely regarded as one of these.

But ideological values, upon close inspection, often prove to be at odds with deeper, more pervasive, though perhaps still potential, values. Mannheim sees the process of cultural history as in a continuous state of greater or lesser tension between the two kinds; thus the crisis of contemporary culture can be depicted as a kind of axiological civil war between inherited ideological values and "utopian" values that more adequately and fundamentally express emerging human goals.

Freedom is again an enlightening symbol. Ideological freedom for Mannheim too often proves to be a shibboleth for a planless, individualistic, competitive "order" that neither works well any longer nor reflects the interests of the great majority who live under it. Utopian freedom, though as yet less articulated, is becoming the goal of more and more groups who begin to see the defects of traditional freedom and who, therefore, grope for a reformulation and for a correlative program and policy that will more completely satisfy their need to be free in the meaningful sense of Malinowski. Progress, by the same token, is no longer a glib slogan for the allegedly increasing benefits of free enterprise; it is a symbol defensible only in terms of reconstructed institutional arrangements that provide ever-widening opportunities to share democratically in control of economic processes and in consumption of the products thereof. Similarly, progress for the critic of ideological freedom is unlikely to mean an increase of nationalism and isolationism, but rather their decrease in favor of world order and international planning.

Although few anthropologists or other culture-theorists have, so far as I know, paid substantial attention to Mannheim's thought, it is not difficult to find fruitful relationships between his and theirs. Kluckhohn's concept of implicit culture, for example, emphasizes the distinction between its verbalized expressions and those that more profoundly express its configurations. I would be taking liberties with his meaning were I to say that the implicit culture is always more utopian, in Mannheim's sense, than it is ideological; only in some cases is this probably true. But Kluckhohn, and Kroeber with him, do lend direct credence to the meaning that Mannheim intends. Thus, in their analogy between a culture and a cathedral, the explicit pattern of a culture suggests the framework and girders; its implicit culture is more like "the architect's conception of the total over-all effects he wishes to achieve."[41] In this sense, the implicit culture reveals more the ideal (or utopian) than the explicit (or ideological) meaning—a distinction which Kroeber sharpens still further (even though his main point is a somewhat different one): "There is thus an unavoidable gap between the ideal or 'pure' picture of the culture and the actuality of how this ideal is lived out by the average adherent of the culture."[42]

Still another way of throwing light upon the problem of freedom by utilizing the concept of ideology is suggested by Edel. It will be remembered that he defends the proposition that some values may be potentially universal even when they are not explicitly recognized as such up to a given time. This point could be turned to support Mannheim's thesis: an explicit and ideological expression of a value does not necessarily indicate that it is as accurate a symbol of the desirable as one that is still implicit and utopian. Or, as Morris could say, an "object value" is one that remains desirable whether or not it is as yet a "conceived value."

What, then, is the usefulness of ideology as a way to clarify further the problem of freedom? Clearly, for Mannheim it is to expose the fallacies and obsolescences in traditional expressions of freedom as a goal of man and to substitute fresh, utopian expressions that more exactly and richly disclose the nature of freedom as an object value worthy of universal attainment. Progress, in turn, is measured by cultural development toward such attainment. Whether freedom of this kind will in fact be attained is not, however, a defensible prediction. The most we can affirm is to say, with Wallis, that men can "have as satisfying a life as they deserve . . ." For in last analysis men are the makers, not the pawns, of their own future.

TOWARD A GOAL-CENTERED EDUCATION-AND-CULTURE

Malinowski leads us to a consideration of the educational import of the issues we have been discussing. Reflecting a mechanistic and behaviorist theory of learning of the type already criticized, he nevertheless states a position (at the cost of still further inconsistency) that is congenial to his general approach:

Exactly as culture gives mankind its integral increment of freedom through evolution, so in the life history of every individual through the stages from animal to infant, to the last word in contemporary culture, education bestows upon him the freedom of his tribal or national culture. Or else it deprives him of certain aspects of this freedom . . . [Human] beings can either be trained to be free, or trained to be rulers, tyrants, or dictators, or else they can be trained to be slaves . . . In this widest sense the course of education transforms the immature, unequipped, and untutored young animal into a social . . . citizen who emerges with abilities to think, act, and to respond in co-operation with other human beings . . . [It] is one of the most powerful instruments of democracy. Its cultural value consists in that, abolishing birthright, it supplies us with the greatest opportunities to mobilize real talent. In making education universal, democracy makes possible the participation of the people in the guidance of their own destinies.[43]

With this statement serving as a kind of target, it is now necessary to subject to more careful scrutiny the role of education as the end and means of freedom.

1. We begin by recalling the struggle of culture-theorists with the relation between descriptive research into values on the one hand, and normative judgments about and choices among values on the other hand. The "validation of the valuational base," to repeat Edel's phrase, is so difficult that few if any culture-theorists are satisfied that it has thus far been accomplished.

The result is, as we anticipated, that the largest contribution of culture-theorists and especially of anthropologists has been to the "valuational base" rather than to its "validation"—that is, to the descriptive treatment of values as realities of culture. Thanks chiefly to the behavioral sciences, we know more today about the values that people hold in the cultures of the world than we have ever known before. We know something about those values that may properly be called universal and those that may not. We can define freedom and progress as values that are more empirically meaningful than they are speculatively arbitrary, because we are coming to understand the dynamics of human experience in its intra- and interpersonal, and its intra- and intercultural, relations. Still, the question persists as to whether, granting that we can describe the meaning of freedom with fairly objective precision, men *ought* to believe in it enough to commit themselves unequivocally both to it as the supreme human goal and to the actions by which they may gain its fullest satisfaction.

While culture-theorists continue to wrestle with the problem, can we say that educational theory is itself any closer to a defensible solution? In some ways, yes. Education differs from a science like anthropology in the respect that, far from even claiming to be a descriptive discipline, it is value-guided throughout. Thus it is, as it has always been, concerned to perpetuate, to enrich, and to attain the values implicit and explicit in any given culture. While of course it describes, education is even more deeply obligated to *prescribe*—to make certain that the goals of the culture it serves will be pursued and won as devotedly and energetically as human and physical resources can possibly ensure.

Let us then inquire, first, whether education *does* thus pursue and win the goal of freedom, and, second, whether it can clearly justify that it *should* do so.

2. The answer to the first question must be equivocal. The record shows plainly that sometimes education does and sometimes it does not. Malinowski has stressed that learning and teaching have been and still are only too commonly harnessed to indoctrinate and habituate the young in authoritarian patterns of life. Moreover, Chapter Two enumerated several ways in which freedom is abrogated or weakened by the educational system of a culture such as our own: the hypocrisy with which schools teach the ideal and ignore the reality of its emasculation by, say, the prejudiced white Southerner; the encouragement of other-directed habits of conformity by teachers holding middle-status standards; the lack of democratic controls in countless school systems both from without and from within; the overt pressures and covert intimidations against honest study of the most disturbing controversial issues of our day.

To these examples might be added others. One is the threat of anti-intellectualism in its numerous forms.[44] Another not unrelated is the kind of learning, considered earlier, that encourages habits of dulling acquiescence and reflexive obedience more often than it does habits of creative, critical participation among growing personalities and cooperating groups.

The debit side is, however, partially counterbalanced. On the credit side is a deep tradition in democratic cultures of education as the ally of enlightened self-government—a tradition which, despite ideological concealments, contains a core of vitality and loyalty that is far from merely verbal. On the credit side, also, is accumulating evidence that educational policies and programs are slowly profiting both by growing scientific knowledge of the human species and by those contemporary philosophic movements that are both conditions and results of this knowledge. With all its weaknesses, education does increasingly utilize learning and teaching based upon functional, organismic principles; it does begin to reflect seriously the newer insights and research of the social sciences; it does engage in critical assessments of its own performance; it does, finally, inquire more conscientiously than hitherto as to the meaning and adequacy of its own goals and of the actions instrumental to them.

These encouraging signs are not enough, of course. Actually, if we accept the judgment of Mumford and others that ours is a revolutionary age, we are forced to assert that the steps thus far taken by education to catch up with the fantastic changes in con-

CULTURAL FOUNDATIONS OF EDUCATION

temporary culture resemble those of a toddling one-year-old. What, then, are some of the next steps?

3. The most important of these steps is to clarify our second question: Granting that education, however humbly, now assists some cultures to approach closer to the goal of freedom, can it justify in any fundamental ways its commitment *to* the goal? Or, again in Edel's terms, can education "validate" its own "valuational base"? I believe that it can, and that such a commitment and such a validation will have the effect of enhancing its influence and power.

One source of support for this belief lies in the universality or near-universality of human goals that are harmonious with freedom in the empirical sense that we have been considering. Most if not all of man's basic goals, in other words, contribute not to his frustration but to his greater satisfaction and richer self-fulfillment. Recall, for example, Edel's evidence of cultural convergence toward the value if not always the reality of health rather than of illness, toward security and abundance rather than insecurity and poverty, toward opportunity for development of human powers rather than spiritual or physical debasement.

The anthropologist Ashley Montagu epitomizes this generalization in terms of the value of health:

The basic test of a value is the extent to which it contributes to the survival of the organism as a healthy and harmonically functioning interdependent whole. Health is the state of being organismically sound: that is, sound according to the requirements of the organism. Health is *the* organismic value, the summation of all the organism's values.[45]

Montagu quotes L. O. Kattsoff in support: "The concept of the 'ought,' like the concept of value . . . has its basis in the very structure of the organism. It is, therefore, an absolute basis for any ethics. . . ."[46] The case for freedom-creating values is indeed impressive.

Yet, does even such an impressive case succeed in proving that education *must* support these values? Can one actually convince any person or any group choosing to endorse life-denying rather than life-affirming goals that their choice is wrong or fallacious? I think that one cannot. On the contrary, it is far more typical of those who, by their actions if not always their words, reveal a preference for hatred, violence, and suffering to deny scientific evidence, to reject logical persuasion, and to fix instead upon their own impenetrable feelings and inscrutible beliefs.

Fortunately, however, the sciences of man already show that the consensus of most people of most cultures is, if not always explicitly or as yet conclusively, overwhelmingly against that kind of preference. Their consensus, rather, is increasingly toward freedom—toward freedom as the quintessence of all values establishing that man-in-culture, as Fromm has said, is not potentially *against* but *for* himself and his fellowmen. Therefore education, *in so far as it serves cultures in their widest rather than their narrowest scope,* is justified in expending its powers, too, in behalf of that consensus.

Here, then, the concept of "social consensus"[47] emerges as indispensable to education's normative task. This is not to say that education should strive for the goal of freedom *simply* because most people wish to strive for it. Counting-of-noses never by itself establishes a value any more than it establishes a truth. Always there is need for searching examination against as well as for every judgment in behalf of freedom. Nor is the mere desire for freedom enough to sanction it; the crucial problem, of course, is to determine the grounds upon which we choose to be free because we find our desire for it preferable to alternative desires. All available evidence of the sciences and arts of man as to what freedom permits him to become, as well as what non-freedom prevents him from becoming, is therefore essential. Equally essential is the fullest possible communication of this evidence—the opportunity to expose it to meticulous examination, to hear all possible doubts, to muster all possible support. So, too, is the need to test out any agreements attained on the basis of such communicated evidence—in short, to determine by cooperative action whether freedom actually provides the satisfactions and fulfillments that its proponents claim.

Can we find additional support for the consensus principle among culture-theorists themselves? It is, I think, already inherent in the views of such authorities on universal values as Linton, Kluckhohn, and Edel. As it becomes more refined with the aid of the philosophy of science,[48] the concept of consensus could thus serve to breach the gap that still prevails between the descriptive and normative perspectives on cultural values (in, say, anthropology) without injury to objective standards of research. Likewise, opportunities for cooperation between the behavioral sciences and education might thereby expand, for then both fields—no longer education merely—could be openly regarded in the normative context which Bidney so strongly urges as a requirement of anthropological maturity.

Herskovits, however, is the only anthropologist thus far encountered who assists us in approaching this frontier with the concept of consensus utilized in any explicit way. Consensus, he shows, always pervades cultural patterns—that is, their coherence and continuity are designs resulting from, yet by no means merely a sum of, individual behavior patterns. For "the nature of any pattern, no matter how minute or particular, or how broad . . . [is] a *consensus* of behavior. . . ."[49] But Herskovits scarcely develops the idea sufficiently to provide the operational precision that is now required.

Meanwhile, this much we can affirm at least for educational theory. *The ultimate justification for our commitment to the goal of freedom lies in the social consensus—a consensus that most of us do or could share—that real people living in real cultures reach in behalf of that commitment.* Those members who, for whatever reasons, continue to oppose it not only have the right to do so but have the parallel right —more, the obligation—to indicate why. But most of us, of course, do not oppose freedom as we have here considered it, for the good reason that when we come to understand it we also come to agree that it is preferable to other goals that may be open to us. And it is we who thus find reasons for uniting on a common platform of normative commitment.

Once we are agreed, the agenda of education in its conscious normative role is ready for reformulation. In broadest terms, such an agenda (related, of course, to the educational proposals considered in Parts II and III) will provide and communicate the cumulative evidence in behalf of freedom; it will expose freedom to critical analysis even to the point of conceivable repudiation; and it will test freedom by continuous practice of learning and teaching both in classroom and community.

4. Let us sketch further our design for what may now be called goal-centered education. The principle determining the selection of all subject-matters, as well as the development of all skills and techniques, is invariably the particular culture's "value-orientation." That the latter varies tremendously both in time and space in no way annuls

the major premise that its common denominator of human freedom remains the same for all cultures.

The objective by which curricula are organized and continually modified is likewise governed by a single principle. Does an established course of study demonstrably add to man's capacity to control nature and himself so that the quality and quantity of freedom are augmented further? If so, then let it remain. If not, then eliminate it and replace it by one that does.

The disciplines that contribute to this over-all objective embrace all of those we have touched upon. The behavioral sciences are, of course, crucial. So too are philosophy, religion, and art. The sciences dealing with nature below and beyond the human level—physics, geology, biology, astronomy—are just as essential as they ever were. But the contents that are included, like the methods of learning these disciplines, are not necessarily those now most common. The latter are more than likely to require drastic alteration when assessed by the dominating goal.

Take as an instance the contributions of psychology. Study of human needs and wants, related as these are to human dynamics, to unconscious and cathectic as well as to conscious and rational processes, is no longer undertaken for its own sake or because of academic convention. It is undertaken because evidence concerning the nature of wants, of the influence of culture in shaping as well as being shaped by wants, of their cross-cultural as well as intra-cultural manifestations, is both directly and indirectly necessary to freedom itself. To determine what we do and do not want, to compare what you or I want with what other people of our culture and of other cultures want, to explore the question of how far present institutions offer or deny opportunity to satisfy our wants, to consider the organismic relations of wants to one another, to recognize the imperative of developing "conceived values" (guided by "phase-rules") that will help attain the maximum of "object values," rather than to indulge in simple assuagement of our immediate, often conflicting "operative values"—these are important contributions that psychology can help to make in partnership with a normatively governed education.

The whole culture-and-personality field is similarly fruitful. Of many implications in our study of that field, Kluckhohn's and Murray's work may be singled out for reiteration. Every personality is goal-seeking, they have told us, though of course goals are immediate as well as long-range. Educationally, this means that students should learn to appreciate both kinds of goals—not, as is now so often true, to magnify the former to the neglect of the latter. Also, the operating construct of an "ego-controlled" personality, as against either an "id-dominated" or "superego-dominated" personality, points directly at the norm of a free personality—one that is neither the anxiety-ridden creature of its conflicting urges nor the slave of cultural compulsions. Rather, it is a personality able to join with other personalities in reflecting upon choices and in guiding their lives by purposeful effort toward the richest possible satisfaction of the choices they make.

The fertility of this general view for education is reinforced from the psychological side by Murphy, Fromm, and Sullivan, and from the anthropological side by Hallowell and Bidney. All of these authorities, among others, appreciate the vast contributions of behaviorist and psychoanalytic theory. All would surely plead for more attention particularly to Freudian theory in the training of teachers and in the curriculum as a whole. But all would also question the inference drawn by, say, Kardiner or Róheim to the effect that freedom of personality is achievable mainly if not entirely through the kind of therapeutic principles associated with that theory. More careful analysis by education of the cultural foundations of human experience would help to demonstrate that while a truly free culture is the macrocosm of free personalities the converse proposition is at least equally true: free personalities are the microcosms of a free culture.

Hence any adequate agenda for education galvanized by the central goal to which it ought to be committed will consider, along with the important evidence of the psychological sciences, comparably important evidence of the social sciences. In Malinowski's terms, education will pay close attention to all "institutions"—familial, political, economic, religious, educational—not merely to describe them but to apprase their merits and demerits according to their "charters." Or, in Kluckhohn's and Murray's terms, education will be guided by an "ideal superego." Does the typical American family, for example, enlarge the scope of freedom? Let us investigate this question comparatively, cross-culturally, with the help of Murdock, Mead, Whiting, and others of like authority. Let us learn from India and Samoa, as well as from the Navahos and the people of Elmtown, how the personality of the American child can be affected toward worse or better development by patterns of parental training, of sexual practice, and of familial responsibilities.

Evaluations of economic and political institutions are carried on intensively with like normative measuring-sticks. How far is Malinowski justified in his anthropological support of democracy as the most desirable political order? How far does Edel's evidence from several other sciences help to substantiate the same ideal? Is capitalism, by and large, a freedom-expanding system or is it a freedom-contracting one? Can we obtain more sophisticated, less prejudiced value judgments of communist lands with the aid of "culture-at-a-distance" explorations?

Education as an institution is itself subjected to critical appraisal. Students are encouraged to observe concrete ways in which their schools and those of other cultures inhibit or enhance the guiding norm. Does typical classroom discipline lead to frustration and aggression, or does it lead rather toward the ordered freedom of "ego-control"? Are typical rules of school administration conducive to cooperation, participation, and recognition among teachers and students, or do such rules tend to generate divisiveness, resentment, and hostility? Do students best learn the cultural heritage, say, by deliberate indoctrination, or do they learn it more effectively by untrammeled investigation, cooperative discussion, uncoerced agreements and disagreements, with opportunities for individual and group activity?

Religion is another major institution. If the religious experience is as universal as Linton, for example, contends, then it too should be studied for its short-range and long-range failures and successes as a way to freedom. The historical record, which education should frankly review, is far from unblemished; yet the contributions that religious institutions have made to man as a goal-seeking, culturally integrated being may also have been momentous. And what kinds of norms might students agree upon for religion in the future culture? Cassirer's keen analyses of the role of myth in human life, the functions of esthetic symbolism, the importance of dedication to encompassing human ideals and to "ways of life" on a planetary scale—

these are aspects of the religious quest which education can no longer honorably by-pass.

Dozens of other steps could be added to this broad agenda.[50] The place of philosophy, to take just one additional example, is a large question. Ethel M. Albert, a philosopher specializing in the value problems of culture-theory, has shown in "The Classification of Values"[51] how great is the need both for fresh examination of the meaning of values as such, and for study of the relations between axiology, metaphysics, epistemology, and other branches of philosophic belief as they are manifested in culture-configurations. The work that she and her colleagues have already accomplished in the Harvard Values Study Project[52] has proved the benefit to be derived from operating upon cultures with more refined philosophic tools; yet how to make this kind of operation accessible to the average student has scarcely been considered. Her comparison of value patterns in selected American Indian and white cultures demonstrates (as Morris demonstrates in a different way) not only the dangers of hasty generalization, not only that marked differences in values prevail among such cultures, but that marked similarities also prevail. Such differences and similarities are by no means adverse, when carefully interpreted, to the value of freedom in the comprehensive sense that we have been considering this universal goal.

The two problematic concepts of progress and ideology, treated earlier in the chapter, are other pertinent examples of philosophy's new responsibilities. Dissection of the role of progress in history will help to dispel the sophomoric optimism of so many Western students; it will force them to question traditional, speculative teleologies, and it will enable them to grasp the painful but necessary truth that freedom as a human goal can be won only if and when they want it enough to struggle and sacrifice to win it. Ideology as a conceptual device explodes the fallacies and distortions chronic in so many explicit contemporary values (progress itself being one, freedom being another). Thus it helps to develop the sort of critical-mindedness that citizens must acquire if they are to choose between spurious and genuine norms.

Before, however, education can move far along the road I have mapped out, it too will have to choose. It will have to choose between a policy of eclectic aimlessness, of "vicious relativism," of irresponsible neutrality, and a policy of normative commitment to the purpose of transcultural freedom, to the multiple satisfactions which this connotes, and to the "modes, means, and ends of action" that fructify that purpose. In this basic sense, education—or rather the human-beings-living-in-cultures that *are* education—confronts a choice that is far-reaching and probably decisive. Whether or not it will have the clarity or courage to choose in time is a question for which only the generations now emerging can provide the answer. Yet upon the answer may depend, not only the survival of whatever precious increment of freedom humanity has gained, but also the convergence toward that infinitely greater freedom which is the goal of culture.

PART V

ORDER, PROCESS, AND GOALS:
A SELECTIVE RECAPITULATION

CHAPTER THIRTEEN

THE STUDY OF CULTURE IN TEACHER EDUCATION

A TIME OF CONFLICT

ONE OF THE bitter conflicts in education is that of the hostility between liberal arts faculties and professional "educationists." The attack upon schools of education and teachers' colleges has often been more prejudiced and emotional than reasoned and dispassionate. The defense has often been more typified by concern to protect vested interests and traditional policies than by deep concern with the best possible professional training.

In certain ways the conflict is salutary. It has called attention to the unfortunate truth that schools of education are overloaded with "busywork," are staffed by instructors too frequently limited in scholarship, and are filled with students below the intellectual average of those in other divisions of the college and university. At the same time, a minority of liberal arts leaders, realizing that perhaps not every indictment is justified, have taken pains to investigate sufficiently to discover that in some instances the professional programs carried on for future teachers are directed by experts of high caliber. And a minority of educationists have, in turn, become more willing to examine and correct the deficiencies that remain in those programs.

Occasionally, too, representatives of both fields have joined forces and learned from each other. The pioneering conference sponsored by Stanford University[1] in which anthropologists and educators explored common interests afforded one opportunity. Another was the symposium on educational theory by academic and educational philosophers under the auspices of the American Philosophical Association, and carried further by the *Harvard Educational Review*.[2] These efforts have revealed widening agreement that the weaknesses pervading teacher education can neither be ignored any longer nor corrected by mutal recriminations. A more patient, tolerant, and fundamental assessment of current policies is now overdue.

Such evaluations, several already launched with the support of foundation grants, are not, however, likely to produce fruitful reconstruction of colleges of education as long as widespread confusion prevails—as it does prevail—over the proper conception of teacher education itself. On the one side, liberal arts spokesmen are confused when they argue that the one paramount objective should be that of providing the teacher with virtually the same equipment that they themselves ostensibly possess—namely, solid knowledge of the academic field or fields in which he is to teach. This attitude has grown in recent influence to the point where various academicians have advocated the virtual liquidation of schools and departments of education. For, after all, "teachers are born, not made," and the skills they need, if any, are easily acquired by a "methods course" or two.[3]

On the other side, educationists are at least equally confused when they support programs of training that inflate the importance of techniques at the expense of scholarship. In principle, no educationist denies that knowledge of the fields in which a teacher is to work is essential. But lip-service to the principle does not negate the fact that this knowledge as provided by the average school of education is often cursory indeed. Most impartial observers would admit, moreover, that typical teacher-training programs are littered with time-wasting, repetitious, and obvious courses in "know-how," many of which could be eliminated without loss except to entrenched instructors of these courses.

These confusions on both sides result from the fact that neither side has sufficiently considered why its approach to the professionalizing of education is defective. The liberal arts approach is defective because teaching is neither the simple process of conveying subject matters to students, nor the kind of intuitive art that many academicians naively if not lazily assume it to be. Those who think that it is one or the other, or both, thereby succeed only in demonstrating their illiteracy in the science and art of teaching—a demonstration only too apparent on liberal arts campuses where some of the most incompetent instruction on any level occurs.

But the educationist approach to teacher-training is likewise defective. As long as teachers are compelled to take course after course in pedagogical gadgetry at the expense of solid learning and research equal to the best that liberal arts curricula afford, we shall continue to have an education that deserves a great part of the denunciations that are heaped upon it. And the chief victims, of course, will be the classroom teachers themselves, or—what is far more serious—the millions of their students.

The conditions accounting for this appalling situation are multiple. One of these conditions, without doubt, is the contemporary crisis in world affairs that we have noticed: perhaps still more sensitively and quickly than most others, education as an institution reacts to the uncertainties and gropings that infect the structure, the changes, and the aims of the wider culture. A more immediate condition is, however, potentially constructive: it consists in the recognition, as yet but partially expressed, that education as a major profession is just coming into being. The teacher throughout Western history has been the "poor relation" among such professionals as doctors, lawyers, engineers, and priests. Typically, he has worked as hard and often harder for a fraction of their compensation (though the priesthood and ministry have been compensated partly by other means than money). Frequently he has taken on other burdens in order to earn enough for his family to survive. Worst of all, he has usually entered upon his duties with limited background. Today, thousands of teachers are placed in charge of classrooms with little more than a second-rate high-school education. The rapid turnover of teaching personnel that results from this situation continues to be one of the great stumbling-blocks in the way of establishing à worthy profession.

As schools have enrolled more and more children, as young adults (in America, at least) continue their formal educations to a later age than formerly, as the demand for leadership, technical proficiency, and civic enlightenment has increased, many thoughtful citizens have come gradually to agree that these traditional weaknesses of the teaching profession must be corrected. Therefore they have started, really for the first time, to inquire with a sense of urgency as to what must now be done. The confusions, hostilities, and counter-proposals that we hear on every side are a natural, immediate symptom of this sense of urgency.

A FRAMEWORK FOR PROFESSIONAL TRAINING

Is there, then, any expectation that education can at last establish itself on a high plane of professional competence? The answer, I believe, requires first that we develop a framework that avoids the limitations and biases of the two chief opposing camps, that recognizes whatever values may be contained in each, but that transcends both. This framework also requires that we learn from other professions that have already attained, or at least approached, the high standards appropriate to their responsibilities. One of these professions—medicine—may be selected for analogy. Its distinguishing feature is, of course, the practice of the art and science of healing, not for its own sake as a means, but for the sake of physical and mental health as its end.

The means and end of medicine are achieved by professional preparation which normatively combines four essential parts. First, the prospective physician receives a general education so that he may understand, harmonize with, and contribute to the wider culture of which he is an important and respected member. Second, he acquires the fullest possible knowledge of all the sciences (such as biology, physiology, and neurology) necessary to his competence—knowledge based upon long centuries of cumulative research and painstaking experimentation. Third, he learns how to apply this knowledge in the art and science of healing—a kind of learning demanding constant observation and abundant firsthand practice. Fourth, he receives a grounding in the history of medicine and in the theory that undergirds it: here, for example, he learns of the long struggle of science to free itself from superstition; he becomes familiar with the nature of scientific method and with the postulates governing research; he becomes aware of his personal goals as a physician and of the values that should govern his professional conduct both toward the individual patient and toward the culture that he serves.

The candidate for a medical degree is qualified to enter practice in so far as all four parts of this program receive substantial, balanced attention. Without adequate general education, he becomes a narrow specialist unaware of and often indifferent either to his civic responsibilities or to the worth of the culture which has created medicine and which medicine benefits. Without the greatest knowledge he can obtain of the investigations and findings that provide the substance of all natural sciences, he cannot hope to deal competently with the welter of problems that he will confront in practice. Without extensive opportunity to become proficient in the skills of operating, medicating, and curing, his knowledge remains untested in actual experience. Finally, without a framework of theory that includes the philosophy, history, and ethics of medicine, the physician will function with obscure notions of what he does or what he should do. In short, medicine is an *applied* science and an *applied* art. As such, it channels the findings of pure scholarship and pure research into the sphere of human experience where it is supremely important for the reason that life and health are supremely important.

Granting that even the best analogies are imperfect because they deal with dissimilar facts and events, we can remove much of the confusion now besetting professional education if we try to relate this conception of physician-training to that of teacher-training. As Thomas Aquinas pointed out in the thirteenth century (though from different philosophic premises), the guiding purpose of teaching is to draw out the potential powers of the human being so that he can obtain his greatest stature. The teacher, in this sense, is a "healer" too—a therapist for the ailment of ignorance and on behalf of physical, spiritual, and social well-being.

It follows that just as the physician is untrained if he lacks the general education that would place his profession in a cultural setting and help him to estimate his relations to people in other professions and roles, so too is the teacher. Just as the physician is deficient if his knowledge of, say, anatomy or the nervous system is superficial, so too is the teacher who lacks thorough knowledge of the foundations of education or of the field of his choice. Just as the physician is unprepared for practice who is insufficiently experienced in multiple methods of healing, so too is the teacher who lacks the skills of teaching. And just as the physician is denied a well-rounded education if meager attention is given to the evolution of science, to the presuppositions that underlie research, or to the ethics of his profession, so too is the teacher who is uninformed in the history and theory of education.

The storm that is raging today between the liberal arts and teacher education is due in large measure to failure on both sides to grasp this quadrangular conception. There would be widest agreement between them with regard to the first part (the need for general education), though even here confusion is rife because popular notions of general education are in turn confused. On the second part (the need for thorough knowledge of subject-matter fields) liberal arts critics are, of course, the chief protagonists, just as on the third (the need of competent methods and skills) educationists are most vociferous. While educationists, more than many of their critics, readily concede the legitimate need of *both* the second and third parts, the fact remains that by the test of practice they exaggerate the third and thereby fail more often than not to satisfy the second. Both groups, accordingly, may be accused of failure to clarify and to agree upon the one paramount objective of the science and art of teaching: to cure the disease of ignorance by *applying* scientific and humanistic knowledge; to make it *operate* in the interests, the life-experiences, of young and old alike; to help them *to transmit, to cope with, and to redirect the orders and processes of culture in behalf of its highest goals.*

This objective brings us directly to the fourth and final part (the need for unified theory) about which, again, neither group is clear or agrees with the other. The liberal arts group is typically concerned to provide academic subject matters but it has a paucity of interest in any harmonizing pattern that could invest them with meaning and purpose. The educationist group is more concerned with providing the trainee with multiple techniques than it is with clarifying the over-all conception that ought to govern them, or to create normative designs for education that alone make techniques important.

If, then, the typical teacher has not begun to achieve a status approaching that of the physician, this is due at least in important measure to the fact that he has not thus far deserved to achieve it. He earns much less on the average because, in terms of present competence, he deserves to earn less. His influence and prestige in the average community are considerably lower because, by comparison with the physician, he is less secure, more easily intimidated, and much less strongly organized either to protect or to advance his legitimate professional interests. He performs less capably because too often his skills are haphazard, untested, and clumsy. He cannot properly serve the human beings he wishes to serve because the knowledge he acquires about them, about himself, or about his own field is frequently careless and superficial. And despite his conscientiousness he is as a rule less certain of either the assumptions that govern or should govern his own profession.

This is not, of course, to say that medical preparation has risen to the heights to which it is exhorted by its own best standards. Typically, it remains weak both in the general education it requires of average physicians-in-training and in its attention to the history, theory, and ethics either of science in general or of medicine in particular. One consequence of this last weakness is the narrowly self-interested policies that have too consistently continued to dominate medical associations. But at least the fourfold conception that guides the education of physicians is increasingly clear to those most responsible for its over-all norms of training. And they are, I am sure, altogether clear in their recognition that medicine as an applied science and art must synthesize the richest possible academic knowledge and research with the widest possible skill-gaining practice.

Such a conception is lacking in the education of teachers. Until it is recognized and implemented, they will continue to remain at or near the bottom of the professional heap—victims of their own ineptitude, of public negligence, and of muddy thinking.

One purpose of this book has been to anticipate the kinds of (1) general education, (2) subject matter, (3) methodology, and (4) unified theory that a reconstructed policy will have to incorporate if teaching is ever to attain the standards outlined here. The study of culture affords an important—or rather, the single most important —illustration of the background, content, method, and design that such a policy demands. If the preceding pages have demonstrated anything, they have demonstrated that the professionalizing of education cannot possibly avoid sustained examination of the problems, assumptions, research, methods, and values with which the foundations of culture deal. The remaining pages draw together the foremost implications for teacher-training derived from our examination. These implications are now considered, not primarily in the form of a review, but as a selective recapitulation in terms of the four major parts of a normative framework for teacher education.

THE FIRST PART: GENERAL EDUCATION

The first of these parts, *general education,* requires a principle of integration within and between the humanities and sciences. Instead of the eclecticism characteristic of, say, the Harvard report on general education,[4] or instead of the sort of program advocated by Robert M. Hutchins based as it is on regressive metaphysical doctrine,[5] I have suggested that general education be reorganized in terms of the fertile meanings connoted by the concept of cultural order. Since education has been shown to be *a,* if not *the,* major agency by which order is attained and maintained in every known culture, these meanings are crucial to the foundational training of education's chief representatives.

Cultural order provides a principle of integration in numerous ways. Concepts such as pattern, theme, configuration, and "way of life" are, we have seen, curricular *gestalten* or frames of total reference: they enable the student to view art, science, religion, and politics as parts of an organic whole rather than as discrete entities. They enable him, also, to recognize the common denominators of human life so that his provincialism is disturbed, his world-view widened.

But such a pattern for general education is by no means devoid of the concrete and specific. Rather, it avoids one of the commonest weaknesses of many current programs: their over-generality. Sapir's and Kluckhohn's interpretations of culture-configurations, Steward's admonition that culture be differentiated according to its levels, Warner's research on social status, the Marxian theory of classes—these are among the contributions proving that the kind of material to be encompassed by the construct of cultural order can be rich in horizontal and vertical content. It includes, in other words, both widening concentric circles of cultural experience—all the way from the interpersonal to the international sphere—and ascending layers of class, caste, power, and other hierarchies typical of cultures. But order is temporal as well as spatial: it embraces the dynamics of cultural emergence and thereby acquaints students with its historical dimensions.

The importance of history to the curriculum of general education is best exemplified by perspectives upon civilization viewed in grand scale—Toynbee's, Spengler's, Kroeber's, and Sorokin's being conspicuous examples. By challenging the unilinear, melioristic assumptions of many conventional history courses, these great overviews not only place civilizations in relationship; they help to reduce the student's ethnocentric biases as to the superiority and invincibility of his own civilization. At the same time they toughen his historical acumen by helping him to avoid easy causal explanations and to be skeptical of "laws" of history that claim to predict an inevitable future.

Cultural order, it will be recalled, also suggests the interdisciplinary character of general education. Once the significance of gestalt and "field" theory is grasped, traditional departments and divisions of the school and college are no longer justified. I do not imply, however, that cultural order in its various components is enough to provide every kind of subject matter that should be included in this part of our program. The natural sciences, for example, deserve more attention than culture-theory, by virtue of its chief interest, pays to them. Yet even these need not and should not be relegated to separate domains. The value of, say, physics and biology, regarded now less as specialized disciplines than as great areas of cultural achievement, is different for the student of general education than to one who majors in them. Moreover, as Kroeber has shown, we may regard the historical and scientific approaches as bipolar ways of viewing culture on a single sliding-scale—a fruitful idea for bringing the two into close partnership.

Just as the guiding principle, then, is not altered by the inclusion of the natural sciences, neither is it altered by the inclusion of abundant resources from art, philosophy, religion, or other fields usually embraced by the term, humanities. These, too, are essential to any program of general education whether for teachers or any one else. Their significance, however, is heightened when they are brought within the compass of cultural order—when they are prized, not as discrete bodies of esoteric learning, but as adventures of the human spirit endlessly engaged in creating "ways of life."

THE SECOND PART: KNOWLEDGE

The second part of the proposed policy is accurately symbolized by *knowledge* itself. If it is here, as liberal arts critics rightly contend, that teacher-training has been weakest, the subject matters studied in preceding chapters prove that it need not, and certainly should not, continue to be so.

Many examples of these subject matters have been introduced by the program of general education. On the professional level, however, some materials are omitted, new ones are included, and all are re-examined more intensively according to their bearing upon the teacher's competence and needs. In addition, opportunity is provided for solid grounding in any field where the teacher plans to concentrate. Since culture-theory does not pretend to embrace all of these fields, I shall omit them from further consideration, while urging the richest possible acquaintance with language, science, mathematics, or whatever the chosen field happens to be.

The point I do wish to underscore is this: just as the chief deputy of physiological and mental health—the physician—must study general physiology before he becomes a neurologist or an obstetrician, so the chief deputy of cultural transmission, continuity, and innovation—the teacher—has equal need to study the anatomy, morphology, and development of culture before he specializes in, say, literature or physics. The comparison applies equally to the general practitioner: some physicians never specialize, and some teachers never do either. But whether or not they do, knowledge of the cultural "body" remains just as indispensable to every qualified teacher as knowledge of the human body remains indispensable to every qualified physician.

Does professional education recognize the validity of this comparison? The curriculum of typical programs proves, unfortunately, that it certainly does not. To be sure, psychology—another area of necessary knowledge—is probably required in every current program; but, aside from the issue of how competently even this subject is treated in the average conventional course, it seldom deals painstakingly enough with learning or emotion in a *cultural* frame of reference. Still worse, the vast majority of trainees are not provided with even a solitary course in anthropology, while almost as many receive teaching licenses with no systematic study of culturally vital areas such as social psychology or political philosophy. Any contact with these areas more often than not is through a smattering of comment in watered-down texts.

By contrast, the kinds of knowledge to which I refer are provided by the representative authorities to whom we have earlier turned. To be sure, most of these authorities exemplify the meaning of pure rather than applied research and scholarship. Many anthropologists, for example, are no more directly interested in the useful effects that their investigations might have upon better human relations in educational practice than is an organic chemist necessarily concerned with the improved health that may eventually result from his discoveries. Yet in both cases the fact that therapeutic application may have little direct relevance does not in itself narrow the importance of their contributions. On the contrary, we know from countless instances in the history of science that often they are widened.

More concretely, what sorts of basic knowledge are appropriate to the second part of the program? I mean a knowledge of the history of culture-theory at least from Tylor through Boas and Kroeber. I mean familiarity with the concepts, questions, and findings gathered together and interrelated under the rubrics of cultural order, cultural process, and cultural goals. I mean intimate acquaintance with frontier areas—with, for example, sophisticated explorations of cultural freedom (both its opportunities and hazards), and with the puzzling questions raised by the relations between descriptive and normative axiology in culture-theory. I mean foundational courses that are completely rather than only partially interdisciplinary, that accordingly synthesize the social *and* psychological sciences after the manner suggested by Frank. I mean the study of cultural history, both methodologically and substantively; the study of cutting-edge issues such as the threat of obliterating violence or the theory and practice of communism; and the study of the fine and applied arts, of the great religions, and of philosophies as these affect and are affected by the dynamics and patterns of culture.

The requirement of knowledge in culture-theory and research is, then, anything but simple. Nor is it one that can be fulfilled quickly or ever with full satisfaction. Nevertheless, the kinds of subject matter appropriate to the study of culture provide the second indispensable norm for teacher education—and they include all of those listed. They will not be included until the faculties of schools of education are at least on a par in scholarly attainment and professional ability with those of other schools that train men and women for responsible service to their fellow citizens.

THE THIRD PART: PRACTICE

We come now to the third part: preparation for the *practice* of teaching. Professional education, we have found, has progressed farther here, though not without serious limitations. One of these limitations is due to the fact that methodology can never be strong while one or more of the other three parts continues to be weak. Teaching skills are not, accurately speaking, separate from the basic knowledge, for example, that they must always utilize. Moreover, practice is itself both an important form of knowledge and a testing-ground for others.

Dozens of instances are available to show how applicable culture-theory is to this part of our design. One conspicuous instance is learning itself. How children become enculturated, and how the school may translate scientific understanding of this process into classroom procedures, is not only perhaps the most pressing question of educational practice but also the most universal. In our review of learning theory as treated by experts in the field of culture-and-personality we have found sharp disagreements: behaviorism, mechanism, Freudianism, gestaltism, transactionism, and combinations of or deviations from these all have their able defenders. In general, however, and despite the continued influence of traditional theories, the trend seems to be toward a conception that encourages goal-centered, creative, participative, and cooperative learning much more than passive absorption of inherited cultural content or indoctrination of pre-scribed rules, beliefs, and habits. Enculturation thereby becomes a continuum of learning how *both* to accept and to reshape culture—a functioning, organismic process that begins in the earliest years of the nursery school and expands in complexity and proficiency with increasing maturation.

Many prospective teachers, emerging as they do from home and school environments where this sort of experience has been minimized, must themselves relearn the nature of learning. By becoming educational interns in laboratory schools (these, of course, are essential adjuncts of all high-standard programs), they can begin with expert supervision to acquire the multiple skills that functional-organismic principles demand. It follows that the practice-teaching now commonly required for certification is often obsolete: much of this practice occurs in classrooms controlled by teachers who, however earnest, are themselves deficient in their grasp of such principles.

In the course of developing competence through methodological experience, opportunity should likewise be provided for trainees to participate in experimental ventures. Group dynamics, based upon Lewin's social psychology, is one of the most promising—a process which, unfortunately, most culture-theorists have as yet assimilated even less than they have contributed directly to the whole problem of culture-change through small-group action. Nevertheless, teachers-in-training should practice with role-playing, sociometric testing, and similar frontier methods. If anthropologists, among other social scientists, could be persuaded that classrooms are fertile testing-grounds in the "fields of forces" that constitute small groups, the value of such experimentation to the teaching intern would be greatly enhanced.

Closely related to these methods are opportunities to utilize the exploratory work now developing around and within the concept of modal personality. Here is the point, more perhaps than at any other, where psychoanalytic theory synthesized with culture-theory should receive close attention in the professional program. As the personality types of teachers and students are delineated more precisely, as the teaching intern discerns the profound influence of early childhood habits in molding every type; as he is sensitized to disparities between his own modal personality (in urban America, at least, this is likely to be middle-status if not middle-class) and those of his typical charges in the public school; as he grows in awareness that the mingling of children from different cultural backgrounds often generates tensions induced, in turn, by the close contact of diverse personality types—as these and other principles become familiar to him, his methodological equipment should become refined.

As a consequence, the teacher-in-training will patiently assess the barriers blocking modification of personality types if and when considered value judgments seem to warrant modification. Operating with the concept of focus, for example, he will search for areas of culture-and-personality that are the most pliable as well as the most rigid. He will become familiar with the validity of "other-direction" and similar current hypotheses of modal personality, taking these into careful account as he works with adolescents. Not, of course, that he can hope to accomplish momentous results while learning to practice in pioneering ways. But, under able guidance, he at least can determine how to enter upon his responsibilities so that mental hygiene, strengthened by the hypotheses and insights of anthropologists like Linton, will function as one important tool of his professional activity.

Teaching and learning in these adventurous ways cannot, obviously, be properly divorced from practice in curriculum planning or in the control of education. Human-relations projects—organized in cores or workshops, designed whenever possible with the direct aid of elementary or secondary students, and constantly enriched by direct contact with citizens' groups—afford one example of how older, often sterile courses in the social studies can be superseded by meaningful experiences that contain at the same time a great deal of content. Other cultural projects could center upon the present world crisis, upon the history of invention, upon the import of religion in past and present cultures, upon the elusive problem of progress, upon the values that should govern young people today, and upon problems *of* the local community crystallized through participation *in* the community. Also, opportunities are needed to test out better ways of controlling the school both within the classroom and on the administrative level—opportunities that include consideration of political proposals toward which prospective teacher-citizens should learn how to be alert and upon which they should seek to exert either opposition or support according to their judgments. In sum, experience in planning, conducting, and evaluating through ways such as these will not only prepare the practitioner on any level (elementary, secondary, college) to undertake more of them later; it will also enlarge both his own knowledge of the contents necessary to their successful operation and his skill in imparting these contents.

This overview of reconstructed principles of effective practice may also profit by several miscellaneous suggestions. One is the need to teach cultural history, not as a mummified record of past events, but as an indispensable resource in the solution of contemporary problems; it is a need that requires history to function in relation to other fields of study, with appreciation of the creative role of the historian as understood by a Collingwood or Muller. A second suggestion is the need for teachers to become involved in cultural affairs, organized labor being one way that will help them to reassess both their actual and potential power in the socio-economic stratum on which they find themselves. A third is the need to practice with skills implied by the several concepts of process examined in Chapter Eight, not merely with the concept of focus mentioned above, but with that of diffusion, acculturation, innovation, causation, indeed each one of the others. Their immense importance—especially for in-service training of teachers preparing to participate in personnel exchange programs sponsored by Unesco, in "human engineering" projects under Point Four auspices, or in communities with many migrant children—can scarcely be overstressed. A fourth suggestion is the need to operate upon beliefs and attitudes with the instrument of ideology—to develop sensitivity, for example, to the cultural premises not only of students but of teachers as well. Related to this is a fifth need: for the paradoxical and subtle skill of teaching with, on the one hand, the descriptive objectivity that is a major axiom of scientific method, yet, on the other hand, normative convictions that are recognized and critically appraised for their lack of objectivity.

Enough examples have, I trust, now been included to establish the third criterion of effective teacher education. Liberal arts proponents are on shaky ground when they contend that such an education is provided by their own preferred academic learnings. Essential as these are, it cannot be provided by them any more than it can be provided, on the other side, by the methodological exaggerations of numerous educationists. Such practices and skills as we have reviewed should become minimum requirements of every program worthy of professional respect.

THE FOURTH PART: UNIFYING THEORY

The fourth and last part, connoted by the term *unifying theory*, includes especially the history and philosophy of education. Their great contribution is to amalgamate professional education into a temporal and spatial, a descriptive and normative design.

This objective reinterprets many of the contents and practices earlier considered, first, by general education, second, by fundamental knowledge, and, third, by methodology. There is much to be said, accordingly, for this final part to serve as a kind of climax. It provides the beginning teacher both with appreciation of the relations between all segments of his training and with an orientation that galvanizes and directs them toward desirable goals.

In contrast with the study of history in other parts of the program, the aim here is to concentrate upon educational history. And there is another contrast: the kind of study I propose is anything but the boresome chronicle that is now more typical than not of textbooks and courses in this field. Educational history cannot properly be divorced from cultural history any more than education can, in fact, be divorced from culture. What should be established are courses that bring education back into the mainstream of the human quest—a quest for emancipation from ignorance, superstition, deprivation, and slavery; a quest that conceives of education in the way that an anthropologist such as Malinowski conceives of it; a quest therefore that is often tragic, sometimes comic, but always the dramatic effort of mankind to discover what it deeply wants and how best to get its wants assuaged.

This synthesis will deal, too, with such deep-seated cultural-educational issues as are raised by the *sui generis* versus operational theory of the superorganic. The growth of secular learning, we remember, has by no means witnessed the disappearance of ecclesiastic or closely related types of schooling, for the good reason that hypostatic ways of symbolizing culture have not disappeared either. The teacher-in-training should realize through historical analysis that just as anthropologists continue to differ on the meaning of cultural reality so too —at least implicitly—do educational theorists and practitioners. Thereby he should come to recognize that Whitehead's "fallacy of misplaced concreteness" is far from being of merely academic interest; it makes a fundamental difference to the way he learns and teaches others about the nature of culture itself.

The issue just cited is enough to demonstrate that only convention separates philosophy from the history of education. So deeply are they intertwined that much is to be said for a concluding, comprehensive course that combines both fields while neglecting neither. If philosophy is regarded as the effort to examine, justify, and often to correct the basic beliefs that underlie nature and man, then it cannot be divorced from their derivation and emergence out of the past, into the present, and toward the future of culture. This is why most of the great issues confronting education-and-culture today have their counterparts in preceding centuries, and why Eastern as well as Western philosophers have long ago given them attention.

Still more is needed, however, than the history of education merged with philosophy. In addition, contemporary philosophic movements, heralded by such developments as the theory of logical empiricism and Cassirer's "philosophical anthropology," ought to enter into the study of education at this concluding stage. Invaluable, too, are studies by anthropologists—Radin's is one—that disclose the philosophic attitudes of "primitive" man and their striking parallels with the philosophic attitudes of "civilized" man. Sapir's insights, refined by his disciples, increases the significance of these studies by revealing more clearly how every culture, including our own, is governed by "metacultural" beliefs concerning reality, truth, and value—how, also, every culture possesses a configuration diffused with beliefs about human orders, processes, and goals.

Mention of goals brings us back to axiology as a philosophic instrument. It is not, to be sure, regarded here merely as the abstract theory of values, though this is important too, but rather as the interpretation of personal and cultural values with meticulous regard for a conception of normative education that can both direct and inspire teachers.

One of the first issues to be confronted by this interpretation is that of relative and universal values. In line with previous discussion, the trainee will consider carefully the arguments of culture-theorists who contend that the problem is not to be resolved by an either-or choice. Thus he will learn, and perhaps eventually teach, that values in one sense *are* relative to particular cultures. He will come to appreciate the plurality of goals, the varieties of moral experience, the diversity of esthetic and political behavior. Not only will he develop personal attitudes of respect for and tolerance of the values of cultures different from his own; he will encourage students to develop like attitudes.

But he will also become critical of the consequences that follow from the "vicious relativism" that Perry justly censures. He will become familiar with the transcultural values that the anthropological research of, say, Murdock, or the philosophic research of Edel and Morris, has sought to establish. He will recognize how easily cultural relativism becomes an apologia for educational laissez-faire and neutrality—the "easy way out" from responsibility and loyalty to any set of universal values or, in Bidney's terms, to any conception of normative culture. And he will consider the challenge in Teilhard's conviction that man must now for the first time in history "become economically, technically, and morally one."

The goal of the entire teacher-training program will thus be the attempt to meet this challenge by crystallizing a philosophy of education committed to a meaningful conception of personal and cultural freedom. Purged of platitudinizing, the aim will be to weigh both the accomplishments of education that expand the forces of freedom and equally those that contract it. The role that education has played as the emasculator of freedom, the role that it now plays as the pawn of totalitarian and other authoritarian orders, must be just as realistically assessed as its alternative democratic roles. Above all, if teachers are to avoid the tender-mindedness so common to ideologists of contemporary education, they must learn to detect and estimate the invisible but enormous power of cultural patterns in conditioning and limiting the role of the school.

At the same time, the disturbing question should be faced squarely as to whether, why, and how cultural freedom, viewed always in its polaristic relations with cultural order, could be established and defended as more desirable than alternative ends. Prospective teachers will therefore search painstakingly for logical and evidential support in behalf of (but also against) any commitment that they may decide to make to this supreme cultural norm. The definition of freedom— as the latent or actual experience of peoples of various races, creeds, and nations trying in their relative ways to deliberate about, to choose among, and then to fulfill by cooperative action the widest available range of their desires—helps to answer this question. Further support is obtained from the concept of social consensus—a concept with which trainees should not only be familiar in educational theory, but with which they should have wide experience as perhaps the single richest way of teaching for freedom in everyday practice.

As the goal of personal freedom (with its institutional concretions on family, community, state, and international levels of order) becomes meaningful to the teacher, it becomes also the chief standard by which all methods and all contents at all stages of education are re-evaluated. Every candidate for a degree will, before graduation, accordingly review his professional years of study. He will inquire as to the issues that have been clarified to his own satisfaction as well as those that have not. He will recognize that culture-theory, in so far as it has been a central concern of his education, is anything but a panacea—that it raises many questions it cannot as yet adequately answer, questions of the kind that I have myself raised especially in Part I and have elaborated in the "preview" chapter of each succeeding Part.

Moreover, he will point to defects and recommend improvements according to whether his exposure to the natural and social sciences, to psychology, to art, philosophy and history, to teaching and administrative practice, have enabled him to move farther away from or closer to the goal of freedom. We may hope that many young teachers will thus begin their professional careers with the rudiments at least of clear commitment to the "ideal superego" of the democratic "charter" —a goal that they can defend because they have reflected seriously upon it, because they have experienced something of its institutional embodiment in their own education, and because they have come to believe that to strive for human freedom will be worth both the hardships and rewards of their chosen life-work.

HONORIFIC AND SCIENTIFIC CULTURE

The requirement of unifying theory as the fourth part of teacher education brings us back to the distinctions and connections discussed in the first chapter between the honorific and scientific conceptions of culture.

The more popular conception has been, of course, the honorific: to be "cultured" is to cultivate, to appreciate, and to share in the "finer things of life." There is nothing wrong with this normative conception: cultures do create and honor "finer things." But, at least from Tylor onward, we have found that the scientific meaning of culture connotes a great deal more—that it is, in fact, the most significant of all descriptive symbols of that "complex whole" which is the human enterprise.

The millennial search for human freedom is, in a penetrating sense, a polaristic fusion of both conceptions of culture. To gain this finest of all things, man must integrate his experience by spatial and vertical *order* evolving through time. He must utilize the diverse *processes* by which cultures undergo flux and gain stability. He must create "value-orientations" as compelling human *goals* that channel and sanction these orders and processes. Education, viewed in such a vista, becomes in turn the central means and central end of man's millennial search—both the way he sometimes expresses and the way he always should express his deepest nature as man.

APPENDIX

PHILOSOPHICAL ANTHROPOLOGY: THE EDUCATIONAL SIGNIFICANCE OF ERNST CASSIRER*

ERNST CASSIRER is a philosopher in the grand manner. His mind roams over the vast terrain of life and nature, encompassing not only the sweep of historical and contemporary experience, but constantly enriching its generalizations with particulars from the sciences, arts, and religions. He proves through his monumental achievements that, even in this most complex and fragmented of civilizations, it is still possible for a superlative intellect to take into consideration the world's infinite multiplicities and yet to weld them into a unified and dynamic outlook.

A brief sketch of his academic life may help to explain why Cassirer so successfully defies our age of super-specialization. Born in Germany in 1874, he was exposed as a young man to the vigorous movement called neo-Kantianism—a movement concerned to revitalize and extend the principles of the Continent's greatest eighteenth-century thinker, Immanuel Kant. As a student of the leading neo-Kantian, Hermann Cohen, Cassirer received his doctorate from Marburg University and at once embarked upon his long career as a productive writer and teacher successively at the Universities of Berlin and Hamburg in Germany, at Goeteborg in Sweden, and from 1941 to his death in 1945, at Yale and Columbia Universities in America. His intellectual roots, therefore, were deep in the traditions of thorough scholarship, and especially in the incredibly fertile soil of German philosophy and literature which, in scarcely more than a century, had produced not only Kant but such giants as Fichte, Schelling, Herder,

* Reprinted by permission of the *Harvard Educational Review,* Vol. 26, 1956. Pp. 207-232.

Hegel, Schopenhauer, and Goethe. Cassirer was both a student and master interpreter of these as well as other important European philosophers, scientists, and artists. In addition, his prodigious memory and capacity for sustained work, his years of first-hand immersion in the cultures of three countries, his suffering as a Jew (it was shortly after Hitler came to power that he left Germany)—these and other factors all contributed to the maturation of a philosophy which, as much as any other that the twentieth century has produced, is at once classical in form and content and continuously absorbed in the profound issues that so grimly beset our time.[1]

In a genuine sense, indeed, Cassirer's thought focuses directly upon the profoundest of these issues: What bases of unity may we discover in an age of conflict? We shall find his answer in his central and certainly most original thesis—namely, that man, no matter what his level of sophistication, is to be differentiated from all other animals as the creator and user of symbols. Through them man obtains not only an articulated world of science but a world of myth, art, religion, and of political and social life. Man knows himself through the various levels of symbolic forms which, though diverse, have their unity in being the unique function of man and in serving his needs.[2] Full recognition of this function is for Cassirer the task which, if accomplished, could serve to bridge the chasm now dividing men from one another because they do not perceive or appreciate sufficiently what they have in common.

It is a task which immediately challenges education as few others could. For, although Cassirer devotes suprisingly little attention to the theory or practice of education as such, yet no institution and no profession are clearly so strategically placed to make the symbolic life more meaningful and more productive of understanding and sympathy among peoples of different creeds, classes, nations, and cultures.

We may already see, then, why Cassirer likes to regard his own position as a "philosophical anthropology." Like the scientific anthropologist, he is concerned first of all with the study of man. Unlike him, however, he is not concerned merely with empirical research into man's cultural experience (though he recognizes and utilizes findings in the human sciences). Rather, his attention is directed to the still more basic problem of the universal premises upon which such research is properly conducted.

The question of whether these premises are entirely adequate will be postponed until we have had opportunity to consider the case for a "philosophical anthropology" grounded in the idea of man as the *animal symbolicum*. We anticipate only enough to say that any weakness discoverable is probably as much that of neo-Kantianism in general as of Cassirer in particular. For neo-Kantianism, with which he must still be associated after all his important amendments are accounted for, is a philosophy of man and the universe no longer sufficient to explain, or give guidance to, a culture-in-crisis such as our own. The educational implications that follow from this philosophy are likewise limited: that we may learn much of value for a reconstructed program of learning cannot be denied; but that we might learn more, given crucial modifications and replacements, cannot be denied either.

Meanwhile, the first step toward interpretation of Cassirer's constructive doctrine is to ask more precisely what is meant by the historic term, neo-Kantianism. For here is both his point of departure and, in a sense, his point of return. It illustrates how a philosophic position which at first seems to the non-philosopher aridly technical and academic may assume very practical significance in the hands of a seminal thinker.

As Cassirer himself points out,[3] neo-Kantianism emerged in Germany in the 1860's primarily as an effort to provide a philosophy of science as underpinning for an extraordinarily productive period in physics, biology, and related fields. The aim was to supplant the arbitrary and often idiosyncratic quality of philosophical systems by strictly impersonal, universal principles applicable to all sorts of scientific inquiry and law—an aim which Kant believed he had achieved particularly in his *Critique of Pure Reason,* but which his followers sought to restate in terms of highly important scientific developments that had occurred subsequently.

It is enough for our purpose to emphasize the central contention that runs through Cohen and other neo-Kantians: the universal principles of science are not derived primarily from some kind of separate and objective reality; they are constructed from and by the rational powers of man. They are conceptually prior to the contents and processes of the outside world, although they take tangible form and become meaningful only as they apply to these contents and processes.

The law of causality, for instance, is a form of understanding which conditions all natural events and is in this sense both subjective and objective. Mind is truly the supreme generator of science; it constantly relates in ever more inclusive ways such elements of experience as perceptions of color or feeling of force. To synthesize these particulars into a reasonable totality is the goal of science—a goal never to be fully achieved, yet one which ever beckons man's insatiable curiosity to know.[4]

And yet, despite its search for scientific universality, neo-Kantianism was torn by dispute among its adherents. The question of just how concrete and orderly are the specific materials given by external nature to man disturbed some of the more realistic, who felt that in Kant and in many of his followers there remained altogether too large a residue of traditional idealism—the doctrine that the world is essentially "ideal" or spiritual. Others tended (as do many positivists of our day) to rule out the entire area of values, contending that these are all very well as poetry or faith but not, strictly speaking, as relevant to that rational enterprise which is alone worthy of philosophy.

Cassirer takes his stand somewhere in the middle of these crosscurrents. Throughout his life he remained deeply interested in the philosophy of science; he kept abreast of the latest discoveries in physics and mathematics; and he wrote extensively on the theory of relativity as well as other revolutionary developments which seemed to him to strengthen, if anything, the Kantian approach to scientific order. He remained interested, likewise, in the question of the reality of objective experience. At the same time, he never rejected or subordinated the problem of values; on the contrary, he insisted that a correct understanding of Kant places ethics in the center rather than on the periphery—that the *Critique of Practical Judgment* (Kant's major work in ethics) is the fulcrum of his entire thought.[5] Cassirer himself, certainly, moves ever closer in his interest to the sphere of human conduct, a trend illustrated by the fact that his first major work was in the theory of knowledge, his last in political philosophy.[6] It is his last work, too, that epitomizes his own exciting refinements and elaborations of neo-Kantianism. Thus we are brought to a more careful examination of his theory of man as the symbol-making animal. For it is here, as we have said, that these refinements and elaborations become most indicative of Cassirer's contribution not only to general philosophy but to the problem of unity.

It is to be expected that *The Philosophy of Symbolic Forms*,[7] as his most definitive work is called, rests squarely upon neo-Kantian doctrine and hence harks back directly to Kant himself. Cassirer paraphrases Kant's position:

Experience, he says, . . . is not a simple fact; it is a compound of two opposite factors, of matter and form. The material factor is given in our sense perceptions; the formal factor is represented by our scientific concepts. These concepts . . . of pure understanding, give to the phenomena their synthetic unity.[8]

Symbols, according to this doctrine, are concepts expressed through language in such a way as to give common meaning to a number of facts in terms of their relations to one another. In this sense, symbols are indispensable to science—indeed, they are its primary tools. The task of science, one might say, is to symbolize nature as objectively and comprehensively as possible. Hence it is easy to understand why mathematics provides by far the most important of all types of scientific symbols, for not only are these devoid of personal or qualitative colorations; they are so general as to embrace all possible examples of similar concrete instances. In this respect, Plato was right in placing mathematics almost at the top of his hierarchy of knowledge.

But Plato was wrong, as most philosophers since have been wrong, in thinking that such abstract scientific symbolism is virtually the only kind worthy of civilized man's full respect or active concern. Kant, more than others up to this time, succeeded in showing that even scientific symbolism is merely verbal so long as it is devoid of the perceptual material with which it must interact in order to become meaningful.

Yet even Kant, no less than his followers, seemed to begin at the wrong end of the evolutionary scale. The fact is that man's symbolic capacity is by no means limited to, or necessarily typified by, his rational activity. Granting the tremendous importance of "pure reason," granting also that it is the highest single achievement of human nature, the portrait of man that has dominated the history of philosophy remains to an alarming extent a one-dimensional portrait. That many philosophers, including Plato, have recognized other sides to man's nature is, of course, true. But for most of them these other sides have been taken for granted, subordinated, or simply dismissed as "ignorance."

What is needed is a study of man that examines other dimensions of the symbolic life with the same care and same respect that have been accorded to rationality. Or, to state the need differently, neo-Kantianism has been much too circumscribed in its radius of concern. Without departing from its great contributions, the labor that must next be performed is to expand the circumference—to interpret man, the symbolic animal, as he functions on *every* plane of his existence— on the scientific, of course, but also on the esthetic, the religious, the mythical. For, on these planes, too, man symbolizes constantly, in fact more constantly, in the sense of much more widely and habitually. What can we learn of how and why he does so? The answer to this question should place us in a better position not only to enter into the spirit of different cultures than our own so-called scientific culture, but to discover ways for theirs to enter into ours. And, in the process, perhaps we shall find that ours, too, is not quite accurately named!

A few sentences from Cassirer sound his theme succinctly:

... in the human world we find a new characteristic which appears to be the distinctive mark of human life. The functional circle of man is not only quantitatively enlarged; it has also undergone a qualitative change. Man has, as it were, discovered a new method of adapting himself to his environment. Between the receptor system and the effector system, which are to be found in all animal species, we find in man a third link which we may describe as the *symbolic system*. This new acquisition transforms the whole of human life. As compared with the other animals man lives not merely in a broader reality; he lives so to speak, in a new *dimension* of reality. There is an unmistakable difference between organic reactions and human responses. In the first case a direct and immediate answer is given to an outward stimulus; in the second case the answer is delayed. It is interrupted and retarded by a slow and complicated process of thought.[9]

And again:

What distinguishes . . . [human responses] from animal reactions is their *symbolic* character. In the rise and growth of human culture we can follow step by step this fundamental change of meaning. Man has discovered a new mode of expression: symbolic expression. This is the common denominator in all his cultural activities: in myth and poetry, in language, in art, in religion, and in science.[10]

If, then, symbolism is indigenous to man always and everywhere, it is indigenous to primitive as well as to civilized man. Instead of disregarding the former, one must approach him with no less care than the latter. And yet, says Cassirer, when we come to explore the theories and evidence of social philosophers and anthropologists we find a welter of conflicting hypotheses about primitive symbolism, many of which imply a kind of pseudo-Platonic dualism: for them, such symbolism is simply pre-scientific and hence totally beyond the scope of serious philosophic consideration.

But Cassirer rejects this easy separation. For him symbolism develops in an evolutionary continuum, and each form is appropriate to its own conditions. Primitive man acts as he does because he has need to do so, and the symbols he fashions are always functional to his own effort to survive and fulfill his interests. Even while he is thinking and acting in mythical ways, moreover, he is already forging the instruments and logic of science. It is incorrect to suppose that he is always purely one thing or the other. In building utensils or boats, in trapping animals or tilling fields, he frequently utilizes crude but nonetheless esentially similar methods to those of more advanced cultures.

This is not to argue, of course, that myth and science are one. What connects them is their symbolic character, but the differences between them remain fundamental. Mythical thinking, in fact, becomes necessary precisely because, in primitive society, man has not yet learned how to meet many of his problems logically. And when we inquire what this different way is we find that the mythical symbol is typified by its emotional glow, by both its concentration upon particular images and its overflowing into others, by its fluidity and mutability, and by its identification with the object or objects it symbolizes. Above all,

The world of myth is a dramatic world—a world of actions, of forces, of conflicting powers. . . . Mythical perception is always impregnated with these emotional qualities. Whatever is seen or felt is surrounded by a special atmosphere—an atmosphere of joy or grief, of anguish, of excitement, of exultation or depression. . . . All objects are benignant or malignant,   friendly or inimical, familiar or uncanny, alluring and fascinating or repellent and threatening.[11]

The fearful, monster-like shape of a bush in the moonlight becomes a real monster because it feels so to the observer's imagination, and simultaneously elicits an image and sooner or later a name appropriate to its appearance. In more technical terms, it follows that primitive man *hypostatizes* his symbols—that is, he attributes objectivity to them. The mythical symbol is not consciously recognized by its user *as* a symbol; rather, it is a reality in and of itself, and possesses a power of its own. Nevertheless it marks the beginning of man's distinctive role in the history of nature—a role without which others of a more sophisticated kind could not have been successively played.

The importance of this theory is such that it is worthwhile to consider several provocative corollaries.

One is that, for Cassirer, myth and language evolve together. Man does not begin with the outside world of things to which he then attaches names. This is the classical explanation, but a false one. He begins with his capacity to react emotionally to the immediate experiences of his environment. Objects of those experiences become focal points of primitive man's concentration when they arouse his attention because of their direct bearing upon his actions and purposes. The moment at which primitive man's emotion in the presence of an object generates in him an awareness that it is an object, at this moment it takes on "meaning" for him—a meaning that is at once mythical and verbal. The bush in the moonlight is objectified as a demon, and when it acquires a name this is likewise objectified because identical with the demon itself. Mythical image and verbal symbol emerge reciprocally; one does not regularly precede the other. The main point, in any case, is that "As soon as the spark has jumped across" from the individual's feelings to the thing or event, ". . . a sort of turning point has occurred in human mentality: the inner excitement which was a mere subjective state has vanished, and has been resolved into the objective form of myth or of speech."[12]

The significance of this "turning point" is, of course, that primitive man now possesses an image which he can and does learn to attach to other things and events that resemble the original. His remarkable capacity to retain a symbol once used enables him gradually to draw it forth from memory and apply it to similar experiences—for example, to name the same god for several functions of comparable importance to him. "What the mind has once created, what has been culled from the total sphere of consciousness, does not fade away again when the spoken word has set its seal upon it and given it definite form."[13] The ground is broken for the germination of logical and scientific symbolism.

A second corollary of Cassirer's theory of language and myth, and likewise one of importance to the understanding not only of primitive but of civilized man, is his interpretation of magic. The magic of symbols derives from belief in their objectivity—in their hypostatic power to cast a spell through their mere utterance, for example. This belief has at least two fruitful consequences. In the first place, the performance of magic gives to primitive man a feeling of his power over nature, of his ability to control rather than merely to bow helplessly before it. In the second place, magic induces a sense of unity with nature: although the magic symbol concentrates upon and is identified with a particular object, yet the latter is never dissevered from other objects, any more than a word is dissevered from the thing it symbolizes. "Sympathetic magic" means for Cassirer sympathy with the whole of events and things encompassed by primitive experience:

. . . man would not think of coming into a magical contact with nature if he had not the conviction that there is a common bond that unites all things—that the separation between himself and nature and between the different kinds of natural objects is, after all, an artificial, not a real one.[14]

A third corollary is the relation of myth to religion. It is to be expected that, in keeping with Cassirer's developmental theory of man, no hard-and-fast line divides these two spheres. The fact is that

. . . mythical and religious thought . . . originate in the same fundamental phenomena of human life. In the development of human culture we cannot fix a point where myth ends or religion begins. In the whole course of its history religion remains indissolubly connected and penetrated with mythical elements. . . . Myth is from its very beginning potential religion.[15]

Cassirer finds the key to religion, no matter what its level of sophistication, in language—especially in the power noted above by which word magic provides man with a sense of pervasive solidarity between himself and his world. Such words as "mana," common to many primitive cultures, are almost impossible to translate because of the complex connotations that civilized languages carry with them. It conveys a vague feeling of the "holy" as against the "profane" or tabooed objects of nature—a mysterious force almost anonymous in character. As man acquires more differentiated functions (tool-making, say), this original nebulosity is superseded by greater definiteness:

It was in fact the division of labor that introduced a new era of religious thought. Long before the appearance of the personal gods we meet with those gods that have been called functional gods. They are not as yet the personal gods of Greek religion. . . . On the other hand they no longer have the vagueness of the primitive mythical conceptions. They are concrete beings; but they are concrete in their actions, not in their personal appearance or existence. They have . . . adjectival names that characterize their special function or activity.[16]

A still higher religious stage is reached when symbols acquire a more general and at the same time more ethical meaning—a process that parallels gradual awareness of the "I" and that finally relates the idea of a supreme or universal Being with the idea of Person or Self. But even here—the stage of monotheism proper—the primitive origin of religion is retained by language. The indefiniteness of mythical religion is supplanted by the generality of sophisticated religion, but language moves in "the middle kingdom between" them:

. . . there are, in the realm of mythic and religious conception, "ineffables" of different order, one of which represents the lower limit of verbal expression, the other the upper limit; but between these bounds, which are drawn by the very nature of verbal expression, language can move with perfect freedom, and exhibit all the wealth and concrete exemplification of its creative power.[17]

The mythical end of the religious spectrum continues to hypostatize its images; the religious end is consciously aware of their symbolic character. (Compare here the naive with the philosophically trained Roman Catholic.) But language is common to both.

The fourth and last corollary we shall note is the esthetic theory that emerges from Cassirer's premises. Art is, of course, a whole species of symbolism. Its language may be verbal, but it may just as well be pictorial, musical, or otherwise expressive of man's creative drive. As in the field of science, Cassirer is at home in the theory and practice of art. And, again as in that field, he rejects the historic view that the human being as artist copies and organizes particular segments of a pre-existent reality. In both science and art, rather, man is the generator not the imitator of nature's forms. The artist differs radically from the scientist, not in his capacity to symbolize, but in the fact that his symbols, while possessing universality of rhythm, pattern, and design, are at the same time filled with the specific and fluid colors, tones, and feelings that he himself perceives in his communion with life. We recall that scientific symbols, on the contrary, are wholly objective, general, and dispassionate. It is here, indeed, that the esthetic level is found to rest squarely on the mythical: in the latter, too, it is the immediate, emotional, mutable character of symbols that distinguishes them most clearly from those of logical or discursive reason.

This is not to say that myth and art are any more identical than are science and art. Mythical experience is typically more conservative, more past-centered, than art: "every great artist in a certain sense makes a new epoch."[18] Still more crucially, the artist unlike the primitive man does not hypostatize his symbols: both actor and audience know that the scene on the stage is not reality, both painter and beholder know that the portrait is not the living person. Yet dramas and paintings have the power to project themselves passionately and imaginatively beyond their media. In short, art may be regarded as intermediate between (though not therefore either "superior" or "inferior" to) science and myth: with science, it seeks to express the universal forms of life and nature as truly and objectively as possible; with myth, it enfuses them with individuality and warmth. But because it accomplishes both ends, it is itself therefore neither. In the sense that art possesses its own character, it is indeed autonomous.

Much more needs to be added before one could claim to have conveyed anything like a complete review of Cassirer's principal ideas. Our purpose, however, has been the more modest one of providing a broad setting within which to select a few implications for educational theory and practice.

The most inclusive of these implications should already be apparent: the effort to find a basis of functional unity for all human experience. If Cassirer is right, invidious distinctions between men and therefore cultures are no longer tenable. To be sure, symbolism, as this basis of functional unity, varies according to the several phases of man's life. But each is appropriate to its own phase. Each, moreover, is clearly appreciated not only as we enter vicariously into its own special manner of expression, but as we view it in the perspective of other phases. The philosophy of symbolic forms is, in this sense, also one of "cultural perspectivism"—a philosophy lending additional support to the growing demand of far-sighted educators for a program of studies that acquaints learners of all ages with the plurality of primitive and civilized cultures of the earth by seeing and feeling them "from the inside." In Cassirer's terms, such a program would extend far beyond the too widely prevailing romantic, "folk-lore" approach that sentimentalizes and superficializes but fails to appreciate fundamentally either institutions and customs or practices and beliefs. If it is to be effective at all, education must come to terms with the underlying motivations, methods, and goals of cultures— with the specific ways that they interpret themselves in relation to the world around them. Above all, it must constantly stress the *continuity* of cultures, the emerging and unfinished evolution of religious, esthetic, scientific symbolism from the mythical. Human life is, truly, a unified *becoming*.

It follows that man can be understood only as we observe him in the work of living. Cassirer therefore rejects any "metaphysical" conception of man and his behavior—that is to say, any interpretation that fits man into an absolute, pre-established system of reality and that requires him to shape himself primarily into a kind of mental facsimile of that reality. On the contrary, it will be recalled that for Cassirer mythical symbolism, for example, is the agent of interest and need, one of the earlier stages of religion being characterized by "functional gods" symbolic of the several practical activities of primitive man. Here a close affinity is revealed to the experimentalist orientation, even to the extent of occasional support from the writings of John Dewey.[19] Such a statement as this is, however, characteristically Cassirer's:

The philosophy of symbolic forms starts from the presupposition that, if there is any definition of the nature or "essence" of man, this definition can only be understood as a functional one, not a substantial one. We cannot define man by any inherent principle which constitutes his meta-physical essence. . . . Man's outstanding characteristic, his distinguishing mark, is not his metaphysical or physical nature—but his work. It is this work, it is the system of human activities, which defines and determines the circle of "humanity".[20]

That such a viewpoint is significant for education is obvious to any one even mildly familiar with the pragmatic-experimentalist approach, in general, or of the movement often called progressivism, in particular. Not only does it provide a guide to the learning process as centered in the present experience of active living rather than of passive contemplation; in terms of Cassirer's special interest, it points the way to radical changes in the school's utilization of such tools or disciplines as language, history, art, and science. Let us consider each in turn.

Cassirer is insistent that "the true unity of language . . . cannot be a substantial one; it must rather be defined as a functional unity."[21] Actually, languages differ extremely, depending upon the "productive and constructive"—not the "reproductive"—task they perform in their respective environments.[22] For it must always be remembered that names "are not designed to refer to substantial things, independent entities which exist by themselves. They are determined rather by human interests and human purposes" that constantly change.[23] "Whatever appears important for our wishing and willing, our hope and our anxiety, for acting and doing: that and only that receives the stamp of verbal 'meaning'."[24] True, the earliest languages are mythical rather than logical; but their source and expression are no less important to those who invent and operate with them. Since, with certain qualifications to be noted later, Cassirer is close to the functional school of semantics, it is reasonable to infer that he would oppose in this context the mental-discipline, formalized type of language instruction that still prevails in secondary and college curriculums. Because language is flexible, because grammars vary widely with different cultures, he would insist rather that language be utilized as a priceless instrument by which men may more effectively interpret and communicate in the on-going process of sharing their experience.

History, likewise, is a kind of semantics. Properly conceived, it is not a photographic copy of the past but a way of constantly revising the past by means of symbols in the hands of present historians. The past which the historian pictures for us can never be merely one of data given to the senses, for the past strictly speaking is gone forever. It must be one he conveys through images, especially images conjured up by words. "In history the interpretation of symbols precedes the collection of facts, and without this interpretation there is no approach to historical truth."[25] And again, in language similar to Dewey's: ". . . the true criterion does not consist in the value of facts but in their practical consequences. A fact becomes historically relevant if it is pregnant with consequences."[26]

Thus, for the same reason that Cassirer would tend to oppose the sterile teaching of languages on the basis of a conventional object-mind, stimulus-response psychology, he would surely oppose the teaching of history as a kind of mind-stuffing of by-gone dates, names, or events. Both are equally inimical to the excitement of virile learning. Both place the mind in the position of spectator rather than actor in the drama of culture and history.

But Cassirer is careful to insist that, although history is equally creative, it is not identical with art. Unlike the latter, history does not freely and pliably shape the forms of nature and man without cautious regard for objective evidence. "It does not go beyond the empirical reality of things and events but molds this reality into a new shape, giving it the ideality of recollection. Life in the light of history remains a great realistic drama, with all its tensions and conflicts . . . its display of energy and passions."[27] While we may assume, therefore, that a school governed by Cassirer's philosophy would provide ample time for art—not as imitation of nature but as the audacious effort to discover new patterns and rhythms through the play of imagination—we may likewise assume that such a school would give scrupulous attention to the canons of exact research in areas like history.

But it is in science that this attention would be most sustained. Here, at the apex of his thought, Cassirer's early motivation as a neo-Kantian receives reaffirmation. "Science," he declares, "is the last step in man's mental development . . . the highest and most characteristic attainment of human culture."[28] As such, it equally challenges education to revise its methods and assumptions, and in at least two important ways.

First, because science goes *to* nature (it never waits *for* nature), the frame of reference through which it is taught should always be as the supreme means of rationally organizing the forces of the universe, animate and inanimate alike. As with language, history, and art, science then is reconstructive rather than merely reproductive of those forces. Like them, also, it stems originally from the needs, interests, and goals of real human beings. To teach science in this perspective is to teach it as an adventure of the spirit—an adventure fraught with disappointments and dangers but also one of magnificent promise and achievements.

Second, and here we return to Cassirer's study of myth, science becomes important to education not merely for what it is but for what it is not. We have seen that, like all other inventions of civilized man, its ancestry lies deep in primitive culture, its bond of kinship being the symbol. We have seen, too, that mythical symbols are typified by certain attributes—by their emotion, for example, and by the habit of primitive minds to hypostatize them as objective things. Cassirer points out that scientific thought replaces mythical thought just in so far as its symbols exclude such attributes. With the coming of science,

The magic function of the word was eclipsed and replaced by its semantic function. The word is no longer endowed with mysterious powers; it no longer has an immediate physical or supernatural influence. It cannot change the nature of things and it cannot compel the will of gods or demons. Nevertheless it is neither meaningless nor powerless. . . . Physically the word may be declared to be impotent, but logically it is elevated to a higher, indeed to the highest rank.[29]

Of course the transition from magic to science is anything but instantaneous. The Pythagorean mathematics of Ancient Greece, to take an instance, possessed an objective and mysteriously potent reality of its own—a reality projected from the fears and hopes of a culture on the threshold of that emotionless and abstract utilization of number as pure concepts without which modern physics and chemistry could not have been born. Yet even today the mythical way of hypostatizing numbers is far from obliterated: witness the widespread practice of "numerology" not only by the "uneducated" but by people in positions of wide influence.

Still more pervasively, a major characteristic of mythical thinking reminds us of Whitehead's "fallacy of misplaced concreteness" with its primitive habit of regarding scientific classifications (say, in biology) as structures fixed in the universe itself, rather than as modifiable instruments of scientific ordering. The habit of objectifying symbols, which originates in this primitive habit, may at a much more sophisticated stage even produce entire systems of philosophy—as in the Thomist system where a Supreme Being rather than man becomes the final hypostatizer of symbols; or as in the Marxian system of dialectical materialism with its special brand of absolute, predetermined history and nature. Educationally, too, the implication is far-reaching: since schools always reflect in greater or lesser degree the beliefs and rituals of the cultures they serve, they are bound also to reflect mythical as well as scientific methods of thought so far as both continue to prevail. Superstition is by no means absent from all classrooms, nor is the fallacy of misplaced concreteness missing from all science curriculums. It is sufficient to recall the enormous influence of dialectical materialism in the schools of Iron Curtain countries; the ponderous weight of Thomism upon parochial education in many other countries; or the subtle indoctrination by innumerable public schools of the democracies in their common "essentialist" belief that the symbols of science are realities already eternally there in the universe to be accepted and obeyed with not less reverence than the laws of God.

One further implication for educational theory and practice deserves more extended attention: Cassirer's treatment of "the myth of the state."[30] Not only does it throw the spotlight of his philosophy directly upon the most menacing of all contemporary disunities—the social-political—but it reveals perhaps more clearly than any other aspect the therapeutic value of his diagnosis and treatment in a practical situation. We have said that, according to Cassirer, Kant's deepest concern even before he wrote much about it was the ethical problem. One might well argue that this is equally Cassirer's. Certainly in his last years, when Hitlerism threatened to shatter his career, he realized from poignant personal experience that totalitarianism jeopardizes the good life as has no other political phenomenon of the modern era.

Characteristically it is by the historical route that he approaches the meaning of totalitarianism. He wishes first to show how a rational—

i.e., a non-mythical—theory of the state slowly emerged from primitive culture. In the latter, man identifies himself so completely with the whole of nature and society that political concepts do not consciously occur to him at all: in the degree that one can even speak of the "state," it becomes like all symbols a reality with which he is indissolubly fused. With Greek philosophy, however, logical analysis of political experience begins in Western civilization—its highest expression being, of course, Plato's *Republic*. In Cassirer's view, Plato clearly distinguishes between mythical and rational thought, a fact supported by the use of the myth in his dialogues to illustrate a conceptual argument through allegory. But as Cassirer continues his historical treatment, it becomes evident, whether he wholly intends it or not, that Platonic theory is by no means devoid of its own kind of primitivism. Not only does it provide a system of hypostatized concepts (the realm of absolute Ideas): through its incorporation by the Aristotelian and, much later, medieval systems it finally grounds its poetic symbols in a vast system of metaphysics the political corollary of which is theocratic absolutism. In modern philosophy, too, Cassirer's review of the evidence shows that the effort to wrest rational political thought from age-old habits of mythology is seldom entirely victorious. Machiavelli is chosen as the thinker who makes perhaps the greatest progress in the Renaissance, but he also provides a mysterious Fortune to guide reality and to limit man's efficacy. In the Enlightenment, for which Cassirer has unbounded admiration,[31] success is highest through such thinkers as Voltaire, Condorcet, Rousseau, Jefferson, and, of course, Kant. Even in them, to be sure, mythical factors are sometimes implicit if not explicit. But here for the first time the principle is clearly enunciated that states must be conceived primarily as agents of conscious, public deliberation and consent.

Still the struggle is far from won. In the eighteenth and nineteenth centuries, a resurgence of the mythical motif is foreshadowed in the tendency of the romantic movement to give priority to feeling over intellect. And with Carlyle, Hegel, and Gobineau, political mythology is not only supported but glorified by some of the most influential minds of the time. Carlyle's doctrine of hero-worship, while not to be identified with current totalitarianism, nevertheless emphasizes some of the same qualities: like fascism, it is more concerned with the "intuition" than with the intelligence of great leaders; like communism (though, unfortunately, Cassirer himself almost totally disregards Marxian theory and practice), Carlyle stresses the deductive structure of history with its inner core of absolute moral purpose. Hegel, of course, carries this latter stress much farther by providing not only a metaphysical apologia for the Prussian state, but some of the most influential premises (though not identical ones) for both the philosophy of fascism, on the right, and of communism, on the left. To be sure, the conclusion of Hegel's philosophy is not apparently consistent with its original intent. Says Cassirer:

> Hegel's logic and philosophy seemed to be the triumph of the rational. The only thought which philosophy brings with it is the simple conception of Reason. . . . But it was the tragic fate of Hegel that he unconsciously unchained the most irrational powers that have ever appeared in man's social and political life. No other philosophical system has done so much for the preparation of fascism and imperialism as Hegel's doctrine of the state. . . .[32]

In Gobineau, finally, hero-worship and state-worship become less important than race-worship. For him, "race" is an objective entity rather that a pliable tool of scientific classification. Also, it typifies the mythical propensity to ignore evidence whenever this fails to fit its own preconceptions. Thus the argument that the "white race" is superior to the "black race" has no scientific support; but this is no more relevant to one who, like Gobineau, denies the sciences of man than it is to the astrologer who denies the science of the stars.

Cassirer punctuates his historical analysis by deepening the psychological roots of mythical behavior. We have noted that, in primitive man, emotion infiltrates every segment of language and myth. But this fact is by no means limited only to primitive man; rather, it is more or less typical at all times and of all men. Cassirer goes so far as to cite approvingly the James-Lange theory which locates the fountainhead of emotion in bodily reaction rather than in some esoteric psychical equipment. Again, while he frowns upon what he considers to be the oversimplified hypothesis of Freud, nevertheless he admits the great contribution of Freudian psychoanalytic theory: its delineation of the "unconscious" in shaping conscious behavior. Indeed, Suzanne Langer, a competent interpreter of Cassirer, has even suggested that

. . . the "dream work" of Freud's "unconscious" mental mechanism is almost exactly the "mythic mode" which Cassirer describes as the primitive form of ideation, wherein an intense feeling is spontaneously expressed in a symbol, an image seen in something or formed for the mind's eye by the excited imagination. Such expression is effortless and therefore unexhausting; its products are images charged with meanings, but the meanings remain implicit, so that the emotions they command seem to be centered on the image rather than on anything it merely conveys; in the image, which may be a vision, a gesture, a sound-form (musical image) or a word as readily as an external object, many meanings may be concentrated, many ideas telescoped and interfused, and incompatible emotions simultaneously expressed.[33]

Now it is this "primitive form of ideation" analyzed in different terms by both Freud and Cassirer that offers a clue to the psychopathology of totalitarianism. Indeed, we find that even the most sophisticated of thinkers may support and at the same time make more difficult of exposure and refutation its mythical character. Of the three precursors cited above, none, to be sure, is a full-fledged advocate. Gobineau is closest in his emotionalized and unscientific objectification of "race." But even in Hegel, the word images he invents are alchemized into metaphysical realities which, in turn, become charged with the consuming nationalisms and burning patriotisms even more chronic to twentieth-century political movements than to his own time.

For these movements are only the culminations of age-old habits which the symbolic animal, man, has never succeeded in conquering. What the cultural psychiatrist, Erich Fromm, has called an "escape from freedom" becomes for the cultural philosopher, Ernst Cassirer, an escape from rationality—the primitive practice of allowing emotion to dominate logical thought, of objectifying and even worshipping symbols as realities, of substituting magical for scientific methods of control. Cassirer puts the matter forthrightly:

Freedom is not a natural inheritance of man. In order to possess it we have to create it. If man were simply to follow his natural instincts he would not strive for freedom; he would rather choose dependence. Obviously it is much easier to depend upon others than to think, to judge, and to decide for himself. That accounts for the fact that both in individual and in political life freedom is so often regarded much more as a burden than a privilege. Under extremely difficult conditions man tries to cast off this burden. Here the totalitarian state and the political myths step in. The new political parties promise, at least, an escape from the dilemma. They suppress and destroy the very sense of freedom; but, at the same time, they relieve men from all personal responsibility.[34]

As does Fromm, Cassirer points out that this regression is most likely to occur in periods of confusion and instability when more reasonable methods of solving social problems seem to have failed. Just as primitive man utilizes a crude scientific technique in coping with ordinary obstacles, but resorts to magic when the unexpected confronts him, so "In desperate situations man will always have recourse to desperate means—and our present-day political myths have been such desperate means. If reason has failed us, there remains always the . . . power of the miraculous and mysterious."[35] In politics, especially,

. . . we are always living on volcanic soil. We must be prepared for abrupt convulsions and eruptions. In all critical moments of man's social life, the rational forces that resist the rise of the old mythical conceptions are no longer sure of themselves. In these moments the time for myth has come again. For myth has not been really vanquished and subjugated. It is always there, lurking in the dark and waiting for its hour and opportunity. This hour comes as soon as the other binding forces of man's social life, for one reason or another, lose their strength and are no longer able to combat the demonic mythical powers. . . . [For] if modern man no longer believes in a natural magic, he has by no means given up the belief in a sort of "social magic."[36]

It is here that Cassirer would be most likely to urge education to assume a new and heavy responsibility. "We should carefully study," he says, "the origin, the structure, the methods, and the technique of the political myths. We should see the adversary face to face in order to know how to combat him."[37] If, in the democracies at least, education is broadly and rightly conceived as the supreme agency of man's intelligent and uncoerced determination of public policy and program, then it has the solemn duty both to strengthen that determination and to expose the primitive propensity that ever tempts him to yield his freedom to powers that he believes to be greater than himself.

What are some of the necessary steps that must be taken by education if American and other democracies, faced in time of crisis by this choice of alternatives, are not to choose the mythical way?

On the negative side, Cassirer would surely answer, first of all, that schools must sensitize citizens to the dangerous allurements that lie concealed behind mythical symbolism when it is used for ulterior political ends. To take an important case: the deification of leadership, after the manner of Carlyle, and now after the manner of a Hitler or Stalin, must be exposed as simply one manifestation of the unconscious wish to escape from freedom. Just as some individuals cannot grow up because of the consuming attraction of a father-image or mother-image, so a society may react in infantile ways to the image of a leader:

This call for leadership only appears when a collective desire has reached an overwhelming strength and when, on the other hand, all hopes of fulfilling this desire, in an ordinary and normal way, have failed. At these times the desire is not only keenly felt but also personified. It stands before the eyes of man in a concrete, plastic, and individual shape. . . . The former social bonds—law, justice, and constitutions—are declared to be without any value. What alone remains is the mystical power and authority of the leader and the leader's will is supreme law.[38]

Obviously very similar projections occur when "race" or "state" is deified. And both are equally destructive of democratic, persuasive methods of social control.

Another danger in mythical thinking which education has the obligation to reveal is the way words may be manipulated by political groups for the purpose of paralyzing the rational capacities of masses of people. Actually, all of the commonest techniques of professional propagandists are designed to stir emotion rather than to encourage logical judgment—name-calling, for example. Use of words like "communist" for the purpose of damaging a person's reputation becomes, in Cassirer's sense, a diabolical device for arousing blindly hateful reactions instead of reasoned ones—reactions typically primitive in their play upon fear, in their failure to discriminate wholes from parts, and in their inability to perceive that individuals are not necessarily communists because certain of their beliefs (racial equality, say) happen to link with those of communists. Closely related to name-calling is the stereotyping process by which an individual Negro or Jew—or college professor!—is rubber-stamped with a set of common attributes solely because he belongs to a certain racial or cultural group. Here again the fallacy is due to inadequate distinction between wholes and parts—the logical fallacy resulting from failure to note, as Alfred Korzybski might put it, the "et ceteras" that must be explicated before any individual can be characterized fairly. Both of these fallacies illustrate, in turn, what Cassirer calls "semantic magic"—the "art" of producing a response by the emotive power of words which do not actually disclose anything like the real thing or event they are supposed to symbolize. In so far as they become substitutes for that thing or event they take on the illusory character of hypostatic symbols—a discovery that Hitler made in *Mein Kampf* and later applied with such tragic results in effecting a kind of mass hypnosis over his millions of followers.

The educational obligation to counteract such "semantic magic" is made vastly more difficult by the ingenious and novel engines of public opinion constructed in recent years. Even in the brief time since Cassirer's death another such engine—television—has made giant advances in its drive upon the homes of countless impressionable children and parents alike. Cassirer's warning thus becomes still more ominous today than at the moment of its utterance in 1945:

Myth has always been described as the result of an unconscious activity and as a free product of imagination. But here we find myth made according to plan. The new political myths do not grow up freely; they are not wild fruits of an exuberant imagination. They are artificial things fabricated by very skilful and cunning artisans. It has been reserved for the twentieth century, our own great technical age, to develop a new technique of myth. Henceforth myths can be manufactured in the same sense and according to the same methods as any other modern weapon—as machine guns or airplanes. That is a new thing—and a thing of crucial importance. It has changed the whole form of our social life.[39]

But education has the task of providing a positive as well as negative approach to the problem. This can only be, as already indicated, the development of a program of learning based upon a philosophy of scientific and esthetic symbolism—a philosophy that is cognizant of the imperative role of myth in primitive cultures, but that at the same time squarely confronts the dire consequences that must follow from the domination of mythical symbolism in an age of technology. Yet Cassirer is not pessimistic about the possibilities. He warns us, but he does not doom us. Rather, he sees in "the tensions and frictions, the strong contrasts and deep conflicts between the various powers of man" a healthful and natural energy which in the long run "may be described as the process of man's progressive self-liberation."[40]

The preceding quotation provides a stepping-stone to the brief critique with which we shall close our interpretation. With all the fruitfulness and even occasional tough-mindedness of his cultural and political analysis, Cassirer appears in long range as a direct descendant of the Enlightenment—as one whose faith therefore rests ultimately in the polite virtues of a cultivated and rational civilization. The sharpest question to be raised does not, however, stem from lack of admiration for such a faith. Indeed, the irrationality and ruthlessness of twentieth-century fanaticisms have spread so swiftly across the earth that we may be thankful for so able a critic of their deeper import. The question, rather, is whether Cassirer builds a sufficiently sturdy foundation upon which man may achieve and expand the rational life as abundantly as possible. We select three reasons for doubt.

1. Despite Cassirer's insistence that only through cultural evolution can we hope to understand man, one fails nevertheless to find in most of his writings anything except the most incidental and casual consideration of the economic, sociological, or other institutional forces that impinge upon those very philosophical, esthetic, religious, and scientific symbols with which he is most concerned.

Consider his study of the Enlightenment. This brilliant history almost entirely ignores the revolutionary transformations heralded by the rise of a new and dynamic system of production with its supporting attitudes and practices. True, Cassirer does not pretend to be an economic or social historian; he is a historian of ideas. True, also, he is convincing in his insistence that the genesis of a concept is not necessarily the index to its meaning. Yet, in keeping with his equal insistence that the relations of phenomena are, like the relations of symbolic levels, requisite to any adequate philosophy of nature and man, one would expect him to be much more attentive to the legitimate and crucial problem of the extent to which, say, economic relations condition the meaning of particular concepts in the philosophy of a Rousseau, a Hegel, or a Diderot.

Cassirer's treatment of freedom illustrates our concern. Notwithstanding the fact that freedom as "self-liberation"—so central to the Enlightenment—may be called the core of his entire thought, nowhere does he inquire in any detail how freedom is variously defined according to the specific cultural configurations within which it operates at specific times. He does not show us how the freedom that John Locke could so persuasively advocate for the England of his age is by no means synonymous with the kind advocated for the same England over a century later by John Stuart Mill, or still later by Harold J. Laski. These kinds of freedom may all be regarded as "rational" enough—that is to say, they are not mythical but logical concepts. Yet each differs in meaning from the others. And it does so not merely because of changes in symbolic function but also because of changes in the milieu of social relations which, in turn, condition that function.

The question we raise here is shared by others. John Herman Randall, Jr., is one who finds in Cassirer a "humanistic" conception of history structured around great intellectual personalities while almost totally ignoring the problem of historical causation. "There is, in fact, no place in Cassirer's discussion where it would be fitting even to raise the problem of a possible influence of technological or economic factors in determining the issues which confront thinkers."[41] Again, David Bidney, whose analysis of Cassirer's "culturology" is perhaps the most thorough to be found in the English language, concludes that the main tenets are so completely faithful to "the higher rationality of humanity" that they overlook "the serious practical problems of cultural conflict and disunity." In last analysis, Cassirer's is a "spiritual anthropology" that "failed to reckon realistically with the power of the objects to which the symbols referred"[42]—objects which, for us, become peculiarly trenchant in the form of political, economic, social, educational institutions and practices engaged variously in the struggle for power and the satisfaction of human wants.

2. A closely related question arises from Cassirer's interpretation of symbols as instruments of interest and work, rather than as verbal copies of antecedent realities. We have seen how, especially in numerous later passages, he sounds very close to Dewey and the pragmatic school in this interpretation. The difficulty here, accordingly, is not so much due to what Cassirer actually says as from what he does not say sufficiently—that is, from a failure to spell out to the limit the be-

havioral mechanisms by which language operates as a means of human expression and control.

More precisely, it may be argued that Cassirer, with all the admiration felt for him by social scientists of the stature of Kurt Lewin,[43] has not given us a completed theory of the development of language through the social interactions of man with man or group with group. Closer acquaintance with the social philosophy of George Herbert Mead, for example, might have helped him to see that symbolism develops simultaneously with the development of selfhood—that it is primarily a device by which gradually the self becomes aware of himself as he becomes aware of other selves, and of their responses to his gestures as well as of his to theirs. A social and evolutionary hypothesis of this sort would not necessarily prove incompatible with most of Cassirer's chief assumptions. It would, however, carry further the functional emphasis already present by denying any cleavage between individual and individual, between primitive and civilized man, or between child and adult—a cleavage that Cassirer, almost despite himself, seems often to deepen rather than to bridge in his insistence upon the spiritual subjectivity of symbols as these refer to concepts rather than to objects of behavior.[44]

3. Both of the above difficulties may be said to stem from and return to a third: Cassirer's neo-Kantian premise that man possesses the faculty of creating spiritual forms which are autonomous—that is, self-generated and self-sufficient. Once this premise governs a point of view, it is unnecessary and even inconsistent to argue either that such cultural forces as economic relations deeply affect man's symbolic life, or that language is a socio-behavioral device to facilitate interaction between one's self, other selves, and nature. Recalling again that Cassirer widens the Kantian boundaries to include not merely the forms of reason but of myth, art, and religion, and that the functional theory of symbols is developed a considerable way, we are forced nonetheless to conclude that he does not reach far enough. He is, as it were, so securely caught in the meshes of his own tradition that he cannot escape, however valiantly he tries at moments to do so.

One consequence is that Cassirer leaves largely unsolved the identical problem he inherited from Kant: *Which* values are we to select as the gauge of the good as against the bad in cultural experience? Kant's answer, that value is an entirely formal canon of "practical reason," is unsatisfactory because it can never be tested empirically: it is left, so to speak, suspended in mid-air as a pure but arid abstraction. To be sure, Cassirer goes much further than Kant, by tracing the development of all symbols, including therefore values, from primitive life. Even here, however, a certain ambiguity remains. We have seen how frequently he leaves the impression that mythical symbols are no less bad or good than logical symbols; they are just as appropriate to certain levels of man's existence as others are of different levels. Yet, in his philosophy of politics he is vehement in condemning the emotional, irrational, magical quality of mythical symbols and of the primitive mentality that utilizes them. In the one mood, he seems to appreciate impartially the values maintained by all types of culture; in the other, he is partial to the values of which he himself is heir—the values of the Enlightenment. Such partiality is, however, paradoxical in that it also bequeaths to us the kind of impartiality that attaches to the dispassionateness and neutrality of rational forms without commitment to the values of any definite type of cultural order or purpose. Here the problem returns once more to Kant: How can we choose among values when, in order to choose, we must "contaminate" their formal purity by bringing them to bear upon the concrete issues of past, present, and future experience? Without an answer to this question, we are left with little upon which to compare the worth of different cultures of the civilized world, other than their claim to be rational—a claim which, even if granted, scarcely warrants equal approval of all of them. Yet, without a clear answer, we may doubt whether the needed formulation of definite ethical goals can hope to succeed.

Such definite ethical goals are so urgently demanded by contemporary culture that the question just raised may be reiterated in a way that bears even more directly upon the problem of cultural unity. It has become commonplace to hear these days that humanity is more torn asunder by conflict, both potential and actual, both in its personal and collective dimensions, than it has seldom if ever experienced in its entire history. Reasons for this condition are numerous, some of which we have seen that Cassirer himself considers. What he does not consider sufficiently is whether man's facility to create and use symbols provides us with any guarantee that disunity will not result from this facility quite as easily and perhaps as frequently as unity. Certainly the record is far from reassuring. Not only do primitive cultures reveal abundant evidence of conflict. Not only does the recent revival of mythical symbolism by demagogues from Hitler to McCarthy prove to be a potent weapon of hatred and alienation. Within more "civilized" symbolic systems, too, we find overwhelming evidence of disunity abetted if not actually instigated by these very systems: witness the struggle between early Christianity and Roman culture, between Protestantism and Catholicism, between monarchy and democracy, between capitalism and communism—to mention four adequately violent examples.

Nor can we say without extensive qualification that, because the *animal symbolicum* has through the ages slowly achieved a large degree of sophistication culminating on the "highest" level as scientific symbolism, therefore human history, by and large, is one of slow but certain progress. For, if progress means at the minimum a movement from worse to better conditions of human existence, then of course one begs the question to assume that man necessarily and universally betters himself as he becomes more scientific. In this Atomic Age, almost everyone fears, on the contrary, that his situation may become immeasurably worse. The venerable issue of the relation of science to normative ends and means presses upon us with a fresh and ominous urgency: far from being merely the academic conundrum that it often is made to appear, its solution now becomes quite literally a life-or-death imperative.

Any adequate theory of symbolism must therefore be one that moves radically beyond Cassirer's formulation. Utilizing his own remarkable analysis and synthesis, the requirement is to develop a theory and program that can show us not only the importance and worth of all symbolic levels from myth through art to science, but in addition can point the way toward a further level of symbolic unity now required to correct the cultural disunities induced at least partly by those other levels. In the present essay, we cannot seek to characterize that further level in any detail. We may only express the belief that the needed theory must, above all, provide an empirically grounded framework for man and society that is definitely goal-centered and strong in its affirmation of clearcut democratic values. Accordingly it must be a theory that comes to focus in some such axiological guiding-star as "social-self-realization," that is delineated through a discipline of normative action, and is geared to institutional designs (from familial to international) constructed out of the vast esthetic, spiritual, scientific, technological resources that are man's to command for the renascence of culture on a worldwide scale.

All three questions that we have raised by way of criticism are relevant, in turn, to education's major role in that renascence. As to the first, is not realistic appraisal of the underlying cultural patterns that condition ideas imperative to any program of learning capable either of coping with them or of understanding the ideas that they reflect and reinforce? As to the second, must not penetrating analysis of the behavioral process of communication become part-and-parcel of the obligation to make such a process the tool of genuine *community* rather than of anarchy and conflict? As to the third, should not educators become more conscious of their premises and, where these are found to stem from such theories as Kant's, try to realize that education is then probably lending its support, inconsistently or not, both to preserving a curriculum close to the genteel tradition of formalized concepts and innocuous ideals, and to a theory-and-practice of means and ends that is normatively inadequate to cope with a cultural crisis such as our own?

But questions like these, impelling though they are, must not overshadow the positive significance for education of the philosophy of symbolic forms. Not only, as earlier noted, do certain other emphases counterbalance the apologia for classical learning which, if only tacitly, neo-Kantianism helps to perpetuate. Not only do these other emphases supplement and strengthen, while also harmonizing, the richest of experimentalist-progressivist beliefs. Not only, finally, does Cassirer encourage education to look upon the cultures of our world, past and present, primitive and civilized, in a much more cosmopolitan and sympathetic perspective. Beyond these contributions, he takes at least two momentous steps that should be taken also by any philosophy of education willing to reconstruct itself in terms of a strongly goal-centered orientation.

One is his regard, not found among most present-day progressivists, for a utopian or future-centered attitude as indispensable to a mature educational outlook. "In our consciousness of time the future is an indispensable element," Cassirer writes. " . . . The future is not only an image; it becomes an 'ideal' . . . an imperative of human life."[45] Educationally, this could well mean that schools have an obligation to stir the imaginations of people to the potentialities of our technological age for abundance, health, co-operation, peace: "The great mission òf the Utopia is to make room for the possible as opposed to a passive acquiescence in the present actual state of affairs."[46] Here, of course, symbols are the learner's most precious tools, for the future can be expressed only in symbols: "It is symbolic thought which overcomes the natural inertia of man and endows him with a new ability, the ability constantly to reshape his human universe."[47] For "To think of the future and to live in the future is a necessary part of his nature."[48]

The second step follows: the constructive role that myth plays in culture. We do not forget Cassirer's warning that myth can and does sometimes play a destructive role as well. But in his conception of religion and art, he suggests new horizons where education could utilize more vitally while strictly regulating the magnetic attraction of mythical experience. Through the great religions, students could grow into citizens instilled with something of the spirit and dedication of the prophets—not by "foretelling" future events (for this, whether in Oswald Spengler's works or in the witch-doctor's rituals, is only a species of magic), but by envisaging the promise of humanity as a mighty ethical adventure. Through art, students could learn to intensify their commitment to that adventure, to release their creative energies deeply and immediately by means of symbolic expression that combines both the qualities of subjective uniqueness and objective universality.

To convey through education a richer sense of that wonderful wholeness and harmony so natural to myth, to enfuse such a sense both with religious vision and poetic intensity, yet to maintain steady consciousness of the paramount value of science and reason, this is the arduous but necessary goal toward which education should aim by means of the most unifying principle of all: the symbolic power of man.

REFERENCES

CHAPTER ONE: CULTURE: THE CONTEXT OF EDUCATION

1. Edward B. Tylor, *Primitive Culture* (London: J. Murray, 5th ed., 1929), p. 1.
2. Franz Boas, "Anthropology," *Encyclopedia of the Social Sciences* (New York: Macmillan Co., 1930-34), Vol. 2.
3. Edward Sapir, "Custom," *Ibid.*, Vol. 4.

CHAPTER TWO: THREE GREAT PROBLEMS OF EDUCATION-AND-CULTURE

1. Cf. George Orwell, *Nineteen Eighty-four* (New York: Harcourt, Brace and Co., 1949).
2. Cf. Gunnar Myrdal, *An American Dilemma* (New York: Harper & Brothers, 1944).

CHAPTER FOUR: CULTURAL ORDER AS REALITY

1. Cf. David Bidney, *Theoretical Anthropology* (New York: Columbia University Press, 1953), pp. 34f.
2. Alfred L. Kroeber, "The Superorganic," reprinted in *The Nature of Culture* (Chicago: University of Chicago Press, 1952), pp. 22ff.
3. Alfred L. Kroeber, *Anthropology* (New York: Harcourt, Brace and Co., 1948), p. 204.
4. Bidney, *op.cit.*, p. 37.
5. In Leslie A. White, *The Science of Culture* (New York: Farrar, Straus and Co., 1949), p. 89f. And in Bidney, *op.cit.*, p. 91. Cf. also Émile Durkheim, *Education and Sociology* (Glencoe [Ill.]: Free Press, 1956).
6. White, *op.cit.*, p. 413.
7. Kroeber, *The Nature of Culture*, *op.cit.*, p. 112.
8. *Ibid.*, pp. 120f (italics added).
9. Alfred L. Kroeber and Clyde Kluckhohn, *Culture: A Critical Review of Concepts and Definitions* (Cambridge: Peabody Museum, 1952), pp. 148f.
10. Kroeber, *The Nature of Culture*, *op.cit.*, pp. 118ff.
11. Cf. Bidney, *op.cit.*, pp. 156ff.
12. Cf. F. S. C. Northrop, *The Meeting of East and West* (New York: Macmillan Co., 1946).
13. White, *op.cit.*, pp. 99f., 407f.
14. In Robert Ulich, *History of Educational Thought* (New York: American Book Co., 1945), pp. 281-287.

CHAPTER FIVE: CULTURAL ORDER AS SPATIAL

1. Melville J. Herskovits, *Man and His Works* (New York: Alfred A. Knopf, 1948), p. 172 (italics deleted).
2. Julian H. Steward, *Theory of Culture Change* (Urbana: University of Illinois Press, 1955), pp. 5f.
3. Alfred L. Kroeber, *Nature of Culture, op.cit.*, pp. 90-93.
4. Alfred L. Kroeber, *Anthropology, op.cit.*, p. 314.
5. Ruth Benedict, *Patterns of Culture* (New York: Mentor Books, 1934), p. 47.
6. Cf. Kurt Lewin, *Principles of Topological Psychology* (New York: McGraw-Hill Book Co., 1936).
7. Benedict, *op.cit.*, p. 42.
8. Cf. Bronislaw Malinowski, *A Scientific Theory of Culture and Other Essays* (Chapel Hill: University of North Carolina Press, 1944). It should be noted that A. R. Radcliffe-Brown is also famous for the functional theory, but that he insisted upon sharp distinctions between his own formulation and Malinowski's. Cf. his *Structure and Function in Primitive Society* (London: Cohen and West Ltd., 1952), Chaps. 9 and 10. For a careful analysis of the concept of function, cf. Raymond Firth, in William L. Thomas, Jr. (ed.), *Current Anthropology* (Chicago: University of Chicago Press, 1955).
9. Benedict, *op.cit.*, p. 45.
10. Malinowski, *op.cit.*, pp. 150, 160f. For a critique of Malinowski relevant here, cf. Horace Friess, in Vergilius Ferm (ed.), *A History of Philosophical Systems* (New York: Philosophical Library, 1950), pp. 588ff.
11. Cf. Robert Redfield, in Alfred L. Kroeber (ed.), *Anthropology Today* (Chicago: University of Chicago Press, 1953), pp. 733ff. Redfield has contributed further to the problem of spatio-temporal models in his influential studies of folk societies, and of the relations of rural-urban cultures. Cf., e.g., his *The Little Community* (Chicago: University of Chicago Press, 1955), which aids our understanding not only of cultural order but also of cultural process and cultural goals. Cf. also Robert Redfield, *The Primitive World and Its Transformation* (Ithaca: Cornell University Press, 1953).
12. Cf. David Bidney, *Theoretical Anthropology, op.cit.*, Chap. 13. Cf. John Gillin, *The Ways of Men* (New York: Appleton-Century-Crofts, 1948), Part 4.
13. Cf. Robert H. Lowie, *The History of Ethnological Theory* (New York: Farrar and Rinehart, 1937), Chap. 6.
14. Lowie, in Herskovits, *op.cit.*, p. 303.
15. Steward, *op.cit.*, pp. 43ff.
16. In Kurt Mayer, "The Theory of Social Classes," *Harvard Educational Review*, Vol. 23, 1953, p. 155. And in W. Lloyd Warner, Robert J. Havighurst, and Martin B. Loeb, *Who Shall Be Educated?* (New

York: Harper & Brothers, 1944), p. 19. Cf. W. Lloyd Warner and P. S. Lunt, *The Social Life of a Modern Community* (New Haven: Yale University Press, 1941).

17. Cf. Kurt Mayer, *op.cit.*

18. Cf. Robert S. Lynd and Helen M. Lynd, *Middletown, a Study in Contemporary American Culture* (New York: Harcourt, Brace and Co., 1929). And C. Wright Mills, *White Collar* (New York: Oxford University Press, 1951). And C. Wright Mills, *The Power Elite* (New York: Oxford University Press, 1956).

19. Cf. Thorstein Veblen, *The Theory of the Leisure Class* (New York: Modern Library, 1934). And Wesley C. Mitchell (ed.), *What Veblen Taught* (New York: Viking Press, 1936). Cf. David Riesman, *Thorstein Veblen: A Critical Interpretation* (New York: Charles Scribner's Sons, 1953).

20. Cf. Karl Mannheim, *Freedom, Power, and Democratic Planning* (New York: Oxford University Press, 1950). And H. H. Gerth and C. Wright Mills (eds.), *From Max Weber: Essays in Sociology* (New York: Oxford University Press, 1946).

21. In Allison Davis, B. B. Gardner, and Mary R. Gardner, *Deep South* (Chicago: University of Chicago Press, 1941), p. 9.

22. Cf. John Dollard, *Caste and Class in a Southern Town* (New Haven: Yale University Press, 1937).

23. Cf. S. F. Nadel, *The Foundations of Social Anthropology* (Glencoe [Ill.]: Free Press, 1951), Chap. 7.

24. In David Mandelbaum (ed.), *Selective Writings of Edward Sapir in Language, Culture and Personality* (Berkeley: University of California Press, 1949), pp. 548f.

25. *Ibid.*, p. 557.

26. Clyde Kluckhohn, in Leslie Spier, A. Irving Hallowell, and Stanley Newman (eds.), *Language, Culture, and Personality* (Menasha [Wis.]: Banta Publishing Co., 1941), pp. 114, 126.

27. Cf. Paul Radin, *Primitive Man as Philosopher* (New York: D. Appleton and Co., 1927).

28. Clyde Kluckhohn, in F. S. C. Northrop (ed.), *Ideological Differences and World Order* (New Haven: Yale University Press, 1949), p. 359.

29. Kroeber, *op.cit.*, p. 294.

30. Cf. Theodore Brameld, "Conceptualizing Human Relations," *Journal of Educational Sociology*, Vol. 23, 1950, pp. 315ff. And Theodore Brameld, "Human Relations: A 'Field of Forces,'" *Ibid.*, Vol. 24, 1951, pp. 329ff.

31. William H. Burton, "Education and Social Class in the United States," *Harvard Educational Review*, Vol. 23, 1953, pp. 248f.

32. Allison Davis, *Social-Class Influences Upon Learning* (Cambridge: Harvard University Press, 1948), p. 85.

33. Cf. *Harvard Educational Review*, Vol. 23, 1953, pp. 149-338.

34. Cf. Warner, Havighurst, and Loeb, *op.cit.*, pp. 147, 171.

35. Foster McMurray, "Who Shall Be Educated for What?" *Progressive Education*, Vol. 27, 1950, p. 112.
36. Sapir, in Madelbaum (ed.), *op.cit.*, pp. 558f.

CHAPTER SIX: CULTURAL ORDER AS TEMPORAL

1. Bronislaw Malinowski, *A Scientific Theory of Culture and Other Essays, op.cit.*, pp. 118, 28f.
2. Cf. David Bidney, *Theoretical Anthropology, op.cit.*, pp. 223ff.
3. M. J. Herskovits, *Man and His Works, op.cit.*, p. 506.
4. In Bidney, *op.cit.*, p. 216.
5. William Duncan Strong, in Alfred L. Kroeber (ed.), *Anthropology Today, op.cit.*, p. 394.
6. Cf. Margaret Mead, *Coming of Age in Samoa* (New York: Mentor Books, 1949). And Margaret Mead, *New Lives for Old* (New York: William Morrow and Co., 1956).
7. Alfred L. Kroeber, *The Nature of Culture, op.cit.*, p. 97.
8. Cf. Herskovits, *op.cit.*, p. 464.
9. In T. K. Penniman, *A Hundred Years of Anthropology* (New York: Macmillan Co., 1936), pp. 183f.
10. Cf. *Ibid.*, pp. 182f.
11. Bidney, *op.cit.*, p. 207.
12. Cf. Strong, in Kroeber (ed.), *op.cit.*, pp. 386-397; Penniman, *op.cit.*; Robert H. Lowie, *The History of Ethnological Theory, op.cit.*; Paul Radin, *Social Anthropology* (New York: McGraw-Hill Book Co., 1932).
13. Cf. Friedrich Engels, *The Origin of the Family* (Chicago: C. H. Kerr, 1902).
14. Cf. Lewis H. Morgan, *Ancient Society* (Chicago: C. H. Kerr, 1877). Cf. V. Gordon Childe, *Social Evolution* (New York: Henry Schuman, 1951), pp. 9f.
15. Cf. Leslie A. White, *The Science of Culture, op.cit.*, p. 3ff.
16. V. Gordon Childe, *Man Makes Himself* (London: Watts and Co., 1936), p. 19.
17. Strong, in Kroeber (ed.), *op.cit.*, p. 392f.
18. Cf. Clyde Kluckhohn, "Some Reflections on the Method and Theory of the Kulturkreislehre," *American Anthropologist*, Vol. 38, 1936, pp. 157ff.
19. Cf. Kluckhohn, *op.cit.*; Lowie, *op.cit.*; Penniman, *op.cit.*; Childe, *Social Evolution, op.cit.*
20. Cf. Herskovits, *op.cit.*, p. 515.
21. Cf. Kroeber, *op.cit.*, Part 1.
22. Cf. Alfred L. Kroeber and Clyde Kluckhohn, *Culture: A Critical Review of Concepts and Definitions, op.cit.*, p. 160.
23. Kroeber, *op.cit.*, p. 123.
24. Kroeber and Kluckhohn, *op.cit.*, p. 161.
25. Cf. Kroeber, *op.cit.*, p. 64.

26. *Ibid.*, p. 79.
27. *Ibid.*, p. 76.
28. In Franz Boas, *Race, Language and Culture* (New York: Macmillan Co., 1940), pp. 305ff.
29. Cf. E. E. Evans-Pritchard, *Social Anthropology* (Glencoe [Ill.]: Free Press, 1951).
30. Bidney, *op.cit.*, p. 280 (italics deleted).
31. Julian H. Steward, *Theory of Culture Change, op.cit.*, pp. 11-29.
32. R. G. Collingwood, *The Idea of History* (Oxford: Clarendon Press, 1946), pp. 209, 215, 225f.
33. Morris R. Cohen, *The Meaning of Human History* (LaSalle [Ill.]: Open Court Publishing Co., 1947), pp. 53, 171.
34. Herbert J. Muller, *The Uses of the Past* (New York: Oxford University Press, 1952), p. 31.
35. *Ibid.*, p. 32.
36. *Ibid.*, p. 38.
37. Alfred L. Kroeber, *Configurations of Culture Growth* (Berkeley: University of California Press, 1944), p. 761.
38. *Ibid.*, p. 839.
39. *Ibid.*, p. 822.
40. *Ibid.*, p. 766.
41. *Ibid.*, p. 765.
42. Cf. Oswald Spengler, *The Decline of the West* (New York: Alfred A. Knopf, 1926).
43. Cf. Pitirim A. Sorokin, *Social Philosophies of an Age of Crisis* (Boston: Beacon Press, 1951).
44. H. Stuart Hughes, *Oswald Spengler* (New York: Charles Scribner's Sons, 1952), p. 165.
45. Cf. Arnold J. Toynbee, *A Study of History* (New York: Oxford University Press, 1947, 1956).
46. Kroeber, *The Nature of Culture, op.cit.*, pp. 373, 377f.
47. Toynbee, *op.cit.*, pp. 552, 554. Cf. Arnold J. Toynbee, *An Historian's Approach to Religion* (New York: Oxford University Press, 1956).
48. Cf. Sorokin, *op.cit.*, pp. 311ff.
49. Cf. Pitirim A. Sorokin, *Social and Cultural Dynamics* (New York: American Book Co., 1937-41).
50. Cf. Pitirim A. Sorokin, *The Crisis of Our Age* (New York: E. P. Dutton and Co., 1941).
51. Sorokin, *Social Philosophies of an Age of Crisis, op.cit.*, pp. 199, 296.
52. Sorokin, *The Crisis of Our Age, op.cit.*, pp. 28f.
53. *Ibid.*, pp. 106, 117, 318 (italics deleted).
54. Cf., e.g., Rushton Coulborn, "Fact and Fiction in Toynbee's *Study of History*," *Ethics*, Vol. 66, 1956, pp. 235ff.
55. Cf. the journals, *Behavioral Science* and *Human Relations* for basic explorations in interdisciplinary theory and research.

CHAPTER SEVEN: CULTURAL PROCESS—PREVIEW OF THE PROBLEM

1. Cf. Malcolm S. MacLean and Edwin A. Lee, *Change and Process in Education* (New York: Dryden Press, 1956).
2. Anatol Rapoport, *Operational Philosophy* (New York: Harper & Brothers, 1953), p. 79.
3. Cf. Alfred L. Kroeber, *Anthropology, op.cit.*, Chap. 9.

CHAPTER EIGHT: SOME MAJOR CONCEPTS OF CULTURAL PROCESS

1. John Gillin, *The Ways of Men, op.cit.*, p. 555.
2. M. J. Herskovits, *Man and His Works, op.cit.*, p. 525 (italics deleted).
3. Alfred L. Kroeber, *Anthropology, op.cit.*, p. 425.
4. Alfred L. Kroeber, *The Nature of Culture, op.cit.*, p. 344.
5. Cf. Ralph Beals, in Alfred L. Kroeber (ed.), *Anthropology Today, op.cit.*, pp. 621ff.
6. *Ibid.*, p. 626.
7. Herskovits, *op.cit.*, pp. 525ff.
8. Beals, in Kroeber (ed.), *op.cit.*, pp. 626f.
9. Cf., e.g., Robert Redfield, *Peasant Society and Culture* (Chicago: University of Chicago Press, 1956). And Redfield, *The Little Community, op.cit.*
10. Cf. Bronislaw Malinowski, "The Pan-American Problem of Culture Contact," *American Journal of Sociology*, Vol. 48, 1943, pp. 649ff. Cf. Bronislaw Malinowski, *The Dynamics of Culture Change* (New Haven: Yale University Press, 1945).
11. Quoted in M. J. Herskovits, *Acculturation: The Study of Culture Contact* (New York: J. J. Augustin, 1938), p. 13.
12. Beals, in Kroeber (ed.), *op.cit.*, p. 627f.
13. Cf. H. G. Barnett, *Innovation: The Basis of Cultural Change* (New York: McGraw-Hill Book Co., 1953).
14. Felix M. Keesing, *Culture Change* (Stanford: Stanford University Press, 1953), pp. 75, 69. Cf. Bernard J. Siegel (ed.), *Acculturation: Critical Abstracts, North America* (Stanford: Stanford University Press, 1955).
15. Barnett, *op.cit.*, pp. 7, 9.
16. Ralph Linton, in Ralph Linton (ed.), *The Science of Man in the World Crisis* (New York: Columbia University Press, 1945), pp. 213-220.
17. Gillin, *op.cit.*, p. 548. Cf. also, Committee on Historiography, *The Social Sciences in Historical Study* (New York: Social Science Research Council, 1954), pp. 120-125.
18. Herskovits, *Man and His Works, op.cit.*, p. 542.
19. M. J. Herskovits, in Linton (ed.), *op.cit.*, pp. 167f.
20. Keesing, *op.cit.*, pp. 84, 88.

21. Reprinted in David Bidney, *Theoretical Anthropology*, *op.cit.*, pp. 345ff.
22. *Ibid.*, pp. 353f.
23. *Ibid.*, pp. 357, 360.
24. Barnett, *op.cit.*, pp. 80-89.
25. *Ibid.*, p. 89.
26. Laura Thompson, *Culture in Crisis* (New York: Harper & Brothers, 1950), p. 16.
27. *Ibid.*, p. 179.
28. *Ibid.*, p. 184.
29. Cf. Bronislaw Malinowski, *Freedom and Civilization* (New York: Roy Publishers, 1944).
30. Clyde Kluckhohn, *Mirror for Man* (New York: McGraw-Hill Book Co., 1949), pp. 255, 256.
31. Morris Opler, "Cultural and Organic Conceptions in Contemporary World History," *American Anthropologist*, Vol. 46, 1944, pp. 448ff.
32. Josiah Royce, *The Spirit of Modern Philosophy* (Boston: Houghton, Mifflin and Co., 1893), p. 216.
33. Lewis Mumford, *The Conduct of Life* (New York: Harcourt, Brace and Co., 1951), p. 3.
34. *Ibid.*, p. 20.
35. Lewis Mumford, *The Condition of Man* (New York: Harcourt, Brace and Co., 1944), p. 14.
36. *Ibid.* Cf. Lewis Mumford, *The Transformations of Man* (New York: Harper & Brothers, 1956).
37. Keesing, *op.cit.*, p. 72.
38. Cf. Committee on Historiography, *op.cit.*
39. Cf. G. J. Renier, *History—Its Purpose and Method* (Boston: Beacon Press, 1950).
40. Cf. Isaiah Berlin, *Historical Inevitability* (New York: Oxford University Press, 1955).
41. Leslie A. White, *The Science of Culture*, *op.cit.*, pp. 364f., 390ff.
42. Cf. Geza Róheim (ed.), *Psychoanalysis and the Social Sciences* (New York: International Universities Press, 1947), pp. 18-22. Cf. also, John J. Honigmann, *Culture and Personality* (New York: Harper & Brothers, 1954), pp. 64-68.
43. Alfred L. Kroeber and Clyde Kluckhohn, *Culture: A Critical Review of Concepts and Definitions*, *op.cit.*, pp. 165-171.
44. Kroeber, *op.cit.*, p. 114. Cf. Bidney, *op.cit.*, p. 33.
45. Kroeber, *op.cit.*, pp. 132f.
46. Kroeber and Kluckhohn, *op.cit.*, p. 168.
47. *Ibid.*, pp. 169f.
48. Julian H. Steward, *Theory of Culture Change*, *op.cit.*, pp. 37f., 180, 183, 191f.

49. In Sol Tax and Others (eds.), *An Appraisal of Anthropology Today* (Chicago: University of Chicago Press, 1953), pp. 371f.
50. Rushton Coulborn, "Causes in Culture," *American Anthropologist,* Vol. 54, 1952, pp. 112ff.
51. Bidney, *op.cit.,* p. 116.
52. Cf. Herskovits, *Man and His Works, op.cit.,* pp. 619, 621.
53. For further discussion of causation, cf. S. F. Nadel, *The Foundations of Social Anthropology, op.cit.,* pp. 207ff.
54. In *American Journal of Sociology,* Vol. 48, 1943, pp. 629-764.
55. Cf. Margaret Mead (ed.), *Cultural Patterns and Technical Change* (New York: New American Library of World Literature, 1955). Cf. also, International Sociological Association, *The Positive Contribution by Immigrants* (Paris: Unesco, 1955).
56. Robert E. Park, "Education and the Cultural Crisis," *American Journal of Sociology,* Vol. 48, 1943, pp. 728ff.
57. Cf. Freeman Butts, *A Cultural History of Western Education* (New York: McGraw-Hill Book Co., 1955).

CHAPTER NINE: PERSONALITY IN CULTURAL PROCESS

1. Alfred L. Kroeber and Clyde Kluckhohn, *Culture: A Critical Review of Concepts and Definitions, op.cit.,* p. 166.
2. *Ibid.,* p. 167.
3. Clyde Kluckhohn and Henry A. Murray, in Clyde Kluckhohn and Henry A. Murray (eds.), *Personality in Nature, Society, and Culture* (New York: Alfred A. Knopf, 1953), p. 56.
4. Kroeber and Kluckhohn, *op.cit.,* p. 58.
5. M. J. Herskovits, *Man and His Works, op.cit.,* p. 39.
6. *Ibid.,* pp. 45f.
7. A. Irving Hallowell, in John Gillin (ed.), *For A Science of Social Man* (New York: Macmillan Co., 1954), pp. 190f.
8. Cf. Hadley Cantril, *The "Why" of Man's Experience* (New York: Macmillan Co., 1950).
9. John Gillin, *The Ways of Men, op.cit.,* Chap. 11.
10. Cf. John Dollard and Neal E. Miller, *Personality and Psychotherapy* (New York: McGraw-Hill Book Co., 1950).
11. Gillin, *op.cit.,* p. 247.
12. Cf. John W. M. Whiting and Irvin L. Child, *Child Training and Personality* (New Haven: Yale University Press, 1953).
13. *Ibid.,* p. 22 (italics deleted).
14. In David Mandelbaum (ed.), *Selected Writings of Edward Sapir in Language, Culture and Personality, op.cit.,* pp. 544ff.
15. Gillin, *op.cit.,* p. 573.
16. Kluckhohn and Murray, in Kluckhohn and Murray (eds.), *op.cit.,* p. 49.
17. John J. Honigmann, *Culture and Personality, op.cit.,* p. 28.
18. *Ibid.,* p. 192.

19. Cf. S. Stansfeld Sargent and Marian W. Smith (eds.), *Culture and Personality* (New York: Viking Fund, 1949).
20. Cf. Gardner Murphy, *Personality* (New York: Harper & Brothers, 1947).
21. Gardner Murphy, in Sargent and Smith (eds.), *op.cit.*, p. 22.
22. Cf. Erich Fromm, *The Sane Society* (New York: Rinehart and Co., 1955). Cf. Harry Stack Sullivan, *Conceptions of Modern Psychiatry* (Washington, D. C.: William Alanson White Psychiatric Foundation, 1947).
23. Erich Fromm, in Sargent and Smith (eds.), *op.cit.*, p. 7.
24. A. Irving Hallowell, *Culture and Experience* (Philadelphia: University of Pennsylvania Press, 1955), p. 313.
25. Cf. A. Irving Hallowell, in Alfred L. Kroeber (ed.), *Anthropology Today*, *op.cit.*, pp. 597ff., and in Gillin (ed.), *op.cit.*, pp. 166ff.
26. Hallowell, in Kroeber (ed.), *op.cit.*, p. 608.
27. Cf. Hallowell, in Gillin (ed.), *op.cit.*, pp. 218f.
28. Hallowell, in Kroeber (ed.), *op.cit.*, p. 612.
29. Hallowell, in Gillin (ed.), *op.cit.*, pp. 224f.
30. Kluckhohn and Murray, in Kluckhohn and Murray (eds.), *op.cit.*, p. 6.
31. *Ibid.*, p. 24.
32. *Ibid.*, p. 28.
33. *Ibid.*, p. 46.
34. *Ibid.*
35. David Bidney, *Theoretical Anthropology*, *op.cit.*, pp. 77, 83.
36. *Ibid.*, p. 342.
37. *Ibid.*, p. 343.
38. Hallowell, in Gillin (ed.), *op.cit.*, p. 197.
39. Cf. Ralph Linton, *The Cultural Background of Personality* (New York: Appleton-Century Co., 1945).
40. Ralph Linton, in Abram Kardiner, *The Psychological Frontiers of Society* (New York: Columbia University Press, 1945), p. vii.
41. *Ibid.*, p. viii.
42. Cf. George Herbert Mead, *Mind, Self, and Society* (Chicago: University of Chicago Press, 1934).
43. Margaret Mead, in Kroeber (ed.), *op.cit.*, p. 651. Cf. Margaret Mead, in Daniel Lerner and Harold D. Lasswell (eds.), *The Policy Sciences* (Stanford: Stanford University Press, 1951), pp. 70ff. Cf. also Margaret Mead and Rhoda Métraux (eds.), *The Study of Culture at a Distance* (Chicago: University of Chicago Press, 1953).
44. Cf. Goeffrey Gorer, in Kluckhohn and Murray (eds.), *op.cit.*, pp. 246ff.; and Otto Klineberg, in Sargent and Smith (eds.), *op.cit.*, pp. 127ff. Cf. also Geoffrey Gorer, *Exploring English Character* (New York: Criterion Books, 1955).
45. Cf. Margaret Mead, *Male and Female* (New York: William Morrow and Co., 1949). Cf. Margaret Mead and Martha Wolfenstein (eds.), *Childhood in Contemporary Cultures* (Chicago: University of Chicago

Press, 1955). And Margaret Mead, in Kluckhohn and Murray (eds.), *op.cit.*, pp. 651ff. And Margaret Mead, *New Lives for Old*, *op.cit.*
46. Cf. David Riesman, *The Lonely Crowd* (New Haven: Yale University Press, 1950).
47. George D. Spindler, "Education in a Transforming American Culture," *Harvard Educational Review*, Vol. 25, 1955, pp. 145ff. But cf. Spindler's conclusions with those of Charles Morris, considered below (Chap. 11).
48. Cf. Honigmann, *op.cit.*, pp. 262ff. Cf. also Georgene Seward, *Psychotherapy and Culture Conflict* (New York: Ronald Press Co., 1956).
49. Linton, in Kardiner, *op.cit.*, p. ix.
50. *Ibid.*, p. xii.
51. Cf. Felix M. Keesing, *Culture Change*, *op.cit.*, pp. 90f.
52. Mead, in Kluckhohn and Murray (eds.), *op.cit.*, pp. 661f.
53. David Riesman, "Teachers Amid Changing Expectations," *Harvard Educational Review*, Vol. 24, 1954, pp. 114, 116.
54. Van Cleve Morris, "The Other-Directed Man," *Teachers College Record*, Vol. 57, 1956, pp. 239f.
55. Cf. Hallowell, in Gillin (ed.), *op.cit.*, pp. 214ff.
56. Cf. David Bidney, in Paul A. Schilpp (ed.), *The Philosophy of Ernst Cassirer* (Evanston: The Library of Living Philosophers, 1949), pp. 465ff.
57. Cf. Theodore Brameld, "Philosophical Anthropology: The Educational Significance of Ernst Cassirer," *Harvard Educational Review*, Vol. 26, 1956, pp. 207ff. Reprinted as *Appendix*, above.
58. Robert Redfield, in Sol Tax and Others, (eds.), *An Appraisal of Anthropology Today*, *op.cit.*, p. 127.
59. Cf. Robert Redfield, *The Educational Experience* (Pasadena: Fund for Adult Education, 1955).
60. Cf., e.g., Lawrence E. Cole and William F. Bruce, *Educational Psychology* (Yonkers: World Book Co., 1950). Cf. also Theodore Brameld, *Philosophies of Education in Cultural Perspective* (New York: Dryden Press, 1955, pp. 130-141. And Theodore Brameld, *Toward a Reconstructed Philosophy of Education* (New York: Dryden Press, 1956), Chap. 7.
61. Cf. Kurt Lewin, *Resolving Social Conflicts* (New York: Harper & Brothers, 1948). Cf. also, J. L. Moreno, *Who Shall Survive?* (Beacon [NY]: Beacon House, 1953). And G. H. Mead, *op.cit.*
62. For an exception, cf. Joseph Bram, "Application of Psychodrama to Research in Social Anthropology," *Transactions* of the New York Academy of Sciences, Vol. 15, Series II, 1953, pp. 253ff.
63. In personal letters to the author.
64. In personal letters to the author. Cf. also, Margaret Mead, "Cultural Discontinuities and Personality Transformation," *Journal of Social Issues*, Supplement Series No. 8, 1943, pp. 3-16.

65. Cf. A. Paul Hare, Edgar F. Borgatta, and Robert F. Bales (eds.), *Small Groups* (New York: Alfred A. Knopf, 1955).
66. Cf. Edward H. Shils, in Lerner and Lasswell (eds.), *op.cit.*, pp. 44ff.
67. Cf. George C. Homans, *The Human Group* (New York: Harcourt, Brace and Co., 1950).
68. Edward A. Kennard and Gordon Macgregor, in Kroeber (ed.), *op.cit.*, pp. 839f.
69. Cf. Ronald Lippitt, "An Experimental Study of the Effects of Democratic and Authoritarian Group Atmospheres," *University of Iowa Studies in Child Welfare*, Vol. 16, 1940, pp. 45-195.
70. Cf. Herbert Thelen,*Dynamics of Groups at Work* (Chicago: University of Chicago Press, 1954).
71. Cf. John Dewey, *Human Nature and Conduct* (New York: Modern Library, 1930).
72. Cf. Boyd Bode, *How We Learn* (New York: D. C. Heath and Co., 1940).
73. Cf. Brameld, *Philosophies of Education in Cultural Perspective, op.cit.*, pp. 188-197.
74. Lawrence K. Frank, *Nature and Human Nature* (New Brunswick: Rutgers University Press, 1951), pp. 156, 158f. Cf. also, Lawrence K. Frank, *Society as the Patient* (New Brunswick: Rutgers University Press, 1948). For a viewpoint with numerous similarities, cf. M. F. Ashley Montagu, *The Direction of Human Development* (New York: Harper & Brothers, 1955).
75. Lawrence K. Frank, *Personality and Culture* (New York: Hinds, Hayden and Eldridge, 1948), pp. 20f.

CHAPTER TEN: CULTURAL GOALS—PREVIEW OF THE PROBLEM

1. Cf. Felix M. Keesing, *Anthropological Contributions to Value Theory* (revised restricted edition) (Stanford: Stanford University Department of Sociology and Anthropology, 1955).
2. Alfred L. Kroeber, *The Nature of Culture, op.cit.*, pp. 137f., 129, 131.
3. Cf. Keesing, *op.cit.*
4. Bronislaw Malinowski, *Freedom and Civilization, op.cit.*, p. 130.

CHAPTER ELEVEN: HUMAN GOALS AS RELATIVE AND UNIVERSAL

1. Ruth Benedict, *Patterns of Culture, op.cit.*, p. 257.
2. Clyde Kluckhohn, "Ethical Relativity: *Sic et non*," *Journal of Philosophy*, Vol. 52, 1955, p. 663. Cf. Clyde Kluckhohn, in Leonard D. White (ed.), *The State of the Social Sciences* (Chicago: University of Chicago Press, 1956), pp. 116ff.
3. Abraham Edel, *Ethical Judgment: The Use of Science in Ethics* (Glencoe [Ill.]: Free Press, 1955), p. 30.
4. In *Human Organization*, Vol. 8, No. 2, 1949, pp. 20f.

5. M. J. Herskovits, "Tender-minded and Tough-minded Anthropology," *Southwestern Journal of Anthropology*, Vol. 7, 1951, p. 30.
6. *Ibid.*, p. 22.
7. M. J. Herskovits, *Man and His Works, op.cit.*, p. 68.
8. *Ibid.*, p. 76.
9. *Ibid.*
10. David Bidney, *Theoretical Anthropology, op.cit.*, p. 424.
11. Herskovits, *op.cit.*, p. 67.
12. In Herskovits, "Tender-minded and Tough-minded Anthropology," *op.cit.*, p. 25.
13. In Alfred L. Kroeber and Clyde Kluckhohn, *Culture: A Critical Review of Concepts and Definitions, op.cit.*, p. 174.
14. *Ibid.*, pp. 174, 178.
15. Kluckhohn, *op.cit.*, p. 669.
16. Clyde Kluckhohn, in *Modern Education and Human Values* (Pitcairn-Crabbe Foundation Lecture Series, Vol. 4; Pittsburgh: University of Pittsburgh Press, 1952), pp. 100f.
17. Kluckhohn, "Ethical Relativity: *Sic et non,*" *op.cit.*, pp. 676f.
18. *Ibid.*, p. 672.
19. Kluckhohn, in *Modern Education and Human Values, op.cit.*
20. Cf. Clark Wissler, *Man and Culture* (New York: Thomas Y. Crowell, 1923), Chap. 5.
21. Kroeber and Kluckhohn, *op.cit.*, p. 176.
22. *Ibid.*, pp. 178f.
23. Kluckhohn, "Ethical Relativity: *Sic et non,*" *op.cit.*, p. 671.
24. Clyde Kluckhohn, in Alfred L. Kroeber (ed.), *Anthropology Today, op. cit.*, p. 511.
25. *Ibid.*, p. 515.
26. Ralph Linton, in Ruth Anshen (ed.), *Moral Principles of Action* (New York: Harper & Brothers, 1952), p. 646.
27. *Ibid.*, p. 660.
28. Ralph Linton, in Robert F. Spencer (ed.), *Method and Perspective in Anthropology* (Minneapolis: University of Minnesota Press, 1954), p. 156.
29. Alfred L. Kroeber, in *Ibid.*, p. 284. Cf. also Alfred L. Kroeber, in William L. Thomas, Jr. (ed.), *Current Anthropology, op.cit.*, p. 298.
30. George P. Murdock, *Social Structure* (New York: Macmillan Co., 1949), p. 10.
31. George P. Murdock, in Ralph Linton (ed.), *The Science of Man in the World Crisis, op.cit.*, p. 124.
32. Richard B. Brandt, *Hopi Ethics* (Chicago: University of Chicago Press, 1954). Cf. especially Chap. 16. For a pioneering study of Navaho ethics, cf. John Ladd, *The Structure of a Moral Code* (Cambridge: Harvard University Press, 1956).
33. Alfred L. Kroeber, in Sol Tax and Others (eds.), *An Appraisal of Anthropology Today, op.cit.*, pp. 375f.

34. Bidney, *op.cit.*, pp. 427f.
35. Ralph Barton Perry, *Realms of Value* (Cambridge: Harvard University Press, 1954), p. 362.
36. F. S. C. Northrop, in Kroeber (ed.), *op.cit.*, p. 675.
37. Cf. F. S. C Northrop, "Ethical Relativism in the Light of Recent Legal Science," *Journal of Philosophy*, Vol. 52, 1955, pp. 649 ff.
38. Northrop, in Kroeber (ed.), *op.cit.*, p. 678.
39. Northrop, "Ethical Relativism in the Light of Recent Legal Science," *op.cit.*, pp. 656ff.
40. Cf. Charles Morris, *Varieties of Human Value* (Chicago: University of Chicago Press, 1956).
41. Cf. Charles Morris, *Paths of Life* (New York: Harper & Brothers, 1942). And Charles Morris, *The Open Self* (New York: Prentice-Hall, 1948).
42. Cf. Morris, *Varieties of Human Value*, *op.cit.*, Chap. 3.
43. *Ibid.*, p. 65.
44. *Ibid.*, p. 69.
45. *Ibid.*, p. 120.
46. *Ibid.*, p. 191.
47. For a summary of findings and implications, cf. Charles Morris, "Varieties of Human Value," *The Humanist*, Vol. 16, 1956, pp. 153 ff.
48. Edel, *op.cit.*, p. 225.
49. *Ibid.*, p. 242.
50. Cf. Theodore Brameld, *Ends and Means in Education* (New York: Harper & Brothers, 1950), pp. 161, 175.
51. Cf. Theodore Brameld, *Toward a Reconstructed Philosophy of Education*, *op.cit.*, pp. 303-311.
52. Cf. Northrop, in Kroeber (ed.), *op.cit.*, pp. 668 ff.
53. Cf. Brameld, *op. cit.*, pp. 220f., and Brameld, *Ends and Means in Education*, *op.cit.*, pp. 40ff.
54. Cf. Brameld, *Ends and Means in Education*, *op.cit.*, pp. 203ff.
55. The philosophers cited have given education only a little more attention than have the anthropologists. Abraham Edel's study of values is briefly applied to education in his "What Should Be the Aims and Content of a Philosophy of Education?" *Harvard Educational Review*, Vol. 26, 1956, pp. 119ff.
56. Kluckhohn, in *Modern Education and Human Values*, *op.cit.*, pp. 87, 89f.
57. *Ibid.*, pp. 89, 93.
58. *Ibid.*, p. 108.
59. Pierre Teilhard de Chardin, in Tax and Others (eds.), *op.cit.*, p. 338. But cf. Julian Steward in Kroeber (ed.), *op.cit.*, pp. 324f.

CHAPTER TWELVE: HUMAN FREEDOM AS CULTURAL GOAL

1. "Love" is the highest value, according to M. F. Ashley Montagu, an anthropologist who has given thoughtful consideration to many of

318 REFERENCES

the problems of this volume. In his *The Direction of Human Development, op.cit.*, he offers this preliminary definition: "Love may be described as the process of communicating to another that you are 'all for' them, that you will support them, not merely that you will accept them, but that you are actively for them." He quotes approvingly Nelson N. Foote: Love is "that relationship between one person and another which is most conducive to the optimal development of both." (pp. 175f.) I believe that, in view of Montagu's conception (cf. also pp. 293ff.), a strong case can be made in behalf of freedom, as it will be considered in this chapter with the help of Malinowski and others, as the genus value, of which love is a species. Optimum freedom includes but is not identical with optimum love.

2. The literature on value theory is, of course, very large. In terms of the concern of this and the preceding chapter, cf. especially, Felix M. Keesing, *Anthropological Contributions to Value Theory, op.cit.;* Kenneth D. Benne and George E. Swanson (eds.), "Values and the Social Scientist," *Journal of Social Issues*, Vol. 6, 1950, pp. 1-80. Cf. bibliographical sources in Abraham Edel, *Ethical Judgment: The Use of Science in Ethics, op. cit.* Cf. also, Marvin K. Opler, *Culture, Psychiatry and Human Values* (Springfield, [Ill.]: Charles C. Thomas, 1956). And Everett W. Hall, *Modern Science and Human Values* (Princeton: D. Van Nostrand Co., 1956). And Frances Jerome Woods, *Cultural Values of American Ethnic Groups* (New York: Harper & Brothers, 1956).

3. Clyde Kluckhohn, in Talcott Parsons and Edward A. Shils (eds.), *Toward a General Theory of Action* (Cambridge: Harvard University Press, 1951), p. 395 (italics deleted).

4. *Ibid.*, p. 399.

5. *Ibid.*, p. 411 (italics deleted).

6. *Ibid.*, p. 428. For a systematic analysis of Kluckhohn's theory by a philosopher, cf. Cornelius Golightly, "Value as a Scientific Concept," *Journal of Philosophy*, Vol. 53, 1956, pp. 233ff. For further refinement of the relation of goals, values, and other axiological concepts, cf. Richard B. Brandt, *Hopi Ethics, op.cit.*, For a systematic application of Kluckhohn's formulation to an actual culture, cf. Ethel M. Albert, "The Classification of Values: A Method and Illustration," *American Anthropologist*, Vol. 58, 1956, pp. 221ff.

7. In Keesing, *op.cit.*, III, 2, 3. Cf. also Alfred L. Kroeber, *The Nature of Culture, op.cit.*, pp. 136-138.

8. Cf. Ralph Barton Perry, *Realms of Value, op.cit.*

9. Charles Morris, *Varieties of Human Value, op.cit.*, pp. 9-12.

10. Edel, *op.cit.*, pp. 46f.

11. *Ibid.*, Chap. 9.

12. Cf. Bronislaw Malinowski, *Freedom and Civilization, op.cit.*, p. 129. Cf., for further development of his basic theory of values, Bronislaw Malinowski, *A Scientific Theory of Culture and Other Essays, op.cit.*

13. Malinowski, *Freedom and Civilization*, *op.cit.*, p. 137.
14. *Ibid.*, p. 126. Cf. Montagu, *op.cit.*, Chaps. 6 and 7.
15. *Ibid.*, p. 39.
16. *Ibid.*, p. 170.
17. Cf. John Dewey, *Freedom and Culture* (New York: G. P. Putnam's Sons, 1939).
18. Malinowski, *op.cit.*, pp. 230f.
19. *Ibid.*, p. 333.
20. *Ibid.*, p. 336.
21. David Bidney, *Theoretical Anthropology*, *op.cit.*, p. 15.
22. *Ibid.*, pp. 416f.
23. *Ibid.*, p. 432.
24. *Ibid.*, p. 447.
25. *Ibid.*, pp. 452f.
26. For a critique of Bidney's position, cf. A. K. Saran, "Theoretical Anthropology and the Cult of Man," *Ethics*, Vol. 66, 1956, pp. 198ff. Cf. Theodore Brameld, review of *Theoretical Anthropology*, by David Bidney, *Philosophical Review*, Vol. 65, 1956, pp. 130ff.
27. Edel, *op.cit.*, p. 18.
28. Cf. *Ibid.*, pp. 137-143.
29. Cf. A. Irving Hallowell, in Sol Tax and Others (eds.) *An Appraisal of Anthropology Today*, *op.cit.*, pp. 334f.; and Montagu, *op.cit.*, pp. 292f.
30. Edel, *op.cit.*, p. 294.
31. *Ibid.*, pp. 300-303.
32. *Ibid.*, p. 339.
33. In Keesing, *op.cit.*, VI, 6.
34. Alfred L. Kroeber, *Anthropology*, *op.cit.*, p. 300.
35. Cf. Ernst Cassirer, *The Myth of the State* (New Haven: Yale University Press, 1946).
36. Wilson D. Wallis, *Culture and Progress* (New York: McGraw-Hill Book Co., 1930), p. 432.
37. *Ibid.*, pp. 440f.
38. *Ibid.*, p. 447.
39. Perry, *op.cit.*, pp. 402-409. From a different background but with many provocative similarities to those cited above, cf. L. L. Whyte, *The Next Development in Man* (New York: Henry Holt and Co., 1948).
40. Cf. Karl Mannheim, *Ideology and Utopia* (Harcourt, Brace and Co., 1936). And Karl Mannheim, *Essays on the Sociology of Culture* (New York: Oxford University Press, 1956). Cf. Theodore Brameld, *Toward a Reconstructed Philosophy of Education*, *op.cit.*, pp. 87-92, 178f., 262-273. Cf. Margaret Fisher, *Leadership and Intelligence* (New York: Bureau of Publications, Teachers College, Columbia University, 1954).

41. Alfred L. Kroeber and Clyde Kluckhohn, *Culture: A Critical Review of Concepts and Definitions, op.cit.,* p. 169.
42. In Keesing, *op.cit.,* III, 10.
43. Malinowski, *op.cit.,* pp. 140f., 150.
44. Cf. S. Stansfeld Sargent and Theodore Brameld (eds.), "Anti-Intellectualism in the United States," *Journal of Social Issues,* Vol. 11, 1955, pp. 1-61.
45. Montagu, *op.cit.,* p. 155.
46. In *Ibid.,* p. 157.
47. Cf. Brameld, *op.cit.,* pp. 92-103, 179-194, 200-208, 346-358.
48. Cf. A. M. Dupois, "Social Consensus and the Scientific Method," *Educational Theory,* Vol. 5, 1955, pp. 242-248.
49. M. J. Herskovits, *Man and His Works, op.cit.,* pp. 202, 575.
50. For fruitful suggestions, cf. George D. Spindler (ed.), *Education and Anthropology* (Stanford: Stanford University Press, 1955). And Montagu, *op.cit.,* pp. 298ff.
51. Cf. Albert, *op. cit.* Cf. Ethel M. Albert, "Similarities and Differences in Value Systems: A Comparative Analysis" (dittoed); (Cambridge: Harvard University Values Study Project, 1956).
52. For a summary of Project, cf. Evon Z. Vogt and John M. Roberts, "A Study of Values," *Scientific American,* Vol. 195, 1956, pp. 25-31.

CHAPTER THIRTEEN: THE STUDY OF CULTURE IN
TEACHER EDUCATION

1. Cf. George D. Spindler (ed.), *Education and Anthropology, op.cit.*
2. Cf. "Symposium: Philosophy of Education," *Journal of Philosophy,* Vol. 52, 1955, pp. 612-633. And "Symposium: The Aims and Content of Philosophy of Education," *Harvard Educational Review,* Vol. 26, 1956, pp. 93-205.
3. This general viewpoint, while more qualified than the statements in in the paragraph, nevertheless is vigorously and influentially defended by Arthur Bestor, a liberal arts historian, in *The Restoration of Learning* (New York: Alfred A. Knopf, 1955).
4. Cf. Harvard Committee on the Objectives of Education in a Free Society, *General Education in a Free Society* (Cambridge: Harvard University Press, 1945). Cf. Theodore Brameld, *Philosophies of Education in Cultural Perspective, op.cit.,* pp. 251f.
5. Cf. Robert M. Hutchins, *The Conflict in Education in a Democratic Society* (New York: Harper & Brothers, 1953). Cf. Brameld, *op.cit.,* Chap. 12.

APPENDIX: PHILOSOPHICAL ANTHROPOLOGY: THE EDUCATIONAL SIGNIFICANCE OF ERNST CASSIRER

1. Cf. Dimitry Gawronsky, in Paul A. Schilpp (ed.), *The Philosophy of Ernst Cassirer, op.cit.,* pp. 3ff.
2. The writer is greatly indebted to Professor Charles W. Hendel of

Yale University for these epitomizing sentences, as well as for a
painstaking critique of the entire essay. *An Essay on Man* was dedicated
to Professor Hendel—probably the leading American authority on
Cassirer.

3. Cf. Ernst Cassirer, "Neo-kantianism," in *Encyclopaedia Britannica,*
   1955, Vol. 16.
4. Cf. Ernst Cassirer, *Language and Myth* (New York: Harper &
   Brothers, 1946), pp. 25-27.
5. Cf. Ernst Cassirer, "Kant," in *Encyclopedia of the Social Sciences, op.-
   cit.,* Vol. 8.
6. Cf. Ernst Cassirer, *Das Erkenntnisproblem in der Philosophe und
   Wissenschaft der neueren Zeit.* (Berlin: Bruno Cassirer, 1906-1907);
   and Ernst Cassirer, *The Myth of the State, op.cit.* Cf. also Ernst Cassirer, *The Problem of Knowledge: Philosophy, Science, and History
   since Hegel* (New Haven: Yale University Press, 1950).
7. Cf. Ernst Cassirer, *The Philosophy of Symbolic Forms,* 2 Vols. (New
   Haven: Yale University Press, 1953-55).
8. Ernst Cassirer, *An Essay on Man* (New Haven: Yale University Press,
   1944), p. 208.
9. *Ibid.,* p. 24.
10. *The Myth of the State, op.cit.,* p. 45.
11. *An Essay on Man, op.cit.,* pp. 76 f.
12. *Language and Myth, op.cit.,* p. 36.
13. *Ibid.,* p. 38.
14. *An Essay on Man, op.cit.,* p. 94.
15. *Ibid,* p. 87.
16. *Ibid.,* pp. 96 f.
17. *Language and Myth, op.cit.,* p. 81.
18. *An Essay on Man, op.cit.,* p. 226.
19. Cf. *Ibid.,* pp. 67, 78.
20. *Ibid.,* pp. 67 f.
21. *Ibid,* p. 130.
22. *Ibid.,* p. 131.
23. *Ibid.,* p. 134.
24. *Language and Myth, op.cit.,* p. 37.
25. *An Essay on Man, op.cit.,* p. 196.
26. *Ibid.*
27. *Ibid.,* p. 205.
28. *Ibid.,* p. 207. Cf. *The Problem of Knowledge: Philosophy, Science,
    and History since Hegel, op.cit.*
29. *Ibid.,* p. 111.
30. *Op.cit.*
31. Cf. Ernst Cassirer, *The Philosophy of the Enlightenment* (Princeton:
    Princeton University Press, 1951).
32. *The Myth of the State, op.cit.,* p. 273.
33. Suzanne Langer, in Schilpp (ed.), *op.cit.,* pp. 395 f.

34. *The Myth of the State, op.cit.*, p. 288.
35. *Ibid.*, p. 279.
36. *Ibid.*, pp. 280f.
37. *Ibid.*, p. 296.
38. *Ibid.*, p. 280.
39. *Ibid.*, p. 282.
40. *An Essay on Man, op.cit.*, p. 228.
41. John Herman Randall, Jr., in Schilpp (ed.), *op.cit.*, pp. 702-704.
42. David Bidney, in Schilpp (ed.), *op.cit.*, pp. 544, 540.
43. Cf. Kurt Lewin, in Schilpp (ed.), *op.cit.*, pp. 269ff.
44. Cf. Bidney, in Schilpp (ed.), *op.cit.*, pp. 502 f.
45. *An Essay on Man, op.cit.*, pp. 53ff.
46. *Ibid.*, p. 62.
47. *Ibid.*
48. *Ibid.*, p. 53.

INDEX

Acceptance, 134
Acculturation, 129-31, 150-51, 165, 196, 268
Age-grade standards, 173
Albert, Ethel M., 250
Alexander, Samuel, 40
American Philosophical Association, xv, 210, 255
Ames, Adelbert, 160, 165
Anti-intellectualism, 243
Aquinas, St. Thomas, 50, 53, 259, 290
Area, culture, 59
Aristotle, 70, 89, 144, 291
Arts, 105
  and myth, 285
Assimilation, 131-32, 151-52, 196
Association, 64
Augustine, St., 89
Authoritarianism, 21, 48, 49-50, 55, 225, 232, 272

Barnett, H. G., 133-35, 138, 141, 152, 153, 174
Basic personality type, see Modal personality
Beals, Ralph, 129, 130, 132
Beethoven, Ludwig van, 105
Behaviorism, 9, 143, 159-61, 162-64, 165, 166, 169, 179
Benedict, Ruth, 42, 60-61, 62, 67, 70, 72, 75, 159, 169, 193, 199, 214
Benne, Kenneth, 182
Bergson, Henri, 83
Berlin, University of, 275
Bidney, David, 87, 91, 99, 101, 133, 141, 144, 154, 298
  and causation, 147-48, 155
  and crisis, 136-37
  and freedom, 230, 233-34, 237, 246, 248
  and goals, 193, 197, 201, 209, 216, 220, 271
  and modes of cultural integration, 62, 75

Bidney, David—(Contd.)
  and personality, 164, 168, 169, 179 ff.
  and superorganic, 40, 43, 45, 46, 51, 52
Boas, Franz, 9, 10, 42, 45, 67, 87-88, 89, 91, 94-95, 98, 100, 102, 113, 122, 159, 194, 197, 199, 229, 237, 238, 265
Bode, Boyd, 184
Bradley, Francis Herbert, 89
Brandt, Richard B., 207-8
Burnet, John, xi
Burton, William H., 77-78
Butts, Freeman, 156

Caesarism, 107
Cantril, Hadley, 160, 165, 210
Capitalism, 49, 217
Carlyle, Thomas, 291-92, 295
Cassirer, Ernst, 10, 165, 180, 237-38, 249, 270
  academic life, 275-76
  basis of unity, 285-90
  critique of, 297-303
  myth of the state, 238, 290-97
  and neo-Kantianism, 277-80
  and symbols, see Symbols, man as creator and user of
Caste, 69-70
Causation and prediction, 141-48, 155-156, 158, 171, 268
Change, cultural, 173
Chapple, E. D., 182
Child, Irvin L., 161
Child-training, 163-64, 170-71, 183
Childe, V. Gordon, 92-93, 100, 113, 122, 194, 236
Circular causality, 143-44, 155
Civilization, defined, 11
Classes, social, 65-70, 77-81, 194, 262
Cohen, Hermann, 275, 277
Cohen, Morris R., 101-2, 103, 113, 114, 237

323